Italian
verb handbook

Carole Shepherd

**Berlitz Publishing /
APA Publications GmbH & Co. Verlag KG,
Singapore Branch, Singapore**

Italian Verb Handbook

CONTACTING THE EDITORS
Every effort has been made to provide accurate information in this publication, but changes are inevitable. The publisher cannot be responsible for any resulting loss, inconvenience, or injury. We would appreciate it if readers would call our attention to any errors or outdated information by contacting Berlitz Publishing, 95 Progress Street, Union, NJ 07083, USA.
Fax: 1-908-206-1103. email: comments@berlitzbooks.com

Published by Berlitz Publishing/Apa Publications GmbH & Co. Verlag KG, Singapore Branch, Singapore

Berlitz Trademark Reg. U.S. Patent Office and other countries. Marca Registrada.
Used under license from Berlitz Investment Corporation.

Cover photo © Andy Sitt/Alamy

Printed in Singapore by Insight Print Services (Pte) Ltd., February 2005

The Author:
Carole Shepherd is an experienced teacher, author, and language consultant.

The Series Editor:
Christopher Wightwick is a former UK representative on the Council of Europe Modern Languages Project and principal Inspector of Modern Languages for England.

CONTENTS

How to Use This Handbook

How to Use This Handbook

This Handbook aims to provide a full description of the Italian verb system for all learners and users of the Italian language. It provides the following information:

• a chapter explaining the verb system in Italian;

• the conjugation of one hundred six verbs, grouped to show the common patterns underlying the system;

• a subject index to The Verb System in Italian;

• a verb index, containing over twenty-two hundred verbs with their English meanings and references to the pattern(s) they follow.

An important feature of the book is that examples, showing many of the verbs in use, are given throughout The Verb System in Italian and the Model Verbs.

THE VERB SYSTEM IN ITALIAN

Use the Contents and Subject Index to find your way around this section, which describes the functions and forms of verbs in general. It provides information on the use of tenses, word order, the way verbs govern other parts of speech, and the way verbs are formed. It also describes methods of avoiding the passive, and it explains features such as the reflexive forms, the subjunctive, and the auxiliary verbs. It explains the main features of predictability and irregularity, and it illustrates key irregular verbs.

MODEL VERBS

Use the Verb Index to find your way around this section, which gives the full conjugation of two key model verbs — i.e., of **lodare,** in both its active and passive voice; and of **entrare,** in its active voice. This section provides models for for all three groups of regular verbs plus the full range of spelling-change verbs, followed by all useful irregular verbs. This makes a total of one hundred six model verbs.

The conjugation of each verb is given in all usable tenses. Tenses that have any irregularity are given in full, with the irregularity in bold type. For tenses that are predictable, particularly compound tenses, only the first person singular form is given, as this is sufficient to enable you to predict the other forms within those tenses. Therefore, if a tense is not given in full, you can assume that it is regular.

For simple tenses, just look at the two model verbs (**lodare** and **entrare**) or at the appropriate verb of the five regular verbs (**parlare, vendere, dormire, finire,** and **lavarsi**) to figure out the endings needed. For compound tenses, check the Verb System in Italian to decide which tense of which auxiliary verb is necessary, then look up the appropriate auxiliary verb (**avere** or **essere**) in the Model Verbs.

Where appropriate, the model verb pages also contain the following:

• A list of other verbs that follow the same pattern. If possible, all such verbs are given. If, however, they are too numerous to list, a selection of the most useful ones is given. There are, of course, verbs that stand alone, having no others following their model.

• Notes indicating the main features of this pattern and any variations or additional features affecting any of the verbs that basically follow that model.

• Short dialogues, narratives, or sentences that illustrate some of the different tenses and usages of these verbs.

For further information on how the verb system works, refer to The Verb System in Italian.

THE SUBJECT INDEX

The Subject Index gives section references for all the main grammatical terms used in The Verb System in Italian.

VERB INDEX

For each of the twenty-two hundred or so verbs listed, the Verb Index gives information on whether it is transitive (*tr*), intransitive (*intr*), or reflexive (*refl*), together with its English meaning. It also lists common secondary meanings and the main idiomatic expressions based on common verbs. Finally, each entry is referred to the model verb whose pattern it follows:

acquistare (*tr*)   acquire, get 3

There are verbs that have more than one predictable or unpredictable variation from the norm. Such verbs have two numbers after them, and both model verb pages should be consulted in these cases.

assorbire (*tr*)   absorb, soak up 5, 6

HOW TO FIND THE INFORMATION YOU WANT

If you want to check on the form, meaning, or use of a verb, look it up in the Verb Index. This shows:

• which verbs are model verbs (indicated by **[M]**);

vendere (*tr*)   sell, retail 4 **[M]**

• which verbs take **essere** (indicated by *)

*andare (*intr*)   go, ride (in car) 21 **[M]**

• which verbs take **avere** when transitive and **essere** when intransitive (indicated by a †)

†salire (*intr/tr*)   go up, climb, mount, come in (of tide) 77 **[M]**

• any preposition normally accompanying the verb;

*abituarsi a (*intr/refl*)   become accustomed to, get used to 7

• whether the verb is transitive (*tr*), intransitive (*intr*), or reflexive (*refl*);

camminare (*intr*)   step, tread, walk 3

• the main English meaning of the verb, along with any important idiomatic uses;

colpire (*tr*)   impress, knock against, shock, smack, strike, hit 6
colpire a morte (*tr*)   shoot dead 6

• a number indicating the model verb, which gives the congugation of the verb, points out its irregularities, and lists verbs that follow a similar pattern.

chiudere (*tr*)   close, shut, zip up 30 **[M]**

If you want further information on the form or use of the verb, turn to the verb reference given.

Note: *The rules regarding the use of accents in Italian require that there should be an acute accent on closed vowels and a grave accent on open vowels [▶Berlitz Italian Grammar Handbook 2a]. However, modern usage tends to prefer the grave accent, particularly on à, ò, ù and ì, and this usage is employed throughout the Handbook.*

A

THE VERB SYSTEM IN ITALIAN

1 What Verbs Do

1a   Full Verbs

The great majority of verbs tell us about the action, state of mind, or changing situation of the subject of the sentence. We call these verbs *full* verbs.

Abito in Italia.	*I live* in Italy.
Abbiamo un appartamento.	*We have* an apartment.

1b   Auxiliary Verbs

A much smaller group of verbs is used to add something to the sense of the full verb — for example, to make a compound tense or to add a comment on an action. These are called *auxiliary* (helping) verbs.

Sto studiando l'italiano.	I am studying Italian.
Ho comprato una macchina.	I (have) bought a car.
Sono andato in città.	I went into town.

1c   Dual-Purpose Verbs

Most auxiliary verbs can be used either with their full meanings or as auxiliaries. For example, the verb **stare** — used mostly to express the position or the state or condition of something or somebody — is also used as an auxiliary verb to form the present progressive tense, which describes an action actually in progress.

Sta in casa.	She is in the house.
Sta preparando da mangiare.	She is preparing something to eat.

2 What Verbs Govern

A sentence can contain many items of information other than what is given by the subject and the main verb. Some of these items depend directly on the main verb and cannot be removed without leaving the sentence incomplete. These are said to be governed by the verb.

2a   Intransitive Verbs

Some verbs do not normally govern an object [▶2c], though the sentence may, of course, contain expressions that add to the meaning. These verbs are called *intransitive* verbs and are usually marked in the verb lists and dictionaries as (intr) or (i).

Torno subito.	I'll come back right away.

'I'll come back' makes sense in itself. The 'right away' gives us some extra information.

2b   Verbs Linking Equals: The Complement

A small number of verbs act as a link between the subject and another word or phrase, which is called the complement of the verb. Usually, the complement is a noun or a phrase referring to the same person or thing as the subject.

Mio padre è dottore.	My father *is* a doctor.

2c   Transitive Verbs

Many verbs take a *direct object*. These verbs are *transitive*. They are usually marked in dictionaries and verb lists as (tr). A direct object answers the question *what?* or *whom?* Intransitive verbs cannot have a direct object.

Giorgio ha comprato un cane.	Giorgio bought *a dog*.

Here the dog is what Giorgio bought, so it is the direct object of 'bought.'

3

THE VERB SYSTEM IN ITALIAN

2d Verbs That Can Be Both Transitive and Intransitive

Many verbs can be both transitive and intransitive in Italian. They may be listed as (intr/tr) in verb lists.

Maria parla troppo.	Maria talks too much.
Giovanni parla inglese.	Giovanni speaks English.

2e Verbs with Two Objects: Direct and Indirect

Some transitive verbs describe the transfer of the direct object to another person (or possibly thing). This person is then the *indirect object* of the verb. With some verbs the idea can be extended to include people indirectly affected by the action of the verb. The indirect object answers the question *to whom?* or *for whom?* However, in English the 'to' or the 'for' is not always stated.

Sandro ha comprato dei fiori per la mamma.	Sandro bought some flowers for his mother.
Le ha comprato dei fiori.	He bought her some flowers.
Ha dato i fiori alla mamma.	He gave the flowers to his mother.
Le ha dato i fiori.	He gave her the flowers.

Here the flowers are the direct object and the mother/her — the recipient — is the indirect object.

2f Reflexive Verbs

(i) Some verbs express an action that is turned back on the subject; in other words, the object is the same person or the same thing as the subject. These are called *reflexive* verbs [➤10]. In English, these verbs may use one of the '-self' pronouns.

Mi diverto sempre in Italia.	I always enjoy myself in Italy.
Ci siamo divertiti molto.	We enjoyed ourselves a lot.

(ii) Sometimes people are doing the action not to themselves but to each other, in which case the subject is usually plural. As a result, it is only possible to use one of the plural forms of the verb — that is, the **noi, voi,** or **loro** form.

Si sono incontrati ieri.	They met (each other) yesterday.
Ci telefoniamo spesso.	We often phone each other.

(iii)   In many cases the Italian reference to '-self' or 'each other' is not expressed in English.

Mi sveglio alle sette.	I wake up at seven.
Mi alzo subito.	I get up immediately.
Mi lavo nel bagno.	I get washed in the bathroom.

(iv)   With some verbs the reflexive idea has largely disappeared in English, but the reflexive grammatical form in Italian still applies.

Me ne sono accorta che l'uomo mi guardava.	I noticed that the man was looking at me.
Non si rende conto che sono straniera.	He does not realize that I am a foreigner.

(v)   Normally reflexive verbs do not have another direct object; but if they do, the past participle agrees with that object rather than the reflexive pronoun, which then becomes an indirect object.

Mi sono tagliato il dito.	I cut my finger.
Mi sono rotta la gamba.	I have broken my leg.
Mi sono lavate le mani.	I washed my hands.

However, usage varies; and you may find that Italians make a past participle agree with the subject even when there is a direct object.

Alberto s'è tolto la camicia.	Alberto took off his shirt.

In these examples, the English uses a possessive adjective whereas Italian uses a reflexive pronoun.

(vi)   Reflexive verbs are often used where a passive would be used in English.

5

THE VERB SYSTEM IN ITALIAN

Qui si vendono mele.	Apples are sold here.
Qui si parla inglese.	English is spoken here.

2g   *Verbs Governing Verbs*

(i)   *Verbs followed by an infinitive*

This is quite a common structure in Italian, which has many expressions based on a *modal* auxiliary verb [▶3].

Vorrei partire alle otto.	*I'd like* to leave at eight.
Devo essere in città alle nove.	*I must* be in town at nine.
Sai nuotare?	*Do you know how to* swim?
Possiamo andare in piscina insieme.	*We can* go to the swimming pool together.

(ii)   *Verbs followed by a preposition and an infinitive*

Italian also has a number of these structures, which are very similar to *(i)*, but with a preposition between the auxiliary verb and the main verb. The Verb Index lists which verbs take which prepositions.

Andiamo a mangiare adesso!	Let's go to eat now!
Cerca di venire stasera.	Try to come tonight.
Ho dimenticato di comprare il giornale.	I forgot to buy the newspaper.
Sono usciti senza salutarmi.	They went out without saying good-bye to me.

(iii)   *Use of the gerund*

As in English, Italian has a way of describing an action in progress. In English the verb 'to be' and the present participle of the verb are used, while in Italian the verb **stare** and the gerund can be used.

Sto studiando l'italiano.	*I am studying* Italian.
Stavo leggendo quando è arrivato Luigi.	*I was reading* when Luigi arrived.

2h   *Position of Verbs in the Sentence*

(i)   *Subject pronouns*

Generally speaking, the position of verbs in an Italian sentence is similar to that in English. However, one important difference is that Italian verbs are usually found without a subject pronoun. This is because each verb ending is clear and distinct, not just in the written but also in the spoken form. However, the pronouns are used when necessary for emphasis, contrast, or clarity.

Io vado in città, ma tu devi rimanere qui.	*I* am going into town, but *you* must stay here.
— **Chi ha rotto il bicchiere?**	— Who broke the glass?
— **L'ha rotto lui, mamma.**	— *He* broke it, mom / mum.

In the last example the pronoun comes after the verb for greater emphasis on the person who broke the glass.

(ii)   *Questions*

Questions in English are usually formed by inverting the verb and the subject or by using the verb 'to do.' Such inversion is not so common in Italian, since the subject pronoun is rarely used except for emphasis, contrast, or clarity. Instead, questions often look exactly the same as statements but are indicated by voice intonation — the voice is raised at the end of the question. In a written form, the question is made visible, as in English, by the question mark.

Tuo padre ha una macchina nuova.	Your father has a new car.
Tuo padre ha una macchina nuova?	Does your father have a new car?
Hai visto Carlo ieri.	You saw Carlo yesterday.
Hai visto Carlo ieri?	Did you see Carlo yesterday?

(iii)   *Negative expressions*

Negative expressions are straightforward in Italian. The English word 'not' is translated by the Italian **non,** which is placed immediately before the verb and any dependent object pronouns.

THE VERB SYSTEM IN ITALIAN

—Non vado al cinema stasera.	—I'm *not* going to the movies / cinema this evening.
—Perchè non ci accompagni?	—Why do*n't* you come with us?
—Non mi sento bene.	—I do*n't* feel well.
Non lo so.	I do*n't* know.

Non can be combined with other negative expressions (**mai, nessuno, niente,** etc.) usually placed after the main verb.

Non vedo nessuno fuori.	I do*n't* see *anyone* outside.
Non è niente, non ti preoccupare.	It's *nothing*, do*n't* worry.
Non ho mai visto quel film.	I have *never* seen that film.

Note: **Nessuno** can begin a sentence, in which case there is no need for the **non.** This does not affect the position of the verb in the sentence.

Nessuno vuole venire.	*Nobody* wants to come.

3 Attitudes to Action: Modal Verbs

3a The Function of Modal Verbs

Modal verbs, as mentioned in 2g(i), modify full verbs to express additional points of view such as possibility, desire, and obligation. They create moods for the verbs that follow. They are used in the appropriate persons and tenses followed by the infinitives of the full verbs.

3b Modal Verbs and Their Meanings

These are the main modal auxiliary verbs used in Italian:

(i) ***potere*** *'can,' 'be able to'*

Non posso venire domani.	*I can*'t come tomorrow.

(ii) ***volere*** *'want to,' 'wish,' 'like'*

Non voleva andarci.	He *didn't want to* go there.

(iii) ***dovere*** *'have to,' 'must,' 'be obliged to,' 'ought to,' 'should'*

Dovete ascoltare il professore.	*You should* listen to the teacher.

(iv) ***sapere*** *'know how to,' 'be able to'*

—**Sai suonare il flauto?**	— *Do you know how to* play the flute?
—**No, ma so giocare a tennis!**	—No, but *I know how to* play tennis!

Note: Object pronouns may precede the modal verb or be attached to the end of the infinitive.

Te lo posso dire adesso.	I can tell *(it to) you* now.
Posso dirtelo adesso.	I can tell *(it to) you* now.

4 Verb Forms Not Related to Time

Verbs are very important words, in that a single verb form will usually give three pieces of information: *what* is happening, *when* it is happening, and *who* is doing it. However, there are some verb forms that do not specify time or person.

4a The Infinitive

The part of the verb that you will find in a verb list or dictionary, and also in the Verb Index of this book, is the *infinitive.* In English this is the word preceded by 'to,' for example, 'to love.' In Italian the infinitive form of all regular verbs ends in one of the following: **-are, -ere, -ire** (for example, **amare, vendere, capire, dormire**).

4b The Participles and the Gerund

(i) The present participle

The present participle in Italian has lost its verbal force and in most cases is used as an adjective or a noun. It is usually formed by adding **-ante** or **-ente** to the stem of the infinitive.

il capitolo seguente	the *following* chapter
gli amanti	the *lovers*

(ii) The present gerund

The present gerund is often used to describe an action in progress. Its most common use is with the auxiliary verb **stare** to form the present, imperfect, and sometimes future progressive tenses. However, it can be used by itself, provided that its subject and that of the verb in the sentence are the same. The gerund is formed by adding **-ando** or **-endo** to the stem of the infinitive, is invariable, and *never* takes a preposition before it. Care must be taken that the action being referred to actually take place at the same time as that of the main verb — i.e., present, past, or future.

Sto finendo l'esercizio.	*I am finishing* the exercise.
Il bambino sta dormendo nella culla.	The baby *is sleeping* in the cradle.
Cosa stavate facendo?	What *were you doing?*
Cammino lungo la strada parlando con Anna.	I walk along the road *while speaking* to Anna.
Papà ci rispose sorridendo.	Father answered us *smiling.*

Note the difference between the following:

Studio l'italiano a scuola.	I study Italian at school.
Sto studiando l'italiano adesso.	I am studying Italian now (i.e., at this precise moment).

(iii) *The past participle*

This form is used to describe an action that is finished. In Italian it ends in **-ato** (**-are** verbs), **-uto** (**-ere** verbs), or **-ito** (**-ire** verbs). It is mainly used with the verb **avere** or the verb **essere** to form the perfect tense and other compound tenses; but it is also used in other ways, including as an adjective and to form the passive. When used with **avere** in compound tenses, it does not agree with the subject, but can agree with a preceding direct object and *must* agree with a preceding direct object *pronoun.*

When used with **essere** it almost always agrees with the subject [but for reflexive usage ➤ 2f(v)].

Ho comprato una casa nuova.	*I have bought* a new house.
Fu costruita da Salvatore.	*It was built* by Salvatore.
L'ho invitata a pranzo.	*I invited* her to lunch
La mia amica è partita alle nove.	My friend *left* at nine.
Ho lasciato la porta aperta.	*I left* the door open.

In the examples given above, the past participle is used as part of the compound tense of the active transitive / intransitive verb of the sentence in all but the second example, where it is used as part of a passive construction. In the final example the second past participle is used as an adjective. When used in a passive construction or as an adjective or with the verb **essere,** the past participle follows the same rules of agreement as an adjective.

11

THE VERB SYSTEM IN ITALIAN

4c   *The Verb* Piacere

piacere *'like,' 'be pleasing to,' 'please'*

The construction of **piacere** is different from that of most other verbs, and it works the other way around than that of its English equivalents 'like' and 'please.' The subject of the verb in Italian becomes the direct object of the verb in English, and the subject of the verb in English becomes the indirect object of the verb in Italian.

Mi piace studiare	I *like* studying (i.e., '*Studying pleases / is pleasing* to me').
Mi piacciono i film di Fellini.	I *like* Fellini's movies (i.e., 'Fellini's movies *please / are pleasing* to me').

If the indirect object of the verb is a noun, it is usually preceded by the preposition **a.**

A mio padre piace molto leggere il giornale.	*My father* likes to read the newspaper a lot. (i.e., 'Reading the newspaper pleases *my father* a lot / is very pleasing to *my father*).

An indirect object pronoun may be accompanied by **a** + a disjunctive pronoun for emphasis.

A me non mi piacciono le banane.	*I* don't like bananas (i.e., Bananas don't please / are not pleasing *to me*).

5 The Use of Tenses

5a What Are Tenses?

Tenses are grammatical structures that record when an event happened. Both the number of tenses and the names given to them vary from language to language. Many tenses are formed from the stem of the infinitive — this is the part that remains when the **-are, -ere,** or **-ire** ending has been removed (for example, the stem of **parlare** is **parl-**). We may speak of simple and compound tenses.

(i) Simple tenses

These are formed by adding specific endings to the stem of the verb, which may also change.

(ii) Compound tenses

These are formed with the help of the auxiliary verbs **avere, essere,** and **stare** plus a participle or a gerund.

Thus a simple tense is a one-word form, while a compound tense is a form of two or more words.

5b Auxiliary Verbs

(i) The progressive tenses

The progressive tenses are used to describe actions that are in progress at the time being referred to — present, past (imperfect), or sometimes future. In English they are easily identifiable, since they are formed by the appropriate form of the verb 'to be' followed by the main verb in the '-ing' form. Italian uses a similar structure with the verb **stare** in the appropriate tense followed by the gerund of the main verb. The two main tenses of **stare** used in Italian are the present and the imperfect. However, you should note that Italian uses these forms less frequently than English does, and only when the action is in progress at the time being described.

Quando è arrivato, stavo leggendo un libro.	When he arrived, *I was reading* a book.

THE VERB SYSTEM IN ITALIAN

Andare is sometimes used to form the progressive tenses when a cumulative progression is indicated.

Gianna andava parlando di questo progetto per ore e ore.	Gianna *went on talking* about this project for hours and hours.

(ii) The compound past tenses

In Italian these tenses are formed with the appropriate forms of the verb **avere** or **essere** and the past participle.

Ho visto Gianluca ieri.	*I saw* Gianluca yesterday.
Aveva incontrato Sara.	*He had met* Sara.
Sono andata in città.	*I went* into town.
Era partito presto.	*He had left* early.

(iii) The past gerund

The past gerund is formed by combining the present gerund of **avere** or **essere** with the past participle of the verb. It is used to translate the perfect participle in English (i.e., having bought, having understood, and so forth).

Avendo comprato il giornale, tornai a casa.	*Having bought* the newspaper, I returned home.
Essendo partite le mie amiche, andai a dormire.	My friends *having left,* I went to sleep.

Note: As in the second example, the past gerund often has a subject of its own, unlike the present gerund used in the present progressive tense.

6 | Statements of Probable Fact: The Indicative

Verb forms and tenses that make a positive statement are said to be in the *indicative.* [Contrast this with the subjunctive ➤ 8.]

In all verbs there are some tenses whose stems and endings can be predicted if you know one of the other parts of the verb. Parts that cannot be predicted in this way have to be learned. It is helpful to know how to obtain the stem, to which the endings for each tense are added, and any spelling adjustments that may need to be made. The following sections tell you how to form each tense, explaining how to get the stem and giving you the endings; and they list the main uses for each one.

6a   *The Present Tenses*

(i)   *The present indicative*

The present indicative of regular verbs is formed as follows:

FIRST CONJUGATION	SECOND CONJUGATION	THIRD CONJUGATION	
amare 'love'	**vendere** 'sell'	**dormire** 'sleep'	**finire** 'finish'
am**o**	vend**o**	dorm**o**	fin**isco**
am**i**	vend**i**	dorm**i**	fin**isci**
am**a**	vend**e**	dorm**e**	fin**isce**
am**iamo**	vend**iamo**	dorm**iamo**	fin**iamo**
am**ate**	vend**ete**	dorm**ite**	fin**ite**
am**ano**	vend**ono**	dorm**ono**	fin**iscono**

Note that the following groups of verbs undergo spelling changes or other modifications, mainly for pronunciation purposes:

• Verbs ending in **-are** whose stems end in **-c** or **-g** insert an **h** before an **i** or an **e.**

| **pagare** | pago, **paghi, paghiamo,** pagate, pagano |
| **cercare** | cerco, **cerchi,** cerca, **cerchiamo,** cercate, cercano |

• Verbs ending in **-iare** have only one **i** in the **tu** form if the **i** of the stem is not stressed.

THE VERB SYSTEM IN ITALIAN

studiare	**studi**	(The stress falls on the first syllable.)

• Verbs ending in **-iare** retain the **i** if the stem is stressed.

sciare	**scii**	(The stress is on the first **i**.)

• Verbs ending in **-durre** are not irregular once the first person singular is known, as this is based on a **-ducere** ending.

produrre	**produco,** etc.
ridurre	**riduco,** etc.
tradurre	**traduco,** etc.

• Verbs **bere, dire,** and **fare** are formed from the obsolete **-ere** infinitives **bevere, dicere,** and **facere;** and if classified as second conjugation verbs, they are regular in some parts of the present tense.

bere (bevere)	bevo, bevi, beve, beviamo, bevete, bevono
dire (dicere)	dico, dici, dice, diciamo, **dite,** dicono
fare (facere)	**faccio, fai, fa, facciamo, fate, fanno**

• Some verbs add another vowel (turning into a diphthong) in the first, second, and third person singular and third person plural.

morire	**muoio, muori, muore,** moriamo, morite, **muoiono**
sedere	**siedo, siedi, siede,** sediamo, sedete, **siedono**

 For irregular verbs, see Model Verbs.

The present tense in Italian can be used to convey the following ideas:

• What the situation is now.

Studio l'italiano a una scuola serale.	I study Italian at a night school.

• What happens sometimes or usually.

Ogni giorno esco alle sette.	I go out every day at seven.

• What is going to happen soon.

Quest'estate vado in Italia.	This summer I am going to Italy.

• What has been happening up to now and may be continuing to happen.

Abito a Firenze da due anni.	I have been living in Florence for two years.
Aspettiamo da una mezz'ora.	We have been waiting for half an hour.

(ii) The present progressive

This is formed by using the present tense of **stare** plus the gerund [▶ 5b(i)].

studiare → **studiando**   prendere → **prendendo**   finire → **finendo**

There are three irregular gerunds formed from obsolete forms of the **-ere** infinitive.

VERB	OBSOLETE INFINITIVE	GERUND
dire	**(dicere)**	**dicendo**
fare	**(facere)**	**facendo**
bere	**(bevere)**	**bevendo**

Sto bevendo un bicchiere di vino.	*I am drinking* a glass of wine.
Sto leggendo il giornale.	*I am reading* the newspaper.

6b   The Past Tenses

(i) The imperfect indicative

The imperfect tense of all verbs is formed by taking off the **-re** ending of the infinitive and adding the following endings:

-vo, -vi, -va, -vamo, -vate, -vano

comprare 'buy'	**vendere** 'sell'	**dormire** 'sleep'
compra**vo**	vende**vo**	dormi**vo**
compra**vi**	vende**vi**	dormi**vi**
compra**va**	vende**va**	dormi**va**
compra**vamo**	vende**vamo**	dormi**vamo**
compra**vate**	vende**vate**	dormi**vate**
compra**vano**	vende**vano**	dormi**vano**

THE VERB SYSTEM IN ITALIAN

The following irregular imperfect tenses are formed from obsolete forms of the infinitive:

Verb	Obsolete Infinitive	Imperfect
dire	(dicere)	dicevo, etc.
fare	(facere)	facevo, etc.
bere	(bevere)	bevevo, etc.

Verbs ending in **-durre:**

produrre	producevo, etc.
tradurre	traducevo, etc.

Verbs ending in **-arre:**

attrarre	attraevo, etc.
distrarre	distraevo, etc.

The verb **essere** is the only verb to have a completely irregular form.

essere	ero, eri, era, eravamo, eravate, erano

The imperfect tense is used for:

- repeated or habitual actions in the past.

- descriptions of things or of people in the past.

- ongoing actions in the past, often as a setting to other actions.

Ogni anno andava in Francia.	*He used to go* to France every year.
Era una ragazza molto povera.	*She was* a very poor girl.
Parlava con Antonio quando sono entrata.	*He was speaking* to Antonio when I came in.

(ii) *The imperfect progressive tense*

This is formed by using the appropriate form of the imperfect tense of **stare** followed by the gerund [for usage ➤5b(i)]:

Stavo scrivendo quando ha telefonato Leonardo.	*I was writing* when Leonardo called / telephoned.

(iii) *The past definite*

The past definite of regular verbs is formed by adding the following endings to the stem of the infinitive.

-are	-ai, -asti, -ò, -ammo, -aste, -arono
-ere	-ei (-etti), -esti, -é (-ette), -emmo, -este, -erono (-ettero)
-ire	-ii, -isti, -í, -immo, -iste, -irono

trovare 'find'	vendere 'sell'	capire 'understand'
trovai	vendei / vendetti	capii
trovasti	vendesti	capisti
trovò	vendé / vendette	capí
trovammo	vendemmo	capimmo
trovaste	vendeste	capiste
trovarono	venderono / vendettero	capirono

Note: There is stress on the ending of the third person plural.

For irregular verbs ➤ Model Verbs 17–106. Although there are a considerable number of verbs that are irregular in the past definite, many of these are irregular only in the first and third person singular and third person plural, as in the following example:

chiedere	chiesi, chiedesti, chiese, chiedemmo, chiedeste, chiesero

Note the irregular past definite of **avere** and **essere.**

avere	essere
ebbi	fui
avesti	fosti
ebbe	fu
avemmo	fummo
aveste	foste
ebbero	furono

The past definite is used to describe completed actions in the past, which have no further correlation to the present. It is mainly used in literary and formal writing, though in some parts of Italy it is an alternative to the perfect tense.

Tornando a casa, incontrai Carlo.	While I was returning home, *I met* Carlo.
Comprai una macchina due mesi fa.	*I bought* a car two months ago.

Note: The verb **nascere** needs special attention: **è nato** is used for someone still living; **era nato** is used for someone who has recently died; **nacque** is used for someone long dead.

THE VERB SYSTEM IN ITALIAN

La bambina è nata stamattina.	The baby girl *was born* this morning.
Il morto era nato novantadue anni fa.	The dead man *was born* ninety-two years ago.
Dante Alighieri nacque secoli fa.	Dante Alighieri *was born* centuries ago.

(iv) Other past tenses

The remainder of the past tenses in Italian are compound tenses. They are formed using the appropriate tense of the auxiliary verb **avere** or **essere** and the past participle of the verb [➤5b(ii)].

(v) The present perfect tense

The present perfect tense is formed in Italian by using the present tense of **avere** or **essere** and the past participle of the verb. To form the past participle of regular verbs, remove the infinitive ending and add the appropriate ending.

-are	-ato
-ere	-uto
-ire	-ito

comprare	vendere	finire
ho comprato	ho venduto	ho finito
hai comprato	hai venduto	hai finito
ha comprato	ha venduto	ha finito
abbiamo comprato	abbiamo venduto	abbiamo finito
avete comprato	avete venduto	avete finito
hanno comprato	hanno venduto	hanno finito

andare	venire	lavarsi
sono andato / a	sono venuto / a	mi sono lavato / a
sei andato / a	sei venuto / a	ti sei lavato / a
è andato / a	è venuto / a	si è lavato / a
siamo andati / e	siamo venuti / e	ci siamo lavati / e
siete andati / e	siete venuti / e	vi siete lavati / e
sono andati / e	sono venuti / e	si sono lavati / e

Note: Most intransitive verbs, most impersonal verbs, and all reflexive verbs take **essere** in the present perfect tense. In the Verb Index these are marked *.

Some of the most common verbs taking **essere** are as follows:

andare (andato)	go		**restare (restato)**	stay
arrivare (arrivato)	arrive		**rimanere (rimasto)**	remain
cadere (caduto)	fall		**riuscire (riuscito)**	succeed
†correre (corso)	run		**salire (salito)**	go up
essere (stato)	be		**scendere (sceso)**	go down
morire (morto)	die		**scoppiare (scoppiato)**	burst
nascere (nato)	be born		**sembrare (sembrato)**	seem
parere (parso)	appear		**tornare (tornato)**	return
partire (partito)	leave		**uscire (uscito)**	go out
piacere (piaciuto)	please		**venire (venuto)**	come

Note: †Correre can take **avere** when used with a direct object.

Giovanni ha corso un grave rischio quel giorno.	Giovanni ran a great risk that day.

All verbs marked † in the Verb Index take **essere** when used intransitively and **avere** when used transitively.

 Many past participles are irregular and will need to be learned.

The perfect tense is used to describe:

• a single completed action in the past.

Ho letto il suo libro.	I read his book.

• an action taking place in the past but continuing up to the present.

Fino adesso Anna ha scritto tre libri.	Up to now Anna has written three books.

• an action that has recently taken place.

Oggi Antonio è venuto a trovarmi.	Antonio came to see me today.
Stamattina sono andata al mercato.	I went to the market this morning.
Abbiamo finito i compiti!	We have finished the homework!
Maria ha scritto due lettere stasera.	Maria has written two letters this evening.

(vi) The pluperfect tense

The pluperfect tense is formed with the imperfect tense of **avere** or **essere** and the past participle of the verb.

comprare	vendere	finire
avevo comprato	avevo venduto	avevo finito
avevi comprato	avevi venduto	avevi finito
aveva comprato	aveva venduto	aveva finito
avevamo comprato	avevamo venduto	avevamo finito
avevate comprato	avevate venduto	avevate finito
avevano comprato	avevano venduto	avevano finito

andare	venire	lavarsi
ero andato / a	ero venuto / a	mi ero lavato / a
eri andato / a	eri venuto / a	ti eri lavato / a
era andato / a	era venuto / a	si era lavato / a
eravamo andati / e	eravamo venuti / e	ci eravamo lavati / e
eravate andati / e	eravate venuti / e	vi eravate lavati / e
erano andati / e	erano venuti / e	si erano lavati / e

The pluperfect tense is used to take a step back in time in the past. It corresponds to the English 'had.'

Antonio aveva scritto due righe.	Antonio had written a note ('two lines').
Avevo mangiato bene.	I had eaten well.
Ero arrivato tardi.	I had arrived late.

(vii) The past anterior

The past anterior has the same meaning as the pluperfect tense. It, too, corresponds to the English 'had' and is formed with the past definite tense of **avere** or **essere** and the past participle of the verb.

comprare	vendere	finire
ebbi comprato	ebbi venduto	ebbi finito
avesti comprato	avesti venduto	avesti finito
ebbe comprato	ebbe venduto	ebbe finito
avemmo comprato	avemmo venduto	avemmo finito
aveste comprato	aveste venduto	aveste finito
ebbero comprato	ebbero venduto	ebbero finito

andare	venire	lavarsi
fui andato / a	fui venuto / a	mi fui lavato / a
fosti andato / a	fosti venuto / a	ti fosti lavato / a
fu andato / a	fu venuto / a	si fu lavato / a
fummo andati / e	fummo venuti / e	ci fummo lavati / e
foste andati / e	foste venuti / e	vi foste lavati / e
furono andati / e	furono venuti / e	si furono lavati / e

 The past anterior is rarely used in speech.

It can only be used in subordinate clauses introduced by a conjunction of time when the verb of the main clause is in the past definite.

Quando ebbi finito, me ne andai.	When I finished, I left.
Non appena fu arrivato, squillò il telefono.	As soon as he arrived, the phone rang.

6c The Future Tenses

(i) The simple future

The present tense in Italian can be used to denote the future.

Dove vai in vacanza?	Where are you going on vacation / holiday?
Vado in Italia quest'estate.	I am going to Italy this summer.
A che ora arriva Paolo?	What time is Paolo arriving?
Arriva alle otto.	He is arriving at eight.

(ii) The future

The future tense in Italian is formed by adding these modified forms of the present tense of **avere** to the infinitive of the verb minus the final **-e.**

-ò, -ai, -à, -emo, -ete, -anno

Note: **-are** verbs change their stems from **-ar** to **-er** in the future.

comprare	vendere	finire
comprer**ò**	vender**ò**	finir**ò**
comprer**ai**	vender**ai**	finir**ai**
comprer**à**	vender**à**	finir**à**
comprer**emo**	vender**emo**	finir**emo**
comprer**ete**	vender**ete**	finir**ete**
comprer**anno**	vender**anno**	finir**anno**

23

THE VERB SYSTEM IN ITALIAN

The verbs **avere** and **essere** have irregular future stems.

avr-	avrò	sar-	sarò

The following verbs have contracted stems (i.e., they lose the characteristic vowel of the infinitive ending).

andare	andrò	potere	potrò
cadere	cadrò	sapere	saprò
dovere	dovrò	vedere	vedrò
morire	morrò	vivere	vivrò

Some verbs and their compounds undergo a slight modification to their spelling so that the stem doubles the **-r**.

bere	berrò	valere	varrò
parere	parrò	venire	verrò
rimanere	rimarrò	volere	vorrò
tenere	terrò		

A few verbs retain the vowel of the infinitive ending.

dare	darò	stare	starò
fare	farò		

Verbs ending in **-ciare** and **-giare** drop the **i** before the **-er** of the future tense.

cominciare	comincerò	mangiare	mangerò

Verbs ending in **-care** or **-gare** add an **h** after the **c** or the **g** throughout the future tense to retain the hard sound.

cercare	cercherò	pagare	pagherò

The future tense is used to refer to what is going to happen.

Andrò a Roma l'anno prossimo.	I shall go to Rome next year.

It is used in dependent clauses that start with **se** or a conjunction of time if the main verb is in the future.

| **Se lo vedrò, glielo spiegherò.** | If I see him, I shall explain it to him. |
| **Quando arriverà, gliene parlerò.** | When he arrives, I shall speak to him about it. |

It can also denote probability.

| Sarà un coltello? | Is it (perhaps) a knife? |
| Saranno i miei genitori alla porta. | It must be my parents at the door. |

(iii) The future perfect

The future perfect tense is used to take a step forward from a time in the past. It expresses the idea of 'will have,' or it indicates probability. It is formed with the future tense of **avere** or **essere** and the past participle of the verb.

comprare	vendere	finire
avrò comprato	avrò venduto	avrò finito
avrai comprato	avrai venduto	avrai finito
avrà comprato	avrà venduto	avrà finito
avremo comprato	avremo venduto	avremo finito
avrete comprato	avrete venduto	avrete finito
avranno comprato	avranno venduto	avranno finito

andare	venire	lavarsi
sarò andato / a	sarò venuto / a	mi sarò lavato / a
sarai andato / a	sarai venuto / a	ti sarai lavato / a
sarà andato / a	sarà venuto / a	si sarà lavato / a
saremo andati / e	saremo venuti / e	ci saremo lavati / e
sarete andati / e	sarete venuti / e	vi sarete lavati / e
saranno andati / e	saranno venuti / e	si saranno lavati / e

Quando avrò finito i compiti, guarderò la televisione.	When I have finished the homework, I shall watch television.
Saranno andati al bar.	They will / must have gone to the bar.
Avrà perso la borsa.	She must have lost her bag.

6d The Conditional

(i) The present conditional

The present tense of the conditional mood is formed by adding the following endings to the future stem:
-ei, -esti, -ebbe, -emmo, -este, -ebbero.

THE VERB SYSTEM IN ITALIAN

comprare	vendere	finire
comprerei	venderei	finirei
compreresti	venderesti	finiresti
comprerebbe	venderebbe	finirebbe
compreremmo	venderemmo	finiremmo
comprereste	vendereste	finireste
comprerebbero	venderebbero	finirebbero

Note: The irregular future stems in 6c also apply to the conditional.

The conditional is used to express an English conditional form.

Dovrei andare a scuola.	*I should* go to school.
Vorrei comprare dei fiori.	*I would like* to buy some flowers.

It is also used to express a wish more politely.

Potrei avere un po' di zucchero?	*Could I* have some sugar?
Mi accompagneresti domani?	*Will you come with* me tomorrow?

The verb **gradire** 'like to,' 'appreciate,' can also be used in the conditional to stress politeness.

Gradirei una risposta alla mia lettera.	*I would like* a reply to my letter.
Gradiremmo sapere i prezzi da Voi praticati.	*We would like* to know your prices.

(ii)   The conditional perfect

The perfect tense of the conditional mood is used to convey the idea of 'would have' or that the statement reported is hearsay. It is formed with the present conditional of **avere** or **essere** and the past participle of the verb.

comprare	vendere	finire
avrei comprato	avrei venduto	avrei finito
avresti comprato	avresti venduto	avresti finito
avrebbe comprato	avrebbe venduto	avrebbe finito
avremmo comprato	avremmo venduto	avremmo finito
avreste comprato	avreste venduto	avreste finito
avrebbero comprato	avrebbero venduto	avrebbero finito

andare	**venire**	**lavarsi**
sarei andato / a	sarei venuto / a	mi sarei lavato / a
saresti andato / a	saresti venuto / a	ti saresti lavato / a
sarebbe andato / a	sarebbe venuto / a	si sarebbe lavato / a
saremmo andati / e	saremmo venuti / e	ci saremmo lavati / e
sareste andati / e	sareste venuti / e	vi sareste lavati / e
sarebbero andati / e	sarebbero venuti / e	si sarebbero lavati / e

Note: According to the sequence of tenses in Italian, when the main verb is in the past tense, any subordinate conditional clause must also be in the past.

Avrei voluto imparare il giapponese.	I would have liked to learn Japanese.
Lasciò detto che sarebbe tornato alle otto.	He left word to say that he would be returning at eight.
A quanto dicono i giornali, la disoccupazione sarebbe cresciuta durante gli ultimi dieci anni.	From what the newspapers say, unemployment has increased during the last ten years.

27

7 | Requests and Commands: The Imperative

7a The Informal Imperative: Tu, Noi, Voi

Apart from the **tu** form of **-are** verbs, the imperative of regular verbs is the same as the present indicative.

tu *form*	**noi** *form*	**voi** *form*
parla	parliamo	parlate
vendi	vendiamo	vendete
dormi	dormiamo	dormite
finisci	finiamo	finite

A few verbs are irregular in the **tu** and, occasionally, the **voi** forms.

andare	va	andate
avere	**abbi**	**abbiate**
dare	dà	date
dire	di'	dite
essere	**sii**	**siate**
fare	fa	fate
sapere	**sappi**	**sappiate**
stare	sta	state

Pronouns are attached to the end of the informal imperative.

Parla alla mamma!	Speak to mom / mum!
Andiamo in Italia!	Let's go to Italy!
Trovate quei libri!	Find those books!
Fammi un piacere!	Do me a favor / favour!
Digli che venga a casa mia.	Tell him to come to my house.

7b Informal Negative Imperative

The informal negative **tu** form of the imperative is formed by adding **non** before the infinitive. Pronouns are attached to the end of the infinitive, which then drops the **-e.**

The informal negative **noi** or **voi** form is formed by placing **non** before the corresponding informal imperative form.

Non vendere quella gonna!	Don't sell that skirt!
Non parlargli!	Don't speak to him!
Non andarci!	Don't go there!
Non facciamo i compiti!	Let's not do our homework!
Non finite l'articolo!	Don't finish the article!

7c   *Polite Imperative:* Lei, Loro

All formal imperatives are formed using the **Lei** or **Loro** form of the present subjunctive. Any irregularity in the present subjunctive will, of course, occur in these imperatives [▶8] as well.

Note: • The formal form **Loro** is now often replaced by the less formal **voi** form, which avoids the use of the subjunctive.

• With the exception of **loro** 'to them,' pronouns come before the imperative form of the verb.

Mi passi il sale, per favore.	(Would you) pass me the salt, please.
Gli dia quella penna per favore.	(Would you) give him that pen, please.
Mi mostri il libro che ha comprato.	(Would you) show me the book you have bought.
Finiscano adesso.	Finish now.

8 | Areas of Uncertainty: The Subjunctive

8a   The Present Subjunctive

(i)   The present subjunctive of regular verbs is formed by adding the following endings to the stem of the infinitive.

-are	**-i, -i, -i, -iamo, -iate, -ino**
-ere	**-a, -a, -a, -iamo, -iate, -ano**
-ire	**-a, -a, -a, -iamo, -iate, -ano** (verbs like **dormire**)
-ire	**-isca, -isca, -isca, -iamo, -iate, -iscano** (verbs like **finire**)

parlare	**vendere**	**dormire**	**finire**
parl**i**	vend**a**	dorm**a**	fin**isca**
parl**i**	vend**a**	dorm**a**	fin**isca**
parl**i**	vend**a**	dorm**a**	fin**isca**
parl**iamo**	vend**iamo**	dorm**iamo**	fin**iamo**
parl**iate**	vend**iate**	dorm**iate**	fin**iate**
parl**ino**	vend**ano**	dorm**ano**	fin**iscano**

(ii)   The present subjunctive of most irregular verbs is formed from the first person singular of the irregular present indicative.

andare	vada, vada, vada, andiamo, andiate, vadano
bere	beva, beva, beva, beviamo, beviate, bevano
dire	dica, dica, dica, diciamo, diciate, dicano
dovere	deva / debba, deva / debba, deva / debba, dobbiamo, dobbiate, devono / debbano
fare	faccia, faccia, faccia, facciamo, facciate, facciano
morire	muoia, muoia, muoia, moriamo, moriate, muoiano
parere	paia, paia, paia, paiamo, paiate, paiano
potere	possa, possa, possa, possiamo, possiate, possano
rimanere	rimanga, rimanga, rimanga, rimaniamo, rimaniate, rimangano
scegliere	scelga, scelga, scelga, scegliamo, scegliate, scelgano
tenere	tenga, tenga, tenga, teniamo, teniate, tengano
tradurre	traduca, traduca, traduca, traduciamo, traduciate, traducano
uscire	esca, esca, esca, usciamo, usciate, escano
venire	venga, venga, venga, veniamo, veniate, vengano
volere	voglia, voglia, voglia, vogliamo, vogliate, vogliano

However, the present subjunctive of some other irregular verbs is formed from the **noi** form of the present indicative.

avere	abbia, abbia, abbia, abbiamo, abbiate, abbiano
dare	dia, dia, dia, diamo, diate, diano
essere	sia, sia, sia, siamo, siate, siano
sapere	sappia, sappia, sappia, sappiamo, sappiate, sappiano
stare	stia, stia, stia, stiamo, stiate, stiano

8b   *The Imperfect Subjunctive*

The imperfect subjunctive of regular verbs is formed by adding the following endings to the stem of the infinitive.

-are	**-assi, -assi, -asse, -assimo, -aste, -assero**
-ere	**-essi, -essi, -esse, -essimo, -este, -essero**
-ire	**-issi, -issi, -isse, -issimo, -iste, -issero**

comprare	**vendere**	**finire**
comprassi	vendessi	finissi
comprassi	vendessi	finissi
comprasse	vendesse	finisse
comprassimo	vendessimo	finissimo
compraste	vendeste	finiste
comprassero	vendessero	finissero

The following verbs are irregular.

dare	**dessi,** etc.	**stare**	**stessi,** etc.
essere	**fossi,** etc.		

All verbs with contracted infinitives revert to their obsolete forms in the imperfect subjunctive.

bere	**bevessi,** etc.	**fare**	**facessi,** etc.
dire	**dicessi,** etc.		

Note also verbs in **-durre** and **-arre.**

produrre	**producessi,** etc.	**trarre**	**traessi,** etc.

8c   *Compound Subjunctive Tenses*

The compound subjunctive tenses are formed by using the appropriate subjunctive tense of the auxiliary verb **avere** or **essere,** followed by the past participle of the main verb.

THE VERB SYSTEM IN ITALIAN

(i) The perfect subjunctive

This is formed by using the present subjunctive of **avere** or **essere** with the past participle of the verb.

parlare   **abbia parlato,** etc.   **capire**   **abbia capito,** etc.
accorgersi **mi sia accorto,** etc.

(ii) The pluperfect subjunctive

The pluperfect subjunctive is formed by using the imperfect subjunctive of **avere** or **essere** with the past participle of the verb.

parlare   **avessi parlato,** etc.
capire   **avessi capito,** etc.
accorgersi **mi fossi accorto,** etc.

8d   Use of the Subjunctive

The subjunctive is used:

• as a polite imperative [>7c].

Mi dia un piatto per favore.	(Would you) give me a plate, please.
Venga pure!	Please do come!

• in many subordinate clauses introduced by **che.**

(i) to express commands, following the verbs:

dire   tell
ordinare   order
proibire   forbid, prohibit

Ha ordinato che io venga con te.	He has ordered that I come with you.
Digli che ci accompagni al teatro.	Tell him to accompany us to the theater.
Proibisco che tu esca stasera.	I forbid you to go out tonight.

(ii) to express preference, desire to, or insistence, following the verbs:

aspettare   await   **attendere**   await
aspettarsi expect   **augurarsi**   wish, hope

desiderare	wish, want		**piacere**	like
impedire	prevent		**preferire**	prefer
insistere	insist		**sperare**	hope
lasciare	let		**suggerire**	suggest
permettere	permit, allow		**volere**	want, wish, like

Ha voluto che si parlasse inglese qui.	He wanted English to be spoken here.
Preferisce che tu rimanga in Italia.	He prefers that you stay in Italy.
Non permetto che tu esca stasera!	I won't allow you to go out tonight!
Impedì che visitassero la nonna.	He prevented them from visiting grandmother.

(iii) *to express opinion, doubt, ignorance, or denial, following the verbs:*

credere	believe		**(non) dire**	(not) say
dubitare	doubt		**negare**	deny
pensare	think		**(non) sapere**	(not) know
ritenere	consider, think			

Penso che Domenico abbia ragione.	I think Domenico is right.
Dubito che Gianni venga stasera.	I doubt that Gianni is coming this evening.
Non dico che Antonia abbia ragione.	I am not saying that Antonia is right.
Non so se abbia molto denaro.	I don't know if he has much money.
Nego che Gianni abbia rotto quella finestra.	I deny that Gianni broke that window.
Non dico che non sia vero.	I am not saying it isn't true.

Note: However, if there is no doubt at all, the indicative may be used with verbs expressing positive opinion.

Credo che Luigi potrà aiutarci.	I believe/am sure that Luigi will be able to help us.

(iv) *to express emotions, following the verbs:*

avere paura	be afraid	**essere sconvolto**	be upset
dispiacere	be sorry, regret	**essere sorpreso**	be surprised
essere arrabbiato	be angry	**essere spiacente**	be sorry
essere contento	be happy, pleased	**essere triste**	be sad
essere deluso	be disappointed	**meravigliarsi**	be amazed
essere felice	be happy, pleased	**rincrescere**	regret
essere infelice	be unhappy, displeased	**stupirsi**	be surprised
essere scontento	be unhappy, displeased	**temere**	fear

Mi dispiace che Giovanni non ci accompagni.	I am sorry that Giovanni is not coming with us.
Sono contenta che tu sia venuta ad incontrarmi.	I am pleased that you have come to meet me.
Mi meraviglio che tu sia riuscito ad aprirla.	I am amazed that you managed to open it.

If the subject is the same in both halves of the sentence, an infinitive construction is preferred.

Sono contenta di incontrarti.	I am pleased to meet you.

• after many impersonal verbs followed by **che.**

accade	it happens	**è peggio**	it is worse
basta	it is enough	**è possibile**	it is possible
bisogna	it is necessary	**è preferibile**	it is preferable
capita	it happens	**è probabile**	it is probable
conviene	it is better / advisable	**è strano**	it is strange
è bene	it is a good thing	**è un peccato**	it is a pity
è difficile	it is difficult	**è utile**	it is useful
è facile	it is easy	**importa**	it matters / is important
è impossibile	it is impossible		
è improbabile	it is unlikely	**occorre**	it is necessary
è inutile	it is useless / pointless	**pare**	it seems / appears
è male	it is a bad thing	**può darsi**	it may be
è meglio	it is better	**sembra**	it seems
è naturale	it is natural	**succede**	it happens
è necessario	it is necessary	**vale la pena**	it is worth it

Note that the verbs are given here in the present tense, but they may well be found in other tenses.

Pare che abbia ragione.	It appears that he/she is right (that you are right).
Bisogna che vadano subito a vedere Giuliana.	They must go to see Giuliana immediately.
È meglio che esca adesso.	It's better that he/she go out (that you go out) now.
È un peccato che tu non sia qui.	It's a pity that you not be here.
Sembrava che avesse già visto quel film.	It seemed that he/she had already seen that film (that you had already seen that film).
Non è possibile che Simone sia uscito a quest'ora.	It is not possible that Simone has gone out at this time.

Note that many of these impersonal expressions may be followed by the infinitive in Italian, as in English.

È meglio uscire adesso.	It is better to go out now.

• after certain conjunctions.

a condizione che	on condition that	**per paura che (non)**	for fear that
a meno che (non)	unless		
a patto che	on condition that	**perché**	so that, in order that
affinché	so that		
benché	although, even though, even if	**prima che**	before
		purché	provided that, on condition that
caso mai	should, in the event that		
		qualora	in case, if
come se	as if	**quand'anche**	even if
finché non	until	**salvo che (non)**	unless, provided that
in maniera che	so that		
in / di modo che	so that	**se, quando,**	if
malgrado che	in spite of the fact that	**sebbene**	although, even though, even if
nel caso che	in case	**senza che**	without
nonostante che	in spite of the fact that	**seppure**	even though, even if
		supponendo che	supposing that

Telefonagli prima che esca.	Call him before he goes out.
Benché piova, voglio partire.	Although it is raining, I want to leave.
Caso mai faccia brutto tempo domani, possiamo andare al cinema.	Should the weather be bad tomorrow, we can go to the movies / cinema.
Gli ho dato i soldi perché andasse al cinema.	I gave him some money so that he could go to the movies / cinema.

Note: • **Perché** takes the indicative when it means 'because.' **In modo che** and **in maniera che** also take the indicative when they mean 'with the result that' (i.e., when the action has clearly happened).

• **Se** often takes the indicative in the present and future tenses, and when it means 'whether;' but it can *never* be followed by a conditional. When the main verb is in the present or perfect conditional, the verb of the **se** conditional clause must be in the imperfect or the pluperfect subjunctive, according to the sense.

Oggi la scuola è chiusa perché è festa nazionale.	Today school is closed because it's a national holiday.
Se mi avesse parlato, avrei detto di sì.	If he had spoken to me, I would have said yes.
Se andasse a trovare la nonna, sarei molto contenta.	If she were to go and see her grandmother, I would be very pleased.

• in indirect statements expressing doubt and in some indirect questions, although it is not always obligatory.

Si dice che il professore sia un uomo alto e bello.	They say that the teacher is a tall, handsome man.
Mi hanno chiesto come fossi venuto in Italia.	They asked me how I had come to Italy.
Il capitano domandò dove andassero i ragazzi.	The captain asked where the boys were going.
Mi domando perché Anna abbia parlato così.	I wonder why Anna spoke like that.
Chi ha chiesto se Antonella potesse venire alla festa?	Who asked whether Antonella could come to the party?

• after indefinite pronouns and adjectives.

chiunque	whoever	**qualunque**	whichever
comunque	however, no matter how	**qualunque cosa**	whatever
dovunque	wherever	**qualsiasi cosa**	whatever

Chiunque venga con me, deve essere disposto a guidare.	Whoever comes with me must be willing to drive.
Qualunque decisione prenda, fammela sapere domani.	Whichever decision you make, let me know tomorrow.
Qualunque cosa lo faccia, trovo sempre difficoltà.	Whatever I do, I always find difficulties.

• after a negative, a comparative, or a superlative in the previous clause.

Non c'è nessuno qui che sappia parlare tedesco.	There is no one here who knows how to speak German.
Questa donna è più intelligente che non sembri.	This woman is more intelligent than she appears.
Giovanni è l'uomo più pigro che io abbia mai conosciuto.	Giovanni is the laziest man I have ever known.
Anna è l'unica persona che sia in grado di scrivere una tale lettera.	Anna is the only person capable of writing such a letter.

Note that, in the second example, the word **non** must be inserted before the verb. Note also that the words **primo, ultimo, unico,** and **solo** are treated as superlatives for this purpose.

• in certain exclamations.

Fossi pazzo!	If I were crazy!
Volesse il cielo!	God willing! ('Would to heaven!')
Fosse possibile!	If only it were possible!

8e *The Sequence of Tenses with the Subjunctive*

The most usual combinations of tenses are as follows:

THE VERB SYSTEM IN ITALIAN

(i)   *Main clause in the present, future, or present perfect indicative* —

subordinate clause in the present or perfect subjunctive.

Spero che tu abbia ragione.	I hope you are right.
Mi ha chiesto come abbiano viaggiato.	He asked me how they had traveled.

(ii)   *Main clause in the imperfect, present perfect, past definite, pluperfect indicative; in the present conditional, conditional perfect* —

subordinate clause in the imperfect or pluperfect subjunctive.

Pensavano che arrivasse alle otto.	They thought he was arriving at eight.
Bisognerebbe che lo studente cambiasse corso.	It would be necessary for the student to change course.
Impedì che venissero domani.	He stopped them from coming tomorrow.
Sperava che fossero partiti l'altro ieri.	He hoped that they had left the day before yesterday.

[For a more detailed explanation ➤ Berlitz *Italian Grammar Handbook.*]

⑨ Things Done to You: The Passive

9a The True Passive

The passive is formed when the object of the sentence becomes the subject.

L'uomo ha costruito la casa.	The man built the house.
La casa è stata costruita dall' uomo.	The house was built by the man.

The object of the first sentence 'the house' has become the subject of the second.

(i) The passive with **essere**

In Italian the passive is usually formed by using an appropriate tense of the verb **essere** and the past participle of the verb. Here are the first person singular forms of the verb **lodare** 'praise' in the passive [▷ **lodare 1** for full passive forms].

PRESENT INDICATIVE sono lodato/a	**PRESENT PERFECT** sono stato/a lodato/a
IMPERFECT ero lodato/a	**PLUPERFECT** ero stato/a lodato/a
PAST DEFINITE fui lodato/a	**PAST ANTERIOR** fui stato/a lodato/a
FUTURE sarò lodato/a	**FUTURE PERFECT** sarò stato/a lodato/a
PRESENT CONDITIONAL sarei lodato/a	**CONDITIONAL PERFECT** sarei stato/a lodato/a
PRESENT SUBJUNCTIVE sia lodato/a	**PERFECT SUBJUNCTIVE** sia stato/a lodato/a
IMPERFECT SUBJUNCTIVE fossi lodato/a	**PLUPERFECT SUBJUNCTIVE** fossi stato/a lodato/a

THE VERB SYSTEM IN ITALIAN

Note: The past participle always agrees in number and gender with the subject of the sentence, as in the following examples:

Il pranzo è servito.	Lunch is (being) served.
La cena è servita.	Supper is (being) served.
La finestra fu rotta ieri.	The window was broken yesterday.
I ladri sono stati visti in città.	The thieves have been seen in town.

(ii) The use of **venire**

With verbs of action **venire** very often replaces **essere** as an auxiliary verb.

La porta era chiusa.	The door was closed. (*state*)
La porta venne chiusa.	The door was (had just been) closed. (*action*)

Venire can act as an auxiliary verb in place of **essere** only in simple tenses, not compound ones.

Io vengo lodato / io sono lodato.	I am praised.
But	
Sono stato lodato.	I have been praised.

Note: Since **sono stato lodato** is a compound tense, **venire** cannot be used.

(iii) The use of **andare**

With verbs of losing, wasting, destroying, **andare** can be used to form the passive.

Una buona parola non va mai sprecata.	A good word is never wasted.
Andarono perduti dei documenti importantissimi.	Important documents were lost / went missing.

However, **andare** is more often used to indicate obligation.

| Quella sedia va messa nell'angolo. | That chair should be put in the corner. |
| Costruirò la scuola come va costruita. | I shall build the school as it should be built. |

9b   Alternatives to the Passive

There are several ways of avoiding the passive.

• By using a reflexive verb.

| Come si scrive il tuo nome? | How do you write your name? |

• By using the indefinite pronoun **si**.

| Si dice che sia fuggito. | It is said (They say) that he has fled. |

• By using the third person plural form of the verb.

| Dicono che la bottega sia aperta oggi. | They say that the shop is open today. |

10 Reflexive Verbs

In section 2f you have encountered a general explanation of reflexive verbs. Many verbs can be used both reflexively and as ordinary transitive verbs.

10a Reflexive Pronouns

The full set of reflexive pronouns can be seen in the present tense of this reflexive verb.

lavarsi	'to wash oneself' / 'get washed'
mi lavo	I wash myself
ti lavi	you wash yourself (*informal*)
si lava	he / she washes her- / himself
	you wash yourself (*formal*)
ci laviamo	we wash ourselves
vi lavate	you wash yourselves
si lavano	they wash themselves

Note: The pronouns can be contracted to **m'**, **t'**, **s'**, in front of a vowel, although this is not obligatory.

10b Position of Reflexive Pronouns

Reflexive pronouns obey the same rules as other pronouns:

• they come *before* the verb in all tenses of the indicative and subjunctive.

• they come after the verb with the infinitive; and with the **tu**, **noi**, and **voi** forms of the imperative.

Mi alzo alle sette ogni mattina.	I get up at seven every morning.
Bisogna alzarsi quando entra il maestro.	You need (It is necessary) to stand up when the teacher comes in.
Siediti qui accanto a me!	Sit down here next to me!
Sedetevi, ragazzi!	Sit down, boys!

10c Reflexive Verbs and Ne

Some verbs are not only reflexive, but they also take **ne** — for example:

andarsene 'to go away' / 'leave'

me	ne	vado
te	ne	vai
se	ne	va
ce	ne	andiamo
ve	ne	andate
se	ne	vanno

Note how the **-i** of the reflexive pronoun becomes an **-e** when followed by **ne.**

Verbs with **ne** are very often used colloquially.

scapparsene   slip away   **starsene seduto / a**   sit

Sono stanca, me ne vado adesso!	I am tired, I am going now!
Se ne sta seduta senza aiutare la mamma!	She just sits there without helping mom / mum!

10d   Other Uses of the Reflexive

(i)   The reflexive is often used in Italian when a possessive adjective would be used in English.

Si lavano le mani.	They wash their hands.
Vi asciugate i capelli.	You dry your hair.

(ii)   Plural reflexive verbs can be used to describe actions done to 'each other.'

Si amano tanto.	They love each other so much.
Si scrivono ogni giorno.	They write to each other every day.

(iii)   A number of idiomatic phrases are formed with the reflexive verb and the feminine pronoun **la:**

Quel professore se la prende con tutti.	That teacher argues with everyone.
Ce la godiamo sempre qui alla spiaggia.	We always enjoy (it) here at the beach.

11 Types of Verbs in Italian

11a   Predictability

Within each tense in Italian there are six different forms of the verb, each one corresponding to a particular person, as follows:

first person singular	**io**	I
second person singular	**tu**	you (*informal singular*)
third person singular	**lui**	he
	lei	she
	Lei	you (*formal singular*)
first person plural	**noi**	we
second person plural	**voi**	you (*informal / formal plural*)
third person plural	**loro**	they
	Loro	you (*formal plural*)

Note: 'He,' 'she,' and 'you' (*formal singular*) share the same verb form. **Loro** is rarely found nowadays and is frequently replaced by **voi.**

11b   Regular Verbs

Regular verbs are those verbs for which you can predict any part of any tense from the spelling of the infinitive. Infinitives in Italian end in **-are, -ere,** and **-ire.** Verbs in which some parts cannot be predicted in this way are said to be *irregular.* Many common **-ere** verbs are irregular in Italian, but often only in their past participle and definite past forms. Some verbs also have an irregular, shortened future stem and an irregular present subjunctive / formal imperative form.

11c   Spelling-Change Verbs

Some verbs make spelling changes in certain tenses.

(i)   Verbs ending in **-care** and **-gare** insert an **h** after the **c** and the **g** when these letters are followed by **e** or **i.**

dimenticare	**dimentichi, dimentichiamo, dimenticherò,** etc.
pregare	**preghi, preghiamo, pregherò,** etc.

(ii)   Verbs ending in **-ciare** and **-giare** drop the **i** before another **i** or an **e.**

lasciare	**lasci, lascerò,** etc.
mangiare	**mangi, mangerò,** etc.
viaggiare	**viaggi, viaggerò,** etc.

(iii)   Other verbs in **-iare** that have an unstressed **i** in the first person singular drop the **i** before another **i.**

fischiare	**fischi, fischiamo,** etc.
studiare	**studi, studiamo,** etc.
imbrogliare	**imbrogli, imbrogliamo,** etc.

(iv)   Verbs in **-iare** that have an unstressed **i** in the first person singular keep the **i** before another **i** when it is stressed.

rinviare	**rinvii,** but **rinviamo,** etc.
sciare	**scii,** but **sciamo,** etc.

(v)   Verbs ending in **-scere** insert an **i** before the **u** of the past participle only.

conoscere	**conosciuto,** but **conoscono,** etc.
mescere	**mesciuto,** but **mescono,** etc.
pascere	**pasciuto,** but **pascono,** etc.

(vi)   Some verbs change their stem vowels in certain persons of the present tense, in order to facilitate pronunciation.

sedersi	**mi siedo, ti siedi, si siede,** ci sediamo, vi sedete, **si siedono**
muoversi	mi muovo, ti muovi, si muove, **ci moviamo, vi movete,** si muovono

11d   *Compound Verbs*

Prefixes can be added to any verb as long as it makes sense.

(i)   The following are the most common prefixes:

• **ri-** can be used to indicate repetition, like 're-' in English.

cominciare	begin	ricominciare	begin again
fare	do	rifare	redo
leggere	read	rileggere	reread

• **s-** can sometimes be added to create the opposite meaning.

chiudere	close	**schiudere**	open
coprire	cover	**scoprire**	uncover, discover
gelare	freeze	**sgelare**	thaw

• **mal-** gives the meaning of 'bad,' 'badly,' or 'evil'.

trattare	treat	**maltrattare**	mistreat
intendere	understand	**malintendere**	misunderstand

(ii)　Some common base verbs have a variety of prefixes, which often correspond to similar prefixes in English.

• The verb **porre** 'place,' 'put,' has many compounds.

comporre	compose	**posporre**	postpone
decomporre	decompose	**presupporre**	presuppose
disporre	dispose	**proporre**	propose
imporre	impose	**supporre**	suppose
opporre	oppose		

• The verb **tenere** 'hold' has many compounds that correspond to the English ending '-tain.'

contenere	contain	**ritenere**	retain
detenere	detain	**sostenere**	sustain
mantenere	maintain	**trattenere**	detain

• Similarly, the verb **venire** 'come' has a number of compounds.

avvenire	happen	**provenire**	come from,
convenire	agree, suit		originate from
divenire	become	**sopravvenire**	arrive, happen
intervenire	intervene	**svenire**	faint

(iii)　Finally, there are a number of verbs ending in **-durre.**

condurre	lead, drive	**ridurre**	reduce
dedurre	deduce	**riprodurre**	reproduce
indurre	induce	**sedurre**	seduce
introdurre	introduce	**tradurre**	translate
produrre	produce		

B

MODEL VERBS

Index of Model Verbs

An * before a verb indicates that this verb takes **essere.**

A † before a verb indicates that this verb takes **essere** when intransitive, but **avere** when transitive.

If the verb is usually used impersonally, this is indicated by (*Imp.*)

THE COMPLETE SYSTEM OF TENSES IN ITALIAN

Model Regular Verbs		Number
lodare	praise	1
***entrare**	enter, come in; get in	2

Regular Verbs

parlare	speak	3
vendere	sell	4
dormire	sleep	5
finire	finish	6
***lavarsi**	wash oneself	7

Verbs with Obsolete Infinitives

bere	drink	8
dire	say	9
fare	do	10

Spelling-Change Verbs

dimenticare	forget	11
mangiare	eat	12
fischiare	whistle	13
***sedersi**	sit down	14
muovere	move	15
nuocere	be bad for, harm	16

Irregular Verbs

accendere	turn on, light	17
affiggere	post / put (up), attach; fix	18
affliggere	suffer from, afflict	19
alludere	allude	20
***andare**	go	21
annettere	attach, add, annex	22

ACTIVE VOICE

Example of a verb using **avere** in the compound tenses

PRESENT GERUND	PAST PARTICIPLE
lodando	lodato

PRESENT INDICATIVE	PRESENT PERFECT
lodo	ho lodato
lodi	hai lodato
loda	ha lodato
lodiamo	abbiamo lodato
lodate	avete lodato
lodano	hanno lodato

PRESENT PROGRESSIVE	IMPERFECT PROGRESSIVE
sto lodando	stavo lodando
stai lodando	stavi lodando
sta lodando	stava lodando
stiamo lodando	stavamo lodando
state lodando	stavate lodando
stanno lodando	stavano lodando

IMPERFECT	PAST DEFINITE
lodavo	lodai
lodavi	lodasti
lodava	lodò
lodavamo	lodammo
lodavate	lodaste
lodavano	lodarono

PLUPERFECT	PAST ANTERIOR
avevo lodato	ebbi lodato
avevi lodato	avesti lodato
aveva lodato	ebbe lodato
avevamo lodato	avemmo lodato
avevate lodato	aveste lodato
avevano lodato	ebbero lodato

IMPERATIVE
loda (tu)   lodi (Lei)   lodiamo (noi)   lodate (voi)   lodino (Loro)

FUTURE	**FUTURE PERFECT**
loderò	avrò lodato
loderai	avrai lodato
loderà	avrà lodato
loderemo	avremo lodato
loderete	avrete lodato
loderanno	avranno lodato

PRESENT CONDITIONAL	**CONDITIONAL PERFECT**
loderei	avrei lodato
loderesti	avresti lodato
loderebbe	avrebbe lodato
loderemmo	avremmo lodato
lodereste	avreste lodato
loderebbero	avrebbero lodato

PRESENT SUBJUNCTIVE	**PERFECT SUBJUNCTIVE**
lodi	abbia lodato
lodi	abbia lodato
lodi	abbia lodato
lodiamo	abbiamo lodato
lodiate	abbiate lodato
lodino	abbiano lodato

IMPERFECT SUBJUNCTIVE	**PLUPERFECT SUBJUNCTIVE**
lodassi	avessi lodato
lodassi	avessi lodato
lodasse	avesse lodato
lodassimo	avessimo lodato
lodaste	aveste lodato
lodassero	avessero lodato

PASSIVE VOICE

For notes on other ways of expressing the passive ➤9b The Verb System in Italian.

PRESENT INDICATIVE
sono lodato / a
sei lodato / a
è lodato / a
siamo lodati / e
siete lodati / e
sono lodati / e

PRESENT PERFECT
sono stato / a lodato / a
sei stato / a lodato / a
è stato / a lodato / a
siamo stati / e lodati / e
siete stati / e lodati / e
sono stati / e lodati / e

IMPERFECT
ero lodato / a
eri lodato / a
era lodato / a
eravamo lodati / e
eravate lodati / e
erano lodati / e

PAST DEFINITE
fui lodato / a
fosti lodato / a
fu lodato / a
fummo lodati / e
foste lodati / e
furono lodati / e

PLUPERFECT
ero stato / a lodato / a
eri stato / a lodato / a
era stato / a lodato / a
eravamo stati / e lodati / e
eravate stati / e lodati / e
erano stati / e lodati / e

PAST ANTERIOR
fui stato / a lodato / a
fosti stato / a lodato / a
fu stato / a lodato / a
fummo stati / e lodati / e
foste stati / e lodati / e
furono stati / e lodati / e

Note: ➤The Verb System in Italian for explanations of the tenses. It is important to remember that all forms have the basic part or stem **lod-**, which contains the meaning of the verb. Many tenses are simple tenses, in which endings are added to this stem to form one word; other tenses are compound tenses, in which an auxiliary verb is used in the appropriate tense and form in front of the appropriate gerund or past participle of the verb.

FUTURE

sarò lodato / a
sarai lodato / a
sarà lodato / a
saremo lodati / e
sarete lodati / e
saranno lodati / e

PRESENT CONDITIONAL

sarei lodato / a
saresti lodato / a
sarebbe lodato / a
saremmo lodati / e
sareste lodati / e
sarebbero lodati / e

PRESENT SUBJUNCTIVE

sia lodato / a
sia lodato / a
sia lodato / a
siamo lodati / e
siate lodati / e
siano lodati / e

IMPERFECT SUBJUNCTIVE

fossi lodato / a
fossi lodato / a
fosse lodato / a
fossimo lodati / e
foste lodati / e
fossero lodati / e

FUTURE PERFECT

sarò stato / a lodato / a
sarai stato / a lodato / a
sarà stato / a lodato / a
saremo stati / e lodati / e
sarete stati / e lodati / e
saranno stati / e lodati / e

CONDITIONAL PERFECT

sarei stato / a lodato / a
saresti stato / a lodato / a
sarebbe stato / a lodato / a
saremmo stati / e lodati / e
sareste stati / e lodati / e
sarebbero stati / e lodati / e

PERFECT SUBJUNCTIVE

sia stato / a lodato / a
sia stato / a lodato / a
sia stato / a lodato / a
siamo stati / e lodati / e
siate stati / e lodati / e
siano stati / e lodati / e

PLUPERFECT SUBJUNCTIVE

fossi stato / a lodato / a
fossi stato / a lodato / a
fosse stato / a lodato / a
fossimo stati / e lodati / e
foste stati / e lodati / e
fossero stati / e lodati / e

Remember that in Italian, the subject pronouns (**io, tu,** etc.) are not normally needed because the verb endings which are very clear in both spoken and written forms, tell you who the subject of the verb is. Pronouns are only used for emphasis, contrast, or clarity.

For notes on other ways of expressing the passive ➤9b The Verb System in Italian.

2 entrare   enter, come in; get in

Example of a verb using **essere** in the compound tenses

PRESENT GERUND	PAST PARTICIPLE
entrando	entrato

PRESENT INDICATIVE
entro
entri
entra
entriamo
entrate
entrano

PRESENT PERFECT
sono entrato / a
sei entrato / a
è entrato / a
siamo entrati / e
siete entrati / e
sono entrati / e

PRESENT PROGRESSIVE
sto entrando
stai entrando
sta entrando
stiamo entrando
state entrando
stanno entrando

IMPERFECT PROGRESSIVE
stavo entrando
stavi entrando
stava entrando
stavamo entrando
stavate entrando
stavano entrando

IMPERFECT
entravo
entravi
entrava
entravamo
entravate
entravano

PAST DEFINITE
entrai
entrasti
entrò
entrammo
entraste
entrarono

PLUPERFECT
ero entrato / a
eri entrato / a
era entrato / a
eravamo entrati / e
eravate entrati / e
erano entrati / e

PAST ANTERIOR
fui entrato / a
fosti entrato / a
fu entrato / a
fummo entrati / e
foste entrati / e
furono entrati / e

Note: 1) Verbs taking **essere** are marked with an * in all the notes to the model verb pages and in the Verb Index.
2) All compound tenses using **essere** require gender agreements of the past participle — this may be masculine singular (**-o**), feminine singular (**-a**), feminine plural (**-e**), or masculine plural (**-i**).

MODEL REGULAR VERBS   entrare 2

IMPERATIVE
entra (tu)   entri (Lei)   entriamo (noi)   entrate (voi)   entrino (Loro)

FUTURE
entrerò
entrerai
entrerà
entreremo
entrerete
entreranno

FUTURE PERFECT
sarò entrato / a
sarai entrato / a
sarà entrato / a
saremo entrati / e
sarete entrati / e
saranno entrati / e

PRESENT CONDITIONAL
entrerei
entreresti
entrerebbe
entreremmo
entrereste
entrerebbero

CONDITIONAL PERFECT
sarei entrato / a
saresti entrato / a
sarebbe entrato / a
saremmo entrati / e
sareste entrati / e
sarebbero entrati / e

PRESENT SUBJUNCTIVE
entri
entri
entri
entriamo
entriate
entrino

PERFECT SUBJUNCTIVE
sia entrato / a
sia entrato / a
sia entrato / a
siamo entrati / e
siate entrati / e
siano entrati / e

IMPERFECT SUBJUNCTIVE
entrassi
entrassi
entrasse
entrassimo
entraste
entrassero

PLUPERFECT SUBJUNCTIVE
fossi entrato / a
fossi entrato / a
fosse entrato / a
fossimo entrati / e
foste entrati / e
fossero entrati / e

Dubito che Gianna sia ancora entrata.
I doubt that Gianna *has come in* yet.

Le ragazze sono entrate in macchina.
The girls *got into* the car.

First conjugation, regular -**are** verb

PRESENT GERUND	PAST PARTICIPLE
parlando	parlato

PRESENT INDICATIVE	PRESENT PERFECT
parlo	ho parlato
parli	hai parlato
parla	ha parlato
parliamo	abbiamo parlato
parlate	avete parlato
parlano	hanno parlato

PRESENT PROGRESSIVE	IMPERFECT PROGRESSIVE
sto parlando	stavo parlando

IMPERFECT	PAST DEFINITE
parlavo	parlai
parlavi	parlasti
parlava	parlò
parlavamo	parlammo
parlavate	parlaste
parlavano	parlarono

Similar verbs

accompagnare	accompany	**guardare**	look, watch
aiutare	help	**lavare**	wash
*****arrivare**	arrive	**lavorare**	work
chiamare	call	**portare**	carry; wear
*****entrare**	enter	**trovare**	find

Note: The regular -**are** verb conjugation is very large. As most regular verbs belong to this conjugation, only a small selection of the most useful verbs of the group are given above. In the Verb Index the main meanings of each verb are given. Several can also be found in the reflexive form, e.g., **lavare** 'to wash,' **lavarsi** 'to get washed.'

The only -**are** verbs that are irregular are **andare, dare, fare, stare**. These are dealt with in the Irregular Verbs section.

IMPERATIVE
parla (tu)   parli (Lei)   parliamo (noi)   parlate (voi)   parlino (Loro)

PLUPERFECT avevo parlato	**PAST ANTERIOR** ebbi parlato
FUTURE parlerò	**FUTURE PERFECT** avrò parlato
PRESENT CONDITIONAL parlerei	**CONDITIONAL PERFECT** avrei parlato
PRESENT SUBJUNCTIVE parli	**PERFECT SUBJUNCTIVE** abbia parlato
IMPERFECT SUBJUNCTIVE parlassi	**PLUPERFECT SUBJUNCTIVE** avessi parlato

— **Con chi stai parlando?**

— Whom *are you speaking* with?

— **Stavo parlando con Gianni. Adesso sto parlando con Antonia.**

— *I was speaking* with Gianni. Now *I am speaking* with Antonia.

— **Hai parlato con Giuseppe?**

— *Have you spoken* with Giuseppe?

— **No, ma gli parlerò domani.**

— No, but *I'll speak* with him tomorrow.

— **Dubito che Giuseppe abbia parlato con tuo fratello.**

— I doubt that Giuseppe *has spoken* with your brother.

— **Guarda, porta una valigia molto pesante.**

— Look, *he is carrying* a very heavy suitcase.

— **Lo chiamerò ... Ti possiamo aiutare?**

— *I'll call* him. . . . Can we *help* you?

— **Sì, grazie, mi accompagnerete a casa?**

— Yes, please, *will you accompany* me home?

Second conjugation, regular **-ere** verb

PRESENT GERUND	**PAST PARTICIPLE**
vendendo	venduto

PRESENT INDICATIVE	**PRESENT PERFECT**
vendo	ho venduto
vendi	hai venduto
vende	ha venduto
vendiamo	abbiamo venduto
vendete	avete venduto
vendono	hanno venduto

PRESENT PROGRESSIVE	**IMPERFECT PROGRESSIVE**
sto vendendo	stavo vendendo

IMPERFECT	**PAST DEFINITE**
vendevo	vendei / vendetti
vendevi	vendesti
vendeva	vendé / vendette
vendevamo	vendemmo
vendevate	vendeste
vendevano	venderono / vendettero

Similar verbs

The following **-ere** verbs are regular and follow the pattern of **vendere**.

battere	beat	**ripetere**	repeat
credere	believe	**temere**	fear
ricevere	receive		

Note: Many verbs of the **-ere** conjugation are either irregular, often in the past participle and past definite forms, or subject to spelling variations. The three verbs **bere, dire, fare,** which are given in full later [➤8, 9, 10], also belong to this conjugation.

IMPERATIVE
vendi (tu)   venda (Lei)   vendiamo (noi)   vendete (voi)   vendano (Loro)

PLUPERFECT	**PAST ANTERIOR**
avevo venduto	ebbi venduto

FUTURE   **FUTURE PERFECT**
venderò   avrò venduto

PRESENT CONDITIONAL   **CONDITIONAL PERFECT**
venderei   avrei venduto

PRESENT SUBJUNCTIVE   **PERFECT SUBJUNCTIVE**
venda   abbia venduto
venda
venda
vendiamo
vendiate
vendano

IMPERFECT SUBJUNCTIVE **PLUPERFECT SUBJUNCTIVE**
vendessi   avessi venduto
vendessi
vendesse
vendessimo
vendeste
vendessero

In addition, many **-ere** verbs can have both a reflexive and a nonreflexive form.

Note that the following present tense endings are the same as those of the **-are** verbs:

• the first person singular and plural
• the second person singular

5 dormire   sleep

Third conjugation, regular **-ire** verb

PRESENT GERUND	PAST PARTICIPLE
dormendo	dormito

PRESENT INDICATIVE	PRESENT PERFECT
dormo	ho dormito
dormi	hai dormito
dorme	ha dormito
dormiamo	abbiamo dormito
dormite	avete dormito
dormono	hanno dormito

PRESENT PROGRESSIVE	IMPERFECT PROGRESSIVE
sto dormendo	stavo dormendo

IMPERFECT	PAST DEFINITE
dormivo	dormii
dormivi	dormisti
dormiva	dormí
dormivamo	dormimmo
dormivate	dormiste
dormivano	dormirono

PLUPERFECT	PAST ANTERIOR
avevo dormito	ebbi dormito

Similar verbs

Some **-ire** verbs conjugate like **dormire,** others like **finire** [▶6]. A few are irregular, and you will find these in the Verb Index.

The most commonly used verbs like **dormire** are:

bollire	boil	***pentirsi**	repent
consentire	consent	**seguire**	follow
*divertirsi	amuse oneself	**sentire**	feel, hear
†fuggire	flee	**servire**	serve
*partire	leave	**soffrire**	suffer

Note: 1) The gerund and the following present tense endings are the same as those of the **-ere** verbs:

IMPERATIVE
dormi (tu)   dorma (Lei)   dormiamo (noi)   dormite (voi)   dormano (Loro)

FUTURE
dormirò

FUTURE PERFECT
avrò dormito

PRESENT CONDITIONAL
dormirei

CONDITIONAL PERFECT
avrei dormito

PRESENT SUBJUNCTIVE
dorma
dorma
dorma
dormiamo
dormiate
dormano

PERFECT SUBJUNCTIVE
abbia dormito

IMPERFECT SUBJUNCTIVE
dormissi
dormissi
dormisse
dormissimo
dormiste
dormissero

PLUPERFECT SUBJUNCTIVE
avessi dormito

- the first person singular and plural
- the second person singular
- the third person singular and plural

2) The verb **riempire,** 'fill,' follows the **dormire** pattern, with the exception of the gerund **riempiendo** and the present tense, where it adds an **i** before the endings of the first and third person singular and the third person plural: riemp**i**o, riempi, riemp**i**e, riempiamo, riempite, riemp**i**ono.

—**Ti senti meglio oggi?**

— *Do you feel* better today?

—**Si, ho dormito molto bene stanotte.**

— Yes, *I slept* very well last night.

Riempie le tasche di caramelle.

He is filling his pockets with candies.

6 finire   finish

Third conjugation, regular **-ire** verb adding **-isc-**

PRESENT GERUND	**PAST PARTICIPLE**
finendo	finito

PRESENT INDICATIVE	**PRESENT PERFECT**
fin**isc**o	ho finito
fin**isc**i	hai finito
fin**isc**e	ha finito
finiamo	abbiamo finito
finite	avete finito
fin**isc**ono	hanno finito

PRESENT PROGRESSIVE	**IMPERFECT PROGRESSIVE**
sto finendo	stavo finendo

IMPERFECT	**PAST DEFINITE**
finivo	finii
finivi	finisti
finiva	finí
finivamo	finimmo
finivate	finisti
finivano	finirono

Similar verbs

Some **-ire** verbs insert **-isc-** between the stem and the ending in the singular and in the third person plural of the present indicative and of the present subjunctive. These are indicated in the Verb Index by 6.

Some **-ire** verbs can follow the pattern of either **dormire** or **finire**. The most common are:

applaudire	applaud	**preferire**	prefer
assorbire	absorb	**smentire**	deny
capire	understand; realize	**spedire**	send, dispatch
inghiottire	swallow	**suggerire**	suggest
mentire	lie	**tossire**	cough
nutrire	nourish		

finisci (tu)   finisca (Lei)   finiamo (noi)   finite (voi)   finiscano (Loro)

PLUPERFECT avevo finito	**PAST ANTERIOR** ebbi finito
FUTURE finirò	**FUTURE PERFECT** avrò finito
PRESENT CONDITIONAL finirei	**CONDITIONAL PERFECT** avrei finito
PRESENT SUBJUNCTIVE finisca finisca finisca finiamo finiate finiscano	**PERFECT SUBJUNCTIVE** abbia finito
IMPERFECT SUBJUNCTIVE finissi finissi finisse finissimo finiste finissero	**PLUPERFECT SUBJUNCTIVE** avessi finito

Finisco i compiti e usciamo.	*I finish* my homework, and we go out.
—Capisci quando parla il tuo corrispondente?	—*Do you understand* your pen pal when he speaks?
—Sì, ma preferisco quando mi spedisce una lettera!	—Yes, but *I prefer* it when *he sends* me a letter!
—Il mio corrispondente ha suggerito un buon dizionario.	—My pen pal *has suggested* a good dictionary.
—Preferirei un buon traduttore. Sarebbe meno lavoro per me!	—*I would prefer* a good translator. It would be less work for me.

Reflexive, regular **-are** verb

PRESENT GERUND	PAST PARTICIPLE
lavandosi	lavato

PRESENT INDICATIVE	PRESENT PERFECT
mi lavo	mi sono lavato / a
ti lavi	ti sei lavato / a
si lava	si è lavato / a
ci laviamo	ci siamo lavati / e
vi lavate	vi siete lavati / e
si lavano	si sono lavati / e

PRESENT PROGRESSIVE	IMPERFECT PROGRESSIVE
mi sto lavando	mi stavo lavando

IMPERFECT	PAST DEFINITE
mi lavavo	mi lavai

Note: Reflexive verbs can be either **-arsi, -ersi,** or **-irsi** verbs. As such, they follow the conjugation of the corresponding nonreflexive verbs — i.e., **-are, -ere,** or **-ire** verbs — whether regular or irregular.

In all cases the pronouns **mi, ti, si, ci, vi, si,** will be used. In front of a vowel these can be contracted to **m', t', s', c', v', s'.** Before another pronoun they change to: **me, te, se, ce, ve, se.**

These pronouns normally precede the verb. However, they follow the verb in the following cases:

- in the **tu, noi,** and **voi** imperative forms
- with the past participle
- with the infinitive
- with the gerund

N.B. All reflexive verbs use **essere** in their compound tenses.

IMPERATIVE
lavati (tu) si lavi (Lei) laviamoci (noi) lavatevi (voi) si lavino (Loro)

PLUPERFECT mi ero lavato / a	**PAST ANTERIOR** mi fui lavato / a
FUTURE mi laverò	**FUTURE PERFECT** mi sarò lavato / a
PRESENT CONDITIONAL mi laverei	**CONDITIONAL PERFECT** mi sarei lavato / a
PRESENT SUBJUNCTIVE mi lavi	**PERFECT SUBJUNCTIVE** mi sia lavato / a
IMPERFECT SUBJUNCTIVE mi lavassi	**PLUPERFECT SUBJUNCTIVE** mi fossi lavato / a

Similar verbs

There are many reflexive verbs. Only some of the most common are listed here:

*abbronzarsi	tan	*interessarsi a / di	take an interest in
*abituarsi	get used to	*perdersi	get lost
*accomodarsi	come in; sit down	*pettinarsi	comb one's hair
*alzarsi	get up, stand up	*preoccuparsi	worry
*arrabbiarsi	get angry	*sbrigarsi	hurry up
*avvicinarsi a	approach	*scusarsi	apologize
*chiamarsi	be called	*sentirsi	feel
*divertirsi	enjoy oneself	*svegliarsi	wake up
*fermarsi	stop	*vergognarsi	be ashamed
*incontrarsi	meet	*vestirsi	get dressed

—Svegliati, Paolo, sono già le sette! — *Wake up,* Paolo, it's seven o'clock already.

—Ma, mamma, non voglio alzarmi! —But mom / mum, I don't want *to get up.*

—Vergognati, lavati e vestiti subito! — *You should be ashamed — wash up* and *get dressed* immediately!

—Mi alzerò alle sette e mezzo. — *I'll get up* at seven-thirty.

8 bere   drink

Obsolete infinitive **bevere**

PRESENT GERUND	PAST PARTICIPLE
bevendo	bevuto

IMPERATIVE
bevi (tu)   beva (Lei)   beviamo (noi)   bevete (voi)   bevano (Loro)

PRESENT INDICATIVE	PRESENT PERFECT
bevo	ho bevuto

PRESENT PROGRESSIVE	IMPERFECT PROGRESSIVE
sto bevendo	stavo bevendo

IMPERFECT
bevevo

PAST DEFINITE
bevvi / bevetti / bevei
bevesti
bevve
bevemmo
beveste
bevvero

PLUPERFECT	PAST ANTERIOR
avevo bevuto	ebbi bevuto

FUTURE	FUTURE PERFECT
berrò	avrò bevuto

PRESENT CONDITIONAL	CONDITIONAL PERFECT
berrei	avrei bevuto

PRESENT SUBJUNCTIVE	PERFECT SUBJUNCTIVE
beva	abbia bevuto

IMPERFECT SUBJUNCTIVE	PLUPERFECT SUBJUNCTIVE
bevessi	avessi bevuto

Note: ➤10 **fare** for notes on verbs with obsolete infinitives.

Obsolete infinitive **dicere**

PRESENT GERUND	PAST PARTICIPLE
dicendo	**detto**

IMPERATIVE
di' (tu)   dica (Lei)   diciamo (noi)   **dite** (voi)   dicano (Loro)

PRESENT INDICATIVE	PRESENT PERFECT
dico	ho detto
dici	
dice	
diciamo	
dite	
dicono	

PRESENT PROGRESSIVE	IMPERFECT PROGRESSIVE
sto dicendo	stavo dicendo

IMPERFECT	PAST DEFINITE
dicevo	**dissi**
	dicesti
	disse
	dicemmo
	diceste
	dissero

PLUPERFECT	PAST ANTERIOR
avevo detto	ebbi detto

FUTURE	FUTURE PERFECT
dirò	avrò detto

PRESENT CONDITIONAL	CONDITIONAL PERFECT
direi	avrei detto

PRESENT SUBJUNCTIVE	PERFECT SUBJUNCTIVE
dica	abbia detto

IMPERFECT SUBJUNCTIVE	PLUPERFECT SUBJUNCTIVE
dicessi	avessi detto

10 fare   do

Obsolete infinitive **facere**

PRESENT GERUND	PAST PARTICIPLE
facendo	**fatto**

PRESENT INDICATIVE	PRESENT PERFECT
faccio	ho fatto
fai	
fa	
facciamo	
fate	
fanno	

PRESENT PROGRESSIVE	IMPERFECT PROGRESSIVE
sto facendo	stavo facendo

IMPERFECT	PAST DEFINITE
facevo	**feci**
	facesti
	fece
	facemmo
	faceste
	fecero

Similar verbs

contraffare	counterfeit
disfare	undo; unpack
soddisfare	satisfy

Note: The three verbs with obsolete infinitives (**bere** 8, **dire** 9, and **fare** 10) are exceptions. As can be seen above, sometimes the stem returns to the obsolete infinitive; other times it doesn't, thus being shorter.

— **Dimmi, cosa hai fatto ieri sera?**	— Tell me, what *did you do* last night?
— **Ho detto a Stefano di venire a trovarmi.**	— *I told* Stefano to come and see me.
— **E cosa avete fatto?**	— And what *did you do*?
— **Abbiamo bevuto una birra e abbiamo mangiato una pizza.**	— *We drank* a beer and ate a pizza.

IMPERATIVE
fa (tu)   faccia (Lei)   facciamo (noi)   **fate** (voi)   facciano (Loro)

PLUPERFECT avevo fatto	**PAST ANTERIOR** ebbi fatto
FUTURE **farò**	**FUTURE PERFECT** avrò fatto
PRESENT CONDITIONAL **farei**	**CONDITIONAL PERFECT** avrei fatto
PRESENT SUBJUNCTIVE **faccia** **faccia** **faccia** **facciamo** **facciate** **facciano**	**PERFECT SUBJUNCTIVE** abbia fatto
IMPERFECT SUBJUNCTIVE facessi	**PLUPERFECT SUBJUNCTIVE** avessi fatto

To say you are having or getting something done, you use **fare** immediately followed by the infinitive. Note the use of **fare** in the following examples:

Ho fatto riparare la macchina.	*I have had* the car repaired.
Hai fatto tradurre quella lettera?	*Have you had* that letter translated?
Gianni mi ha fatto aspettare un'ora!	Gianni *made* me wait one hour.
Fammi vedere!	*Let me* see!
Le faccio entrare?	*Shall I let* them in?

Verbs ending in **-care / -gare**

PRESENT GERUND	PAST PARTICIPLE
dimenticando	dimenticato

PRESENT INDICATIVE	PRESENT PERFECT
dimentico	ho dimenticato
dimenti**chi**	
dimentica	
dimenti**chiamo**	
dimenticate	
dimenticano	

PRESENT PROGRESSIVE	IMPERFECT PROGRESSIVE
sto dimenticando	stavo dimenticando

IMPERFECT	PAST DEFINITE
dimenticavo	dimenticai

Similar verbs

cercare	search, look for	**pagare**	pay
leccare	lick	**pregare**	pray

Note: Verbs ending in **-care** or **-gare** insert an **h** after the **c** and the **g** when these letters are followed by **e** or **i.** In all other respects these verbs are regular.

IMPERATIVE

dimentica (tu)   dimenti**chi** (Lei)   dimenti**chiamo** (noi)
dimenticate (voi) dimenti**chino** (Loro)

PLUPERFECT
avevo dimenticato

PAST ANTERIOR
ebbi dimenticato

FUTURE
dimenti**cherò**

FUTURE PERFECT
avrò dimenticato

PRESENT CONDITIONAL
dimenti**cherei**

CONDITIONAL PERFECT
avrei dimenticato

PRESENT SUBJUNCTIVE
dimenti**chi**

PERFECT SUBJUNCTIVE
abbia dimenticato

IMPERFECT SUBJUNCTIVE
dimenticassi

PLUPERFECT SUBJUNCTIVE
avessi dimenticato

Ho dimenticato dove ho messo la penna.

I have forgotten where I put my pen.

Ho cercato dappertutto.

I have searched everywhere.

Chi mi pagherà una nuova se l'ho persa?

Who *will pay* for a new one for me if I lost it?

Adesso pregherò.

Now *I shall pray.*

12 mangiare
eat

Verbs ending in **-ciare / -giare**

PRESENT GERUND	**PAST PARTICIPLE**
mangiando	mangiato

PRESENT INDICATIVE	**PRESENT PERFECT**
mangio	ho mangiato
mangi	
mangia	
mang**iamo**	
mangiate	
mangiano	

PRESENT PROGRESSIVE	**IMPERFECT PROGRESSIVE**
sto mangiando	stavo mangiando

IMPERFECT	**PAST DEFINITE**
mangiavo	mangiai

Similar verbs

cominciare	begin	**pronunciare**	pronounce
lasciare	leave; allow	**viaggiare**	travel

Note: Verbs ending in **-ciare** or **-giare** drop the **i** before another **i** or before an **e**.

IMPERATIVE
mangia (tu)   mangi (Lei)   mangiamo (noi)   mangiate (voi)   mangino (Loro)

PLUPERFECT
avevo mangiato

PAST ANTERIOR
ebbi mangiato

FUTURE
mangerò

FUTURE PERFECT
avrò mangiato

PRESENT CONDITIONAL
mangerei

CONDITIONAL PERFECT
avrei mangiato

PRESENT SUBJUNCTIVE
mangi

PERFECT SUBJUNCTIVE
abbia mangiato

IMPERFECT SUBJUNCTIVE
mangiassi

PLUPERFECT SUBJUNCTIVE
avessi mangiato

—Viaggi spesso in Italia?

—Sì, so che ci mangerò molto bene.

—Lasci i figli a casa?

—No, viaggiamo tutti insieme.

—*Do you travel* to Italy often?

—Yes, I know that *I will eat* very well there.

—*Do you leave* your children at home?

—No, *we* all *travel* together.

13 fischiare — whistle

Verbs ending in **-iare**

PRESENT GERUND	PAST PARTICIPLE
fischiando	fischiato

PRESENT INDICATIVE	PRESENT PERFECT
fischio	ho fischiato
fisch**i**	
fischia	
fisch**iamo**	
fischiate	
fischiano	

PRESENT PROGRESSIVE	IMPERFECT PROGRESSIVE
sto fischiando	stavo fischiando

IMPERFECT	PAST DEFINITE
fischiavo	fischiai

Similar verb

pigliare   take, catch

Note: Verbs in **-iare** drop the **i** before another **i**.

IMPERATIVE
fischia (tu)   fischi (Lei)   fischiamo (noi)   fischiate (voi)   fischino (Loro)

PLUPERFECT	**PAST ANTERIOR**
avevo fischiato	ebbi fischiato

FUTURE	**FUTURE PERFECT**
fischierò	avrò fischiato

PRESENT CONDITIONAL	**CONDITIONAL PERFECT**
fischierei	avrei fischiato

PRESENT SUBJUNCTIVE	**PERFECT SUBJUNCTIVE**
fischi	abbia fischiato

IMPERFECT SUBJUNCTIVE	**PLUPERFECT SUBJUNCTIVE**
fischiassi	avessi fischiato

Perché fischi?	Why *are you whistling?*
Chi dorme non piglia pesci. (Proverbio)	The early bird *catches* the worm. (*Lit.* He who sleeps *catches* no fish.) (*Proverb*)

14 sedersi   sit down

Verb ending in **-ersi** with a change of vowel in the present indicative
and present subjunctive

PRESENT GERUND	PAST PARTICIPLE
sedendosi	seduto

PRESENT INDICATIVE	PRESENT PERFECT
mi siedo / seggo	mi sono seduto / a
ti siedi	
si siede	
ci sediamo	
vi sedete	
si siedono / seggono	

PRESENT PROGRESSIVE	IMPERFECT PROGRESSIVE
mi sto sedendo	mi stavo sedendo

IMPERFECT	PAST DEFINITE
mi sedevo	mi sedei / sedetti

Similar verbs

possedere	possess, have
sedere	be seated, sit

Note: The main irregular features of the verb are

   • the present indicative and the present subjunctive tenses

IMPERATIVE
siediti (tu)   **si sieda** (Lei)   sediamoci (noi)   sedetevi (voi)   **si siedano** (Loro)

PLUPERFECT	**PAST ANTERIOR**
mi ero seduto / a	mi fui seduto / a
FUTURE	**FUTURE PERFECT**
mi sederò	mi sarò seduto / a
PRESENT CONDITIONAL	**CONDITIONAL PERFECT**
mi sederei	mi sarei seduto / a
PRESENT SUBJUNCTIVE	**PERFECT SUBJUNCTIVE**
mi sieda / segga	mi sia seduto / a
ti sieda / segga	
si sieda / segga	
ci sediamo	
vi sediate	
si siedano / seggano	
IMPERFECT SUBJUNCTIVE	**PLUPERFECT SUBJUNCTIVE**
mi sedessi	mi fossi seduto / a

—**Siediti qui accanto a me!**

—*Sit* here next to me!

—**No, grazie, non mi siedo, ho fretta.**

—No thank you, *I'll* not *sit down,* I'm in a hurry.

—**Mi dispiace che non ti sieda, ho tanto da dirti.**

—I am sorry that *you won't sit down,* I have a lot to tell you.

Possiede una memoria prodigiosa.

He has an exceptional memory.

Giovanni sedeva in una poltrona vicino alla finestra.

Giovanni *was sitting* in an armchair near the window.

Verb ending in **-ere** with a change of vowel in the present indicative, past definite, present subjunctive, and past participle

PRESENT GERUND	PAST PARTICIPLE
muovendo	**mosso**

PRESENT INDICATIVE	PRESENT PERFECT
muovo	ho mosso
muovi	
muove	
moviamo	
movete	
muovono	

PRESENT PROGRESSIVE	IMPERFECT PROGRESSIVE
sto muovendo	stavo muovendo

IMPERFECT	PAST DEFINITE
muovevo	**mossi**
	movesti
	mosse
	movemmo
	moveste
	mossero

Similar verbs

commuovere	move, affect
promuovere	promote, pass (*exams*)
smuovere	shift; dissuade

Note: A few verbs change their vowels like **muovere**. These are indicated in the Verb Index by 15.

IMPERATIVE
muovi (tu)   muova (Lei)   **moviamo** (noi)   **movete** (voi)   muovano (Loro)

PLUPERFECT	**PAST ANTERIOR**
avevo mosso	ebbi mosso
FUTURE	**FUTURE PERFECT**
muoverò	avrò mosso
PRESENT CONDITIONAL	**CONDITIONAL PERFECT**
muoverei	avrei mosso
PRESENT SUBJUNCTIVE	**PERFECT SUBJUNCTIVE**
muova	abbia mosso
muova	
muova	
moviamo	
moviate	
muovano	
IMPERFECT SUBJUNCTIVE	**PLUPERFECT SUBJUNCTIVE**
muovessi	avessi mosso

Ci moviamo?	*Shall we move?*
Nessuno si è mosso.	No one *moved*.
Mosse la sedia.	*He moved* the chair.
Era veramente commossa.	*She was* really *moved*.
Non fu promosso quest'anno.	*He did* not *pass* this year.
Promosse il nuovo progetto.	*He promoted* the new project.
Se Stefano ha deciso è difficile smuoverlo.	If Stefano has decided, it is difficult to *dissuade him*.

Verb ending in **-ere** with a change of vowel in the present indicative, past definite, and present subjunctive

PRESENT GERUND	PAST PARTICIPLE
nocendo / nuocendo	**nociuto** / nuociuto

PRESENT INDICATIVE	PRESENT PERFECT
noccio / nuoccio	ho nociuto / nuociuto
nuoci	
nuoce	
nociamo / nuociamo	
nocete / nuocete	
nocciono / nuocciono	

PRESENT PROGRESSIVE	IMPERFECT PROGRESSIVE
sto nuocendo	stavo nuocendo

IMPERFECT	PAST DEFINITE
nocevo / nuocevo	**nocqui**
	nocesti / nuocesti
	nocque
	nocemmo
	noceste
	nocquero

IMPERATIVE
nuoci (tu) **noccia** (Lei) **nociamo** (noi) **nocete** (voi) **nocciano** (Loro)

PLUPERFECT avevo nociuto / nuociuto	**PAST ANTERIOR** ebbi nociuto / nuociuto
FUTURE nocerò / nuocerò	**FUTURE PERFECT** avrò nociuto / nuociuto
PRESENT CONDITIONAL nocerei / nuocerei	**CONDITIONAL PERFECT** avrei nociuto / nuociuto
PRESENT SUBJUNCTIVE **noccia** / nuoccia **noccia** **noccia** **nociamo** **nociate** **nocciano**	**PERFECT SUBJUNCTIVE** abbia nociuto / nuociuto
IMPERFECT SUBJUNCTIVE nocessi / nuocessi	**PLUPERFECT SUBJUNCTIVE** avessi nociuto / nuociuto

Dubito che il gelato noccia al bambino.	I doubt that the ice cream *will be bad for* the child.
Non nuoce a nessuno.	He *harms* no one.
Non gli nocerei.	I *would* not *harm* him.
Non nuocerà ripeterglielo.	It *won't hurt* to tell him again.

Verbs ending in **-endere**

PRESENT GERUND	PAST PARTICIPLE
accendendo	**acceso**

PRESENT INDICATIVE	PRESENT PERFECT
accendo	ho acceso

PRESENT PROGRESSIVE	IMPERFECT PROGRESSIVE
sto accendendo	stavo accendendo

IMPERFECT	PAST DEFINITE
accendevo	**accesi**
	accendesti
	accese
	accendemmo
	accendeste
	accesero

Similar verbs

appendere	hang	**offendere**	offend
difendere	defend	**sospendere**	suspend
dipendere	depend on	**spendere**	spend
intendere	intend		

For **prendere, rendere, scendere,** and their compounds ➤Model
Verbs 66, 71, and 79.

Note: The main irregular features of the verb are

   • the past definite tense
   • the past participle

IMPERATIVE

accendi (tu)	accenda (Lei)	accendiamo (noi)
accendete (voi)	accendano (Loro)	

PLUPERFECT
avevo acceso

PAST ANTERIOR
ebbi acceso

FUTURE
accenderò

FUTURE PERFECT
avrò acceso

PRESENT CONDITIONAL
accenderei

CONDITIONAL PERFECT
avrei acceso

PRESENT SUBJUNCTIVE
accenda

PERFECT SUBJUNCTIVE
abbia acceso

IMPERFECT SUBJUNCTIVE
accendessi

PLUPERFECT SUBJUNCTIVE
avessi acceso

Accese la luce.	*He turned on* the light.
Hai acceso il gas?	*Have you turned on* the gas?
Difesero la patria dal nemico.	*They defended* their country from the enemy.
Sa difendere la sua opinione.	He knows how to *hold his own*.
Ho difeso la causa del ragazzo ferito.	*I pleaded* the case for the injured boy.
Non credo che abbiano difeso la città.	I don't think that *they defended* the city.
Ho speso 50 euro oggi.	*I spent* 50 euros today.
Spese 80 euro per quella collana.	*He spent* 80 euros on that necklace.
Sospesi la lampada al soffitto.	*I hung* the lamp from the ceiling.
L'affare fu sospeso a causa della sua partenza.	The business *was adjourned* because of his departure.

PRESENT GERUND affiggendo	PAST PARTICIPLE **affisso**
PRESENT INDICATIVE affiggo	PRESENT PERFECT ho affisso
PRESENT PROGRESSIVE sto affiggendo	IMPERFECT PROGRESSIVE stavo affiggendo
IMPERFECT affiggevo	PAST DEFINITE **affissi** affiggesti **affisse** affiggemmo affiggeste **affissero**

Note: The main irregular features of the verb are

• the past definite tense
• the past participle

IMPERATIVE
affiggi (tu)   affigga (Lei)   affiggiamo (noi)   affiggete (voi)   affiggano (Loro)

PLUPERFECT avevo affisso	**PAST ANTERIOR** ebbi affisso
FUTURE affiggerò	**FUTURE PERFECT** avrò affisso
PRESENT CONDITIONAL affiggerei	**CONDITIONAL PERFECT** avrei affisso
PRESENT SUBJUNCTIVE affigga	**PERFECT SUBJUNCTIVE** abbia affisso
IMPERFECT SUBJUNCTIVE affiggessi	**PLUPERFECT SUBJUNCTIVE** avessi affisso

Affisse lo sguardo sul cane.   *He fixed* his gaze on the dog.

Cosa ha affisso?   What did *he put up?*

— Affiggo il poster qui?   *— Should I put up* the poster here?

— Lo affiggerei laggiù.   *— I would put it up* down there.

PRESENT GERUND	PAST PARTICIPLE
affliggendo	**afflitto**

PRESENT INDICATIVE	PRESENT PERFECT
affliggo	ho afflitto

PRESENT PROGRESSIVE	IMPERFECT PROGRESSIVE
sto affliggendo	stavo affliggendo

IMPERFECT	PAST DEFINITE
affliggevo	**afflissi**
	affliggesti
	afflisse
	affliggemmo
	affliggeste
	afflissero

Similar verbs

friggere	fry	**soffriggere**	fry lightly
infliggere	inflict	**trafiggere**	run through, pierce
sconfiggere	defeat		

Note: The main irregular features of the verb are

- the past definite tense
- the past participle

IMPERATIVE
affliggi (tu)   affliggiamo (noi)   affliggete (voi)   affligga (Lei)   affliggano (Loro)

PLUPERFECT avevo afflitto	**PAST ANTERIOR** ebbi afflitto
FUTURE affliggerò	**FUTURE PERFECT** avrò afflitto
PRESENT CONDITIONAL affliggerei	**CONDITIONAL PERFECT** avrei afflitto
PRESENT SUBJUNCTIVE affligga	**PERFECT SUBJUNCTIVE** abbia afflitto
IMPERFECT SUBJUNCTIVE affliggessi	**PLUPERFECT SUBJUNCTIVE** avessi afflitto

Dubito che sia afflitto dai reumatismi.	I doubt that *he suffers from* rheumatism.
Sono afflitta dalla sinusite.	*I suffer from* sinusitis.
Inflisse una pena al colpevole.	He *inflicted* a penalty on the guilty man.
Gli ha inflitto un colpo.	He *inflicted* a blow on him.
Ho soffritto l'olio nella padella.	I *fried* the oil lightly in the pan.
L'olio frigge nella padella.	The oil *is frying* in the pan.
Il nemico lo trafisse con la spada.	The enemy *pierced* him with a sword.
Le parole le trafissero il cuore.	The words *pierced* her heart.

PRESENT GERUND	PAST PARTICIPLE
alludendo	**alluso**

PRESENT INDICATIVE	PRESENT PERFECT
alludo	ho alluso

PRESENT PROGRESSIVE	IMPERFECT PROGRESSIVE
sto alludendo	stavo alludendo

IMPERFECT	PAST DEFINITE
alludevo	**allusi**
	alludesti
	alluse
	alludemmo
	alludeste
	allusero

Similar verbs

accludere	enclose, attach	**eludere**	elude, evade
concludere	conclude, achieve	**escludere**	exclude
deludere	disappoint, frustrate	**illudere**	deceive, delude, fool
disilludere	disillusion	**includere**	include

Note: The main irregular features of the verb are

- the past definite tense
- the past participle

IMPERATIVE
alludi (tu)   alluda (Lei)   alludiamo (noi)   alludete (voi)   alludano (Loro)

PLUPERFECT avevo alluso	**PAST ANTERIOR** ebbi alluso
FUTURE alluderò	**FUTURE PERFECT** avrò alluso
PRESENT CONDITIONAL alluderei	**CONDITIONAL PERFECT** avrei alluso
PRESENT SUBJUNCTIVE alluda	**PERFECT SUBJUNCTIVE** abbia alluso
IMPERFECT SUBJUNCTIVE alludessi	**PLUPERFECT SUBJUNCTIVE** avessi alluso

Si alludeva a questo durante la discussione ieri.	This *was alluded to* during the discussion yesterday.
Accludiamo un listino prezzi.	We *enclose* a price list.
Inclusi Giovanni nel numero degli invitati.	I *included* Giovanni in the guest list.
Ho escluso alcuni nomi.	I *excluded* some names.
Fu escluso dall'elenco.	He *was excluded* from the list.
Non abbiamo concluso niente oggi.	We haven't *achieved* anything today.
La faccenda fu conclusa.	The matter *was concluded*.

PRESENT GERUND	PAST PARTICIPLE
andando	andato

PRESENT INDICATIVE	PRESENT PERFECT
vado	sono andato / a
vai	sei andato / a
va	è andato / a
andiamo	siamo andati / e
andate	siete andati / e
vanno	sono andati / e

PRESENT PROGRESSIVE	IMPERFECT PROGRESSIVE
sto andando	stavo andando

IMPERFECT	PAST DEFINITE
andavo	andai

Note: **andare** is the only verb of this type. The main irregular features of the verb are

• the present indicative and the present subjunctive tenses
• the future stem

IMPERATIVE
va (tu)   **vada** (Lei)   andiamo (noi)   andate (voi)   **vadano** (Loro)

PLUPERFECT ero andato	**PAST ANTERIOR** fui andato / a
FUTURE **andrò**	**FUTURE PERFECT** sarò andato / a
PRESENT CONDITIONAL **andrei**	**CONDITIONAL PERFECT** sarei andato / a
PRESENT SUBJUNCTIVE **vada** **vada** **vada** andiamo andiate **vadano**	**PERFECT SUBJUNCTIVE** sia andato / a
IMPERFECT SUBJUNCTIVE andassi	**PLUPERFECT SUBJUNCTIVE** fossi andato / a

— **Vado in città, vuoi venire anche tu?**

— *I'm going* to town, do you want to come too?

— **Grazie no, sono già andata ieri.**

— No thanks, *I* already *went* yesterday.

— **Va', andiamoci insieme.**

— *Go on, let's go* together.

— **Certo è un peccato che tu vada da sola.**

— It's certainly a pity that *you are going* alone.

— **Penso che Gianna sia andata oggi in città.**

— I think Gianna *went* to town today.

— **Sarà andata senz'altro al mercato.**

— *She must have gone* to the market for sure.

91

PRESENT GERUND	PAST PARTICIPLE
annettendo	**annesso**

PRESENT INDICATIVE	PRESENT PERFECT
annetto	ho annesso

PRESENT PROGRESSIVE	IMPERFECT PROGRESSIVE
sto annettendo	stavo annettendo

IMPERFECT	PAST DEFINITE
annettevo	annettei / **annessi**
	annettesti
	annetté / **annesse**
	annettemmo
	annetteste
	annetterono / **annessero**

Similar verb

connettere   connect

Note: The main irregular features of the verb are

- the past definite tense
- the past participle

IMPERATIVE
annetti (tu)   annetta (Lei)   annettiamo (noi)   annettete (voi)   annettano (Loro)

PLUPERFECT	**PAST ANTERIOR**
avevo annesso	ebbi annesso
FUTURE	**FUTURE PERFECT**
annetterò	avrò annesso
PRESENT CONDITIONAL	**CONDITIONAL PERFECT**
annetterei	avrei annesso
PRESENT SUBJUNCTIVE	**PERFECT SUBJUNCTIVE**
annetta	abbia annesso
IMPERFECT SUBJUNCTIVE	**PLUPERFECT SUBJUNCTIVE**
annettessi	avessi annesso

Annettiamo un pieghevole.	*We attach* a brochure.
Dubito che sia stato annesso.	I doubt that *it has been annexed.*
Questi fatti sono strettamente connessi.	These facts *are* closely *linked.*
Giovanni connesse i due fili.	Giovanni *connected* the two wires.

PRESENT GERUND	PAST PARTICIPLE
apparendo	**apparso**

PRESENT INDICATIVE
appaio / apparisco
appari / apparisci
appare / apparisce
appariamo
apparite
appaiono / appariscono

PRESENT PERFECT
sono apparso / a

PRESENT PROGRESSIVE
sto apparendo

IMPERFECT PROGRESSIVE
stavo apparendo

IMPERFECT
apparivo

PAST DEFINITE
apparvi / apparii / apparsi
apparisti
apparve / apparí / apparse
apparimmo
appariste
apparvero / apparirono / apparsero

Similar verbs

*comparire	appear
*scomparire	disappear, die; to cut a poor figure
*trasparire	shine through

Note: The verb **apparire** follows a similar pattern to the verb **finire,** but is irregular in the past participle and past definite tenses as well as having optional spelling changes in the present indicative and present subjunctive tenses.

IMPERATIVE

apparisci / **appari** (tu)	apparisca / **appaia** (Lei)	appariamo (noi)
apparite (voi)	appariscano / **appaiano** (Loro)	

PLUPERFECT	**PAST ANTERIOR**
ero apparso/a	fui apparso / a
FUTURE	**FUTURE PERFECT**
apparirò	sarò apparso / a
PRESENT CONDITIONAL	**CONDITIONAL PERFECT**
apparirei	sarei apparso / a
PRESENT SUBJUNCTIVE	**PERFECT SUBJUNCTIVE**
appaia / apparisca	sia apparso / a
appaia / apparisca	
appaia / apparisca	
appariamo	
appariate	
appaiano / appariscano	
IMPERFECT SUBJUNCTIVE	**PLUPERFECT SUBJUNCTIVE**
apparissi	fossi apparso / a

Gli studenti appaiono intelligenti.	The students *appear* to be intelligent.
Dubito che i cantanti appaiano in televisione questa sera.	I doubt that the singers *will appear* on television tonight.
Non credo che appaiano pigri.	I don't think *they appear* lazy.
Apparvero alla riunione.	*They appeared* at the reunion.
Giovanni è scomparso due giorni fa.	Giovanni *disappeared / died* two days ago.
La luce traspariva dalla finestra.	The light *shone* through the window.

PRESENT GERUND	PAST PARTICIPLE
aprendo	**aperto**

PRESENT INDICATIVE	PRESENT PERFECT
apro	ho aperto

PRESENT PROGRESSIVE	IMPERFECT PROGRESSIVE
sto aprendo	stavo aprendo

IMPERFECT	PAST DEFINITE
aprivo	aprii / **apersi**
	apristi
	aprí / **aperse**
	aprimmo
	apriste
	aprirono / **apersero**

Similar verbs

coprire	cover	**scoprire**	discover, uncover
offrire	offer	**soffrire**	suffer
ricoprire	cover, cover again		

Note: **aprire** and the similar verbs follow the pattern of **dormire** except for the irregular past participle and optional past definite forms.

IMPERATIVE
apri (tu)　apra (Lei)　apriamo (noi)　aprite (voi)　aprano (Loro)

PLUPERFECT	**PAST ANTERIOR**
avevo aperto	ebbi aperto

FUTURE	**FUTURE PERFECT**
aprirò	avrò aperto

PRESENT CONDITIONAL	**CONDITIONAL PERFECT**
aprirei	avrei aperto

PRESENT SUBJUNCTIVE	**PERFECT SUBJUNCTIVE**
apra	abbia aperto

IMPERFECT SUBJUNCTIVE	**PLUPERFECT SUBJUNCTIVE**
aprissi	avessi aperto

— Apri la finestra, per piacere.	— *Open* the window please.
— Perché? Ho già aperto la porta.	— Why? *I have* already *opened* the door.
— Copri il bambino, per piacere.	— *Cover* the baby, please.
— Perché? Chi l'ha scoperto?	— Why? Who *uncovered* him?
Hai scoperto l'America!	Aren't you clever! (*Lit. You have discovered* America.)
La neve ricopriva la cima delle montagne.	The snow *covered* the mountain tops.
Quell'uomo ha sofferto tanto.	That man *has suffered* so much.
— Gianni ti ha offerto da mangiare?	— *Did* Gianni *offer* you something to eat?
— Penso che mi abbia offerto da mangiare.	— I think *he offered* me something to eat.
— Beh, io ti offrirei da mangiare e da bere.	— Well, *I would offer* you something to eat and drink.

Verbs with irregular past participles

PRESENT GERUND	PAST PARTICIPLE
assistendo	**assistito**

PRESENT INDICATIVE	PRESENT PERFECT
assisto	ho assistito

PRESENT PROGRESSIVE	IMPERFECT PROGRESSIVE
sto assistendo	stavo assistendo

IMPERFECT	PAST DEFINITE
assistevo	assistetti / **assistei**
	assistesti
	assistette / **assisté**
	assistemmo
	assisteste
	assistettero / **assisterono**

Similar verbs

25A   All verbs ending in **-istere**

*consistere di	consist	**insistere su**	insist (on)
esistere	exist		

Note: The main irregular features of these verbs are in the past participle and the past definite.

25B   In addition to verbs ending in **-istere**, there are a number of other verbs that are irregular only in the past participle. These verbs are marked **25B** in the Verb Index:

devolvere	(devoluto)	transfer
esigere	(esatto)	demand, require
evolvere	(evoluto)	evolve
flettere	(flesso)	bend
redigere	(redatto)	write, compile
riflettere	(riflesso)	reflect
seppellire	(sepolto)	bury [>6 **finire**]
spandere	(spanto)	spread, spill
transigere	(transatto)	compromise

IMPERATIVE
assisti (tu)   assista (Lei)   assistiamo (noi)   assistete (voi)   assistano (Loro)

PLUPERFECT avevo assistito	**PAST ANTERIOR** ebbi assistito
FUTURE assisterò	**FUTURE PERFECT** avrò assistito
PRESENT CONDITIONAL assisterei	**CONDITIONAL PERFECT** avrei assistito
PRESENT SUBJUNCTIVE assista	**PERFECT SUBJUNCTIVE** abbia assistito
IMPERFECT SUBJUNCTIVE assistessi	**PLUPERFECT SUBJUNCTIVE** avessi assistito

Vi assisterò come posso.   *I will help* you as best I can.

Giovanni ha assistito ad una partita di calcio.   Giovanni *attended* a soccer match.

Di che cosa è consistito?   What *did it consist of?*

Insisti perché lei venga!   *Insist* that she come!

Ho insistito sulla necessità di leggere il libro prima di vedere il film.   *I insisted on* the necessity of reading the book before seeing the movie / film.

PRESENT GERUND assumendo	PAST PARTICIPLE **assunto**

PRESENT INDICATIVE assumo	PRESENT PERFECT ho assunto
PRESENT PROGRESSIVE sto assumendo	**IMPERFECT PROGRESSIVE** stavo assumendo
IMPERFECT assumevo	**PAST DEFINITE** **assunsi** assumesti **assunse** assumemmo assumeste **assunsero**

Similar verbs

desumere   infer, deduce; gather
presumere   presume; rely

Note: The main irregular features of the verb are

- the past definite tense
- the past participle

IMPERATIVE
assumi (tu) assuma (Lei) assumiamo (noi) assumete (voi) assumino (Loro)

PLUPERFECT avevo assunto	**PAST ANTERIOR** ebbi assunto
FUTURE assumerò	**FUTURE PERFECT** avrò assunto
PRESENT CONDITIONAL assumerei	**CONDITIONAL PERFECT** avrei assunto
PRESENT SUBJUNCTIVE assuma	**PERFECT SUBJUNCTIVE** abbia assunto
IMPERFECT SUBJUNCTIVE assumessi	**PLUPERFECT SUBJUNCTIVE** avessi assunto

Assunse un'aria da innocente.	*He assumed* an air of innocence.
Ho assunto un impiegato ieri.	*I hired* a clerk yesterday.
Fu assunto al Pontificato.	*He was raised* to the Papacy.
Penso che sia assunto in cielo.	I think that *he was raised* to Heaven.
Da quanto mi dite desumo che siete rientrati tardi ieri sera.	From what you tell me, *I gather* that you came home late last night.
Presumevo che Stefano fosse ricco.	*I presumed* that Stefano was rich.
Presume troppo dalle sue forze.	*He relies* too much on his strength.

PRESENT GERUND	PAST PARTICIPLE
avendo	avuto

PRESENT INDICATIVE	PRESENT PERFECT
ho	ho avuto
hai	
ha	
abbiamo	
avete	
hanno	

PRESENT PROGRESSIVE	IMPERFECT PROGRESSIVE
sto avendo	stavo avendo

IMPERFECT	PAST DEFINITE
avevo	**ebbi**
avevi	avesti
aveva	**ebbe**
avevamo	avemmo
avevate	aveste
avevano	**ebbero**

Note: **avere** is both a full verb unto itself — meaning 'have,' 'own,' 'possess' — and an auxiliary verb. As an auxiliary verb, it is used to form compound tenses of verbs conjugated with **avere** [▶1b and 1c].

Ho un fratello e due sorelle.	*I have* one brother and two sisters.
Ho ventidue anni.	*I am* twenty-two years old. (*Lit. I have* twenty-two years.)
Ho due paia di scarpe.	*I have* two pairs of shoes.

IMPERATIVE
abbi (tu) **abbia** (Lei) abbiamo (noi) **abbiate** (voi) **abbiano** (Loro)

PLUPERFECT	PAST ANTERIOR
avevo avuto	ebbi avuto

FUTURE	FUTURE PERFECT
avrò	avrò avuto

PRESENT CONDITIONAL	CONDITIONAL PERFECT
avrei	avrei avuto

PRESENT SUBJUNCTIVE
abbia
abbia
abbia
abbiamo
abbiate
abbiano

PERFECT SUBJUNCTIVE
abbia avuto

IMPERFECT SUBJUNCTIVE	PLUPERFECT SUBJUNCTIVE
avessi	avessi avuto

— **Dubito che Carlo abbia spedito quella lettera.**

—I doubt whether Carlo *has sent* that letter.

— **Penso che tu abbia ragione.**

—I think *you are right.*

— **Comunque ha detto che viene domani.**

—However, *he said* he is coming tomorrow.

— **Avremo tempo a convincerlo allora.**

— *We'll have time to* convince him, then.

— **Hai intenzione di spiegargli tutto?**

— *Do you intend to* explain everything to him?

— **Ho paura di dirgli la verità.**

— *I am afraid of* telling him the truth.

— **Ma non aveva il diritto di agire così.**

—But *he did* not *have the right to* act like that.

PRESENT GERUND cadendo	**PAST PARTICIPLE** caduto

PRESENT INDICATIVE cado	**PRESENT PERFECT** sono caduto / a
PRESENT PROGRESSIVE sto cadendo	**IMPERFECT PROGRESSIVE** stavo cadendo
IMPERFECT cadevo	**PAST DEFINITE** **caddi** cadesti **cadde** cademmo cadeste **caddero**

Similar verbs

*accadere	happen
*ricadere	fall again
*scadere	be due, expire

Note: The main irregular features of the verb are

- the past definite tense
- the future stem

IMPERATIVE
cadi (tu)   cada (Lei)   cadiamo (noi)   cadete (voi)   cadano (Loro)

PLUPERFECT	**PAST ANTERIOR**
ero caduto / a	fui caduto / a
FUTURE	**FUTURE PERFECT**
cadrò	sarò caduto / a
PRESENT CONDITIONAL	**CONDITIONAL PERFECT**
cadrei	sarei caduto / a
PRESENT SUBJUNCTIVE	**PERFECT SUBJUNCTIVE**
cada	sia caduto / a
IMPERFECT SUBJUNCTIVE	**PLUPERFECT SUBJUNCTIVE**
cadessi	fossi caduto / a

I prezzi cadevano rapidamente.	The prices *were falling* quickly.
Gli sono caduti i capelli.	*He has lost* his hair.
— Cosa è accaduto?	— What *has happened?*
— Ho paura che Chiara sia ricaduta.	— I am afraid that Chiara *might have fallen again.*
Ho paura che la fattura scada domani.	I am afraid that the invoice *is due* tomorrow.

PRESENT GERUND	PAST PARTICIPLE
chiedendo	**chiesto**

PRESENT INDICATIVE	PRESENT PERFECT
chiedo	ho chiesto

PRESENT PROGRESSIVE	IMPERFECT PROGRESSIVE
sto chiedendo	stavo chiedendo

IMPERFECT	PAST DEFINITE
chiedevo	**chiesi**
	chiedesti
	chiese
	chiedemmo
	chiedeste
	chiesero

Similar verb

richiedere   request, ask for

Note: The main irregular features of the verb are

- the past definite tense
- the past participle

IMPERATIVE
chiedi (tu)   chieda (Lei)   chiediamo (noi)   chiedete (voi)   chiedano (Loro)

PLUPERFECT avevo chiesto	**PAST ANTERIOR** ebbi chiesto
FUTURE chiederò	**FUTURE PERFECT** avrò chiesto
PRESENT CONDITIONAL chiederei	**CONDITIONAL PERFECT** avrei chiesto
PRESENT SUBJUNCTIVE chieda	**PERFECT SUBJUNCTIVE** abbia chiesto
IMPERFECT SUBJUNCTIVE chiedessi	**PLUPERFECT SUBJUNCTIVE** avessi chiesto

Cosa ha chiesto Luigi?	What *did* Luigi *ask?*
Mi chiese di uscire con loro.	*He asked* me to go out with them.
Chiederò al professore domani.	*I shall ask* the teacher tomorrow.
Ho paura che Carlo abbia richiesto l'impossibile.	I am afraid that Carlo *has asked for* the impossible.

PRESENT GERUND	PAST PARTICIPLE
chiudendo	**chiuso**

PRESENT INDICATIVE	PRESENT PERFECT
chiudo	ho chiuso

PRESENT PROGRESSIVE
sto chiudendo

IMPERFECT PROGRESSIVE
stavo chiudendo

IMPERFECT
chiudevo

PAST DEFINITE
chiusi
chiudesti
chiuse
chiudemmo
chiudeste
chiusero

Similar verbs

dischiudere	disclose; open
racchiudere	contain; imply
richiudere	close again
rinchiudere	shut in, shut up
schiudere	open, disclose
socchiudere	half-close, leave . . . ajar

Note: The main irregular features of the verb are

- the past definite tense
- the past participle

IMPERATIVE
chiudi (tu)   chiuda (Lei)   chiudiamo (noi)   chiudete (voi)   chiudano (Loro)

PLUPERFECT	**PAST ANTERIOR**
avevo chiuso	ebbi chiuso
FUTURE	**FUTURE PERFECT**
chiuderò	avrò chiuso
PRESENT CONDITIONAL	**CONDITIONAL PERFECT**
chiuderei	avrei chiuso
PRESENT SUBJUNCTIVE	**PERFECT SUBJUNCTIVE**
chiuda	abbia chiuso
IMPERFECT SUBJUNCTIVE	**PLUPERFECT SUBJUNCTIVE**
chiudessi	avessi chiuso

Ho paura che Antonio abbia chiuso a chiave.	I am afraid that Antonio *has locked* up.
Cosa ha chiuso?	What *did he close?*
Socchiuse la porta	*He half-closed* the door.
Chiuderei alle otto.	*I would close* at eight.
Quella domanda racchiude già la risposta.	That question already *implies* the answer.
Elena fu rinchiusa nella casa.	Elena *was shut up* in the house.

-iere verbs

PRESENT GERUND	PAST PARTICIPLE
cogliendo	**colto**

PRESENT INDICATIVE	PRESENT PERFECT
colgo	ho colto
cogli	
coglie	
cogliamo	
cogliete	
colgono	

PRESENT PROGRESSIVE	IMPERFECT PROGRESSIVE
sto cogliendo	stavo cogliendo

IMPERFECT	PAST DEFINITE
coglievo	**colsi**
	cogliesti
	colse
	cogliemmo
	coglieste
	colsero

Similar verbs

accogliere	welcome
disciogliere	dissolve
distogliere	dissuade, distract
prescegliere	choose from
raccogliere	gather, pick
scegliere	choose
sciogliere	untie; dissolve
togliere	remove

Note: The main irregular features of these verbs are

- the present indicative and subjunctive tenses
- the past definite tense
- the past participle

IMPERATIVE
cogli (tu)   **colga** (Lei)   **cogliamo** (noi)   cogliete (voi)

PLUPERFECT	**PAST ANTERIOR**
avevo colto	ebbi colto
FUTURE	**FUTURE PERFECT**
coglierò	avrò colto
PRESENT CONDITIONAL	**CONDITIONAL PERFECT**
coglierei	avrei colto

PRESENT SUBJUNCTIVE
colga
colga
colga
cogliamo
cogliate
colgano

PERFECT SUBJUNCTIVE (column)

PERFECT SUBJUNCTIVE
abbia colto

IMPERFECT SUBJUNCTIVE
cogliessi

PLUPERFECT SUBJUNCTIVE
avessi colto

Colgono i fiori.	*They are gathering* flowers.
Lo colsi sul fatto.	*I caught* him in the act / red-handed.
Anna sciolse la corda.	Anna *untied* the rope.
—Aspetta, ti sciolgo subito.	—Wait, *I'll untie* you right away.
—Grazie, è molto meglio sciolto!	—Thank you, it is much better *untied*.
—Quale camicia scegliete?	—Which shirt are you *choosing*?
—Scegliamo quella blu, è carina.	—*We're choosing* the blue one, it's nice.
—Io avrei scelto quella rossa!	—I *would have chosen* the red one!
—Adesso non sappiamo quale scegliere!	—Now I don't know which *to choose*.

PRESENT GERUND	PAST PARTICIPLE
comprimendo	**compresso**

PRESENT INDICATIVE	PRESENT PERFECT
comprimo	ho compresso

PRESENT PROGRESSIVE	IMPERFECT PROGRESSIVE
sto comprimendo	stavo comprimendo

IMPERFECT	PAST DEFINITE
comprimevo	**compressi**
	comprimesti
	compresse
	comprimemmo
	comprimeste
	compressero

Similar verbs

deprimere	depress	***imprimersi**	remain impressed
*deprimersi	become depressed	**opprimere**	oppress
esprimere	express	**reprimere**	repress
imprimere	impress; stamp	**sopprimere**	abolish; eliminate; suppress

Note: The main irregular features of the verb are

- the past definite tense
- the past participle

La macchina l'ha compresso.	The machine *compressed* it.
Vorrei esprimerti quanto siamo grati.	I would like to *express to you* how grateful we are.

IMPERATIVE

comprimi (tu)	comprima (Lei)	comprimiamo (noi)
comprimete (voi)	comprimano (Loro)	

PLUPERFECT avevo compresso	**PAST ANTERIOR** ebbi compresso
FUTURE comprimerò	**FUTURE PERFECT** avrò compresso
PRESENT CONDITIONAL comprimerei	**CONDITIONAL PERFECT** avrei compresso
PRESENT SUBJUNCTIVE comprima	**PERFECT SUBJUNCTIVE** abbia compresso
IMPERFECT SUBJUNCTIVE comprimessi	**PLUPERFECT SUBJUNCTIVE** avessi compresso

Il governo soppresse il giornale.	The government *suppressed* the newspaper.
L'avvocato ha soppresso quella clausola.	The lawyer *eliminated* that clause.
Questo tempo lo deprime.	This weather is *depressing* him.
Laura si è tanto depressa oggi.	Laura *has become* so *depressed* today.
Il tiranno oppresse il popolo.	The tyrant *oppressed* the people.
Il lavoro mi opprimeva.	Work *was getting* me *down*.
Ha impresso un timbro sul foglio.	*He put* a stamp *on* the paper.
Le sue parole si impressero nella sua mente.	His words *remained impressed* in her mind.

PRESENT GERUND	PAST PARTICIPLE
concedendo	**concesso** / conceduto

PRESENT INDICATIVE
concedo

PRESENT PERFECT
ho concesso

PRESENT PROGRESSIVE
sto concedendo

IMPERFECT PROGRESSIVE
stavo concedendo

IMPERFECT
concedevo

PAST DEFINITE
concessi / concedei / concedetti
concedesti
concesse / concedé / concedette
concedemmo
concedeste
concessero/ concederono / concedettero

Similar verbs

*accedere   approach; access; comply with
*succedere   happen; succeed

Note: The main irregular features of the verb are

- the past definite tense
- the past participle

IMPERATIVE

concedi (tu)   conceda (Lei)   concediamo (noi)
concedete (voi)   concedano (Loro)

PLUPERFECT	**PAST ANTERIOR**
avevo concesso	ebbi concesso
FUTURE	**FUTURE PERFECT**
concederò	avrò concesso
PRESENT CONDITIONAL	**CONDITIONAL PERFECT**
concederei	avrei concesso
PRESENT SUBJUNCTIVE	**PERFECT SUBJUNCTIVE**
conceda	abbia concesso
IMPERFECT SUBJUNCTIVE	**PLUPERFECT SUBJUNCTIVE**
concedessi	avessi concesso

—**Cosa ti è successo?**   —What *happened* to you?
—**Non mi è successo niente.**   —Nothing *happened* (to me).

—**Concedi tutto?**   — *Do you concede* everything?
—**Concederei tutto per amore.**   — *I would concede* all for love.

PRESENT GERUND	PAST PARTICIPLE
conoscendo	conos**ci**uto

PRESENT INDICATIVE	PRESENT PERFECT
conosco	ho conosciuto

PRESENT PROGRESSIVE
sto conoscendo

IMPERFECT PROGRESSIVE
stavo conoscendo

IMPERFECT
conoscevo

PAST DEFINITE
conobbi
conoscesti
conobbe
conoscemmo
conosceste
conobbero

Similar verb

riconoscere   recognize

Note: It is important to distinguish between the verbs **conoscere** and **sapere**. **Conoscere** means to know a person or a place, whereas **sapere** means to know a fact or to know how to do something.

The main irregular feature of the verb is

• the past definite tense
• the spelling change in the past participle [➤11c(v)]

IMPERATIVE

conosci (tu)	conosca (Lei)	conosciamo (noi)
conoscete (voi)	conoscano (Loro)	

PLUPERFECT
avevo conosciuto

PAST ANTERIOR
ebbi conosciuto

FUTURE
conoscerò

FUTURE PERFECT
avrò conosciuto

PRESENT CONDITIONAL
conoscerei

CONDITIONAL PERFECT
avrei conosciuto

PRESENT SUBJUNCTIVE
conosca

PERFECT SUBJUNCTIVE
abbia conosciuto

IMPERFECT SUBJUNCTIVE
conoscessi

PLUPERFECT SUBJUNCTIVE
avessi conosciuto

—**Conosci Roma?**

— *Do you know* Rome?

—**Conosco Roma molto bene.**

— *I know* Rome very well.

—**Conoscevo una vecchia signora a Roma.**

— *I used to know* an old lady in Rome.

—**Non so se la signora abiti ancora a Roma.**

—I do not know whether the lady still lives in Rome.

Note: In the last example the verb **sapere** is used because the meaning is 'to know a fact.'

PRESENT GERUND	PAST PARTICIPLE
correndo	**corso**

PRESENT INDICATIVE	PRESENT PERFECT
corro	ho corso / sono corso / a

PRESENT PROGRESSIVE	IMPERFECT PROGRESSIVE
sto correndo	stavo correndo

IMPERFECT	PAST DEFINITE
correvo	**corsi**
	corresti
	corse
	corremmo
	correste
	corsero

Similar verbs

† **accorrere**	run, rush	† **ricorrere**	resort to, turn to
† **discorrere**	talk, discuss	† **scorrere**	flow
† **incorrere**	incur	† **soccorrere**	aid, assist
† **occorrere**	be necessary (*impersonal*)	† **trascorrere**	spend (*time*)
† **percorrere**	cover, go along, scour		

Note: The main irregular features of the verb are

- the past definite tense
- the past participle

When used transitively, **correre** takes **avere** in its compound tenses; otherwise it takes **essere.**

IMPERATIVE
corri (tu)   corra (Lei)   corriamo (noi)   correte (voi)   corrano (Loro)

PLUPERFECT avevo corso / ero corso / a	**PAST ANTERIOR** ebbi corso / fui corso / a
FUTURE correrò	**FUTURE PERFECT** avrò corso / sarò corso / a
PRESENT CONDITIONAL correrei	**CONDITIONAL PERFECT** avrei corso / sarei corso / a
PRESENT SUBJUNCTIVE corra	**PERFECT SUBJUNCTIVE** abbia corso / sia corso / a
IMPERFECT SUBJUNCTIVE corressi	**PLUPERFECT SUBJUNCTIVE** avessi corso / fossi corso / a

Ho paura che Antonia sia corsa troppo velocemente.	I am afraid that Antonia *ran* too fast.
Corri ad avvisarlo!	*Run* to warn him!
La strada corre lungo il fiume.	The road *runs* alongside the river.
Il fiume scorre vicino alia casa.	The river *flows* near the house.
Corrono voci poco rassicuranti sul tuo conto.	*There are* some less-than-reassuring rumors about you.
Abbiamo corso il rischio di morire.	*We ran* the risk of dying.
Abbiamo percorso tutti gli Stati Uniti.	*We have traveled* all over the United States.
La polizia percorse la città in cerca dei ladri.	The police *scoured* the town in search of the thieves.
Ne discorreremo dopo cena.	*We shall discuss* it after dinner.

PRESENT GERUND	PAST PARTICIPLE
crescendo	cresciuto

PRESENT INDICATIVE	PRESENT PERFECT
cresco	sono cresciuto / a

PRESENT PROGRESSIVE	IMPERFECT PROGRESSIVE
sto crescendo	stavo crescendo

IMPERFECT	PAST DEFINITE
crescevo	**crebbi**
	crescesti
	crebbe
	crescemmo
	cresceste
	crebbero

Similar verbs

*accrescere	increase
*decrescere	decrease, go down
*rincrescere	regret, be sorry; mind

Note: The main irregular features of the verb are

- the past definite tense
- the spelling change in the past participle [➤11c(v)]

IMPERATIVE
cresci (tu)   cresca (Lei)   cresciamo (noi)   crescete (voi)   crescano (Loro)

PLUPERFECT ero cresciuto / a	**PAST ANTERIOR** fui cresciuto / a
FUTURE crescerò	**FUTURE PERFECT** saròcresciuto / a
PRESENT CONDITIONAL crescerei	**CONDITIONAL PERFECT** sarei cresciuto / a
PRESENT SUBJUNCTIVE cresca	**PERFECT SUBJUNCTIVE** sia cresciuto / a
IMPERFECT SUBJUNCTIVE crescessi	**PLUPERFECT SUBJUNCTIVE** fossi cresciuto / a

I miei capelli non crescono molto.	My hair *does* not *grow* much.
Antonio è cresciuto molto!	Antonio *has grown* a lot.
L'albero è cresciuto poco.	The tree *has grown* very little.
Antonella è cresciuta in Sardegna.	Antonella *grew up* in Sardinia.
I prezzi non decrescono mai!	Prices never *go down*!
Le rincresce di non potervi aiutare.	*She regrets* not being able to help you.
Ti rincrescerebbe aprire la porta?	*Would you mind* opening the door?

PRESENT GERUND	PAST PARTICIPLE
cocendo	**cotto**

PRESENT INDICATIVE	PRESENT PERFECT
cuocio	ho cotto
cuoci	
cuoce	
cociamo	
cocete	
cuociono	

PRESENT PROGRESSIVE	IMPERFECT PROGRESSIVE
sto cuocendo / cocendo	stavo cuocendo / cocendo

IMPERFECT	PAST DEFINITE
cocevo	**cossi**
	cocesti
	cosse
	cocemmo
	coceste
	cossero

Note: The main irregular features of the verb are

• the present indicative and subjunctive tenses
• the past definite tense
• the past participle
• the gerund

IMPERATIVE
cuoci (tu)   **cuocia** (Lei)   **cociamo** (noi)   **cocete** (voi)   cuociano (Loro)

PLUPERFECT avevo cotto	**PAST ANTERIOR** ebbi cotto
FUTURE cocerò	**FUTURE PERFECT** avrò cotto
PRESENT CONDITIONAL cocerei	**CONDITIONAL PERFECT** avrei cotto
PRESENT SUBJUNCTIVE cuocia cuocia cuocia cociamo cociate cuociano	**PERFECT SUBJUNCTIVE** abbia cotto
IMPERFECT SUBJUNCTIVE cocessi	**PLUPERFECT SUBJUNCTIVE** avessi cotto

—**Che cosa hai cotto?**
—What *have you cooked*?

—**Il sugo è cotto, ma sto ancora cocendo la pasta.**
—The sauce *is cooked*, but *I am* still *cooking* the pasta.

—**Ma questa pasta è stracotta!**
—But this pasta *is overcooked*.

PRESENT GERUND	PAST PARTICIPLE
dando	dato

PRESENT INDICATIVE	PRESENT PERFECT
do	ho dato
dai	
dà	
diamo	
date	
danno	

PRESENT PROGRESSIVE	IMPERFECT PROGRESSIVE
sto dando	stavo dando

IMPERFECT	PAST DEFINITE
davo	**diedi / detti**
	desti
	diede / dette
	demmo
	deste
	diedero / dettero

Note: The main irregular features of the verb are

- the present indicative and subjunctive tenses
- the past definite tense
- the future stem

IMPERATIVE
da' / dai (tu)   dia (Lei)   diamo (noi)   date (voi)   dìano / díeno (Loro)

PLUPERFECT avevo dato	**PAST ANTERIOR** ebbi dato
FUTURE darò	**FUTURE PERFECT** avrò dato
PRESENT CONDITIONAL darei	**CONDITIONAL PERFECT** avrei dato
PRESENT SUBJUNCTIVE dia dia dia diamo diate diano	**PERFECT SUBJUNCTIVE** abbia dato
IMPERFECT SUBJUNCTIVE dessi	**PLUPERFECT SUBJUNCTIVE** avessi dato

— **Dammi un po' di pane, per favore.**

— *Would you give* me some bread please.

— **Mah, ti ho già dato il pane.**

— But *I have* already *given* you the bread.

— **Io te ne darei senza tante storie!**

— *I would give* you some without all this fuss.

— **Va bene, te lo do, basta che stai zitto.**

— O.K., *I'll give* it to you, as long as you keep quiet.

PRESENT GERUND decidendo	PAST PARTICIPLE **deciso**

PRESENT INDICATIVE decido	PRESENT PERFECT ho deciso

PRESENT PROGRESSIVE
sto decidendo

IMPERFECT PROGRESSIVE
stavo decidendo

IMPERFECT
decidevo

PAST DEFINITE
decisi
decidesti
decise
decidemmo
decideste
decisero

Similar verbs

coincidere	coincide
incidere	cut, carve
recidere	cut off, amputate

Note: The main irregular features of the verb are

- the past definite tense
- the past participle

IMPERATIVE
decidi (tu)   decida (Lei)   decidiamo (noi)   decidete (voi)   decidano (Loro)

PLUPERFECT avevo deciso	**PAST ANTERIOR** ebbi deciso
FUTURE deciderò	**FUTURE PERFECT** avrò deciso
PRESENT CONDITIONAL deciderei	**CONDITIONAL PERFECT** avrei deciso
PRESENT SUBJUNCTIVE decida	**PERFECT SUBJUNCTIVE** abbia deciso
IMPERFECT SUBJUNCTIVE decidessi	**PLUPERFECT SUBJUNCTIVE** avessi deciso

Dubito che Marco abbia già deciso.	I doubt whether Marco *has decided* yet.
Cosa ha deciso Carla?	What *has* Carla *decided*?
Decise di partire subito.	*He decided* to leave immediately.
Decisi sul rosso.	*I decided on* the red.
Incise il nome di Maria sull'albero.	*He carved* Maria's name on the tree.

PRESENT GERUND
dirigendo

PAST PARTICIPLE
diretto

PRESENT INDICATIVE
dirigo

PRESENT PERFECT
ho diretto

PRESENT PROGRESSIVE
sto dirigendo

IMPERFECT PROGRESSIVE
stavo dirigendo

IMPERFECT
dirigevo

PAST DEFINITE
diressi
dirigesti
diresse
dirigemmo
dirigeste
diressero

Similar verbs

*dirigersi   make one's way towards, head (for)
erigere   erect

Note: The main irregular features of the verb are

• the past definite tense
• the past participle

IMPERATIVE
dirigi (tu)   diriga (Lei)   dirigiamo (noi)   dirigete (voi)   dirigano (Loro)

PLUPERFECT avevo diretto	**PAST ANTERIOR** ebbi diretto
FUTURE dirigerò	**FUTURE PERFECT** avrò diretto
PRESENT CONDITIONAL dirigerei	**CONDITIONAL PERFECT** avrei diretto
PRESENT SUBJUNCTIVE diriga	**PERFECT SUBJUNCTIVE** abbia diretto
IMPERFECT SUBJUNCTIVE dirigessi	**PLUPERFECT SUBJUNCTIVE** avessi diretto

Diresse la nave verso il porto.	*He steered* the boat towards the port.
La nave era diretta a Livorno.	The ship *was headed* for Livorno.
La lettera era diretta a mio padre.	The letter *was addressed* to my father.
Ho diretto lo sguardo verso il mare.	*I turned* my gaze towards the sea.
Lucia dirige un'orchestra.	Lucia *conducts* an orchestra.
Mio padre dirige una grande società.	My father *manages* a large company.
Eresse un gran monumento.	*He erected* a large monument.
Si diresse verso il paese.	*He headed* towards the village.

129

PRESENT GERUND	PAST PARTICIPLE
discutendo	**discusso**

PRESENT INDICATIVE
discuto

PRESENT PERFECT
ho discusso

PRESENT PROGRESSIVE
sto discutendo

IMPERFECT PROGRESSIVE
stavo discutendo

IMPERFECT
discutevo

PAST DEFINITE
discussi / discutéi
discutesti
discusse / discuté
discutemmo
discuteste
discussero / discuterono

Similar verb

incutere   strike, rouse

Note: The main irregular features of the verb are

- the past definite tense
- the past participle

IMPERATIVE
discuti (tu)   discuta (Lei)   discutiamo (noi)   discutete (voi)   discutano (Loro)

PLUPERFECT	**PAST ANTERIOR**
avevo discusso	ebbi discusso
FUTURE	**FUTURE PERFECT**
discuterò	avrò discusso
PRESENT CONDITIONAL	**CONDITIONAL PERFECT**
discuterei	avrei discusso
PRESENT SUBJUNCTIVE	**PERFECT SUBJUNCTIVE**
discuta	abbia discusso
IMPERFECT SUBJUNCTIVE	**PLUPERFECT SUBJUNCTIVE**
discutessi	avessi discusso

—Ho paura che Carlo abbia discusso il problema con Carla.

—I am afraid that Carlo *has discussed* the problem with Carla.

—Cosa hanno discusso Carlo e Carla?

—What *did* Carlo and Carla *discuss?*

—Discussero l'inquinamento.

— *They discussed* pollution.

Discuterò il tema domani.

I shall discuss the essay tomorrow.

Incusse terrore nell'anima di Giovanni.

He struck terror into Giovanni.

PRESENT GERUND	PAST PARTICIPLE
distinguendo	**distinto**

PRESENT INDICATIVE	PRESENT PERFECT
distinguo	ho distinto

PRESENT PROGRESSIVE
sto distinguendo

IMPERFECT PROGRESSIVE
stavo distinguendo

IMPERFECT
distinguevo

PAST DEFINITE
distinsi
distinguesti
distinse
distinguemmo
distingueste
distinsero

Similar verb

estinguere   extinguish

Note: The main irregular features of the verb are

- the past definite tense
- the past participle

IMPERATIVE
distingui (tu)   distingua (Lei)   distinguiamo (noi)
distinguete (voi)   distinguano (Loro)

PLUPERFECT
avevo distinto

PAST ANTERIOR
ebbi distinto

FUTURE
distinguerò

FUTURE PERFECT
avrò distinto

PRESENT CONDITIONAL
distinguerei

CONDITIONAL PERFECT
avrei distinto

PRESENT SUBJUNCTIVE
distingua

PERFECT SUBJUNCTIVE
abbia distinto

IMPERFECT SUBJUNCTIVE
distinguessi

PLUPERFECT SUBJUNCTIVE
avessi distinto

Al telefono non distinguo la tua voce da quella di tua madre.

On the telephone *I can't tell the difference* between your voice and your mother's.

Non riuscivo a distinguere chi c'era.

I was not able *to make out* who was there.

I vigili del fuoco estinsero le fiamme.

The firemen *put out* the flames.

Distinse un uomo all'orizzonte.

He made out a man on the horizon.

PRESENT GERUND	PAST PARTICIPLE
dividendo	**diviso**

PRESENT INDICATIVE	PRESENT PERFECT
divido	ho diviso

PRESENT PROGRESSIVE	IMPERFECT PROGRESSIVE
sto dividendo	stavo dividendo

IMPERFECT	PAST DEFINITE
dividevo	**divisi**
	dividesti
	divise
	dividemmo
	divideste
	divisero

Similar verbs

condividere   share
dividersi   separate

Note: The main irregular features of the verb are

- the past definite tense
- the past participle

IMPERATIVE
dividi (tu)   divida (Lei)   dividiamo (noi)   dividete (voi)   dividano (Loro)

PLUPERFECT avevo diviso	**PAST ANTERIOR** ebbi diviso
FUTURE dividerò	**FUTURE PERFECT** avrò diviso
PRESENT CONDITIONAL dividerei	**CONDITIONAL PERFECT** avrei diviso
PRESENT SUBJUNCTIVE divida	**PERFECT SUBJUNCTIVE** abbia diviso
IMPERFECT SUBJUNCTIVE dividessi	**PLUPERFECT SUBJUNCTIVE** avessi diviso

Dividete la torta fra di voi!	*Divide* the cake among you!
Il marmo si divise in tre parti.	The marble *broke up* into three parts.
Il Po si divide alla foce.	The Po *divides* at its mouth.
Le lotte interne dividono il partito.	Internal disputes *are tearing* the party *apart*.
I bambini condividevano le caramelle.	The children *shared* the candies.

PRESENT GERUND	**PAST PARTICIPLE**
dolendo	doluto

PRESENT INDICATIVE	**PRESENT PERFECT**
dolgo	sono doluto / a
duoli	
duole	
doliamo / dogliamo	
dolete	
dolgono	

PRESENT PROGRESSIVE	**IMPERFECT PROGRESSIVE**
sto dolendo	stavo dolendo

IMPERFECT	**PAST DEFINITE**
dolevo	**dolsi**
	dolesti
	dolse
	dolemmo
	doleste
	dolsero

Similar verb

*condolersi   sympathize, condole with

Note: The main irregular features of the verb are

- the present indicative and subjunctive tenses
- the past definite tense
- the future stem

IMPERATIVE
duoli (tu)   dolga (Lei)   dogliamo / doliamo (noi)   dolete (voi)   dolgano (Loro)

PLUPERFECT ero doluto / a	**PAST ANTERIOR** fui doluto / a
FUTURE **dorrò**	**FUTURE PERFECT** sarò doluto / a
PRESENT CONDITIONAL **dorrei**	**CONDITIONAL PERFECT** sarei doluto / a
PRESENT SUBJUNCTIVE **dolga** **dolga** **dolga** doliamo / dogliamo doliate / dogliate **dolgano**	**PERFECT SUBJUNCTIVE** sia doluto / a
IMPERFECT SUBJUNCTIVE dolessi	**PLUPERFECT SUBJUNCTIVE** fossi doluto / a

---

— **Mi duole molto la testa.**	— My head *is hurting* a lot.
— **Mi dispiace che ti dolga tanto.**	— I am sorry that *it is hurting* you so much.
— **Mi doleva anche ieri sera.**	— *It was* also *aching* yesterday evening.
Si condolsero con lui.	*They sympathized* with him.

PRESENT GERUND	PAST PARTICIPLE
dovendo	dovuto

PRESENT INDICATIVE	PRESENT PERFECT
devo / debbo	ho dovuto / sono dovuto / a
devi	
deve	
dobbiamo	
dovete	
devono / debbono	

PRESENT PROGRESSIVE	IMPERFECT PROGRESSIVE
sto dovendo	stavo dovendo

IMPERFECT	PAST DEFINITE
dovevo	dovei / dovetti

Note: The main irregular features of this modal verb are

• the present indicative and subjunctive tenses
• the future stem

dovere takes **avere** or **essere** according to which one the dependent infinitive takes. However, in practice the auxiliary **avere** is frequently used in speech, when the emphasis is on obligation.

IMPERATIVE
(There is none.)

PLUPERFECT	**PAST ANTERIOR**
avevo dovuto / ero dovuto / a	ebbi dovuto / fui dovuto / a

FUTURE
dovrò

FUTURE PERFECT
avrò dovuto / sarò dovuto / a

PRESENT CONDITIONAL
dovrei

CONDITIONAL PERFECT
avrei dovuto / sarei dovuto / a

PRESENT SUBJUNCTIVE
deva / debba
deva / debba
deva / debba
dobbiamo
dobbiate
devano / debbano

PERFECT SUBJUNCTIVE
abbia dovuto / sia dovuto / a

IMPERFECT SUBJUNCTIVE
dovessi

PLUPERFECT SUBJUNCTIVE
ebbi dovuto / fossi dovuto / a

Devono essere le otto.	*It must* be eight.
Il treno deve arrivare tra poco.	The train *should* arrive soon.
Avrei dovuto parlare con la mamma prima di partire.	*I should have spoken* with my mother before leaving.
Dovrei tornare a casa ora.	*I should* go home now.
Antonio è dovuto andare a casa presto.	Antonio *had* to go home early.

PRESENT GERUND espellendo	**PAST PARTICIPLE** **espulso**

PRESENT INDICATIVE espello	**PRESENT PERFECT** ho espulso
PRESENT PROGRESSIVE sto espellendo	**IMPERFECT PROGRESSIVE** stavo espellendo
IMPERFECT espellevo	**PAST DEFINITE** **espulsi** espellesti **espulse** espellemmo espelleste **espulsero**

Note: The main irregular features of the verb are

• the past definite tense
• the past participle

IMPERATIVE
espelli (tu)   espella (Lei)   espelliamo (noi)   espellete (voi)   espellano (Loro)

PLUPERFECT avevo espulso	**PAST ANTERIOR** ebbi espulso
FUTURE espellerò	**FUTURE PERFECT** avrò espulso
PRESENT CONDITIONAL espellerei	**CONDITIONAL PERFECT** avrei espulso
PRESENT SUBJUNCTIVE espella	**PERFECT SUBJUNCTIVE** abbia espulso
IMPERFECT SUBJUNCTIVE espellessi	**PLUPERFECT SUBJUNCTIVE** avessi espulso

— **Hanno espulso quel ragazzo?**
— **Fu espulso dalla scuola ieri.**

— **Io l'avrei espulso l'anno scorso!**
— **Sì, ma non è facile espellere alunni.**

— *Have they expelled* that boy?
— *He was expelled* from the school yesterday.

— *I would have expelled* him last year.
— Yes, but it is not easy *to expel* students.

PRESENT GERUND	**PAST PARTICIPLE**
esplodendo	**esploso**

PRESENT INDICATIVE	**PRESENT PERFECT**
esplodo	sono esploso / a

PRESENT PROGRESSIVE	**IMPERFECT PROGRESSIVE**
sto esplodendo	stavo esplodendo

IMPERFECT	**PAST DEFINITE**
esplodevo	**esplosi**
	esplodesti
	esplose
	esplodemmo
	esplodeste
	esplosero

Similar verbs

ardere	burn
corrodere	corrode
rodere	gnaw

Note: The main irregular features of the verb are

• the past participle
• the past definite tense

IMPERATIVE
esplodi (tu) esploda (Lei) esplodiamo (noi) esplodete (voi) esplodano (Loro)

PLUPERFECT ero esploso	**PAST ANTERIOR** fui esploso / a
FUTURE esploderò	**FUTURE PERFECT** sarò esploso / a
PRESENT CONDITIONAL esploderei	**CONDITIONAL PERFECT** sarei esploso / a
PRESENT SUBJUNCTIVE esploda	**PERFECT SUBJUNCTIVE** sia esploso / a
IMPERFECT SUBJUNCTIVE esplodessi	**PLUPERFECT SUBJUNCTIVE** fossi esploso / a

---

—**La bomba sarà esplosa al mercato.**	—The bomb *must have exploded* at the market.
—**No, è esplosa nel negozio.**	—No, *it went off* in the shop.
Esplosi in una risata.	*I burst out* laughing.
Poi la sua ira esplose.	Then his anger *exploded*.
Ardevano i lumi.	The lights *were shining*.
Il sole ha arso la terra.	The sun *has burned* the ground.
I topi hanno roso il libro.	The mice *have gnawed* at the book.

PRESENT GERUND	PAST PARTICIPLE
essendo	**stato**

PRESENT INDICATIVE	PRESENT PERFECT
sono	sono stato / a
sei	sei stato / a
è	è stato / a
siamo	siamo stati / e
siete	siete stati / e
sono	sono stati / e

PRESENT PROGRESSIVE	IMPERFECT PROGRESSIVE
sto	stavo

IMPERFECT	PAST DEFINITE
ero	**fui**
eri	**fosti**
era	**fu**
eravamo	**fummo**
eravate	**foste**
erano	**furono**

Note: It is important that you learn all tenses of **essere** as it is used in so many compound tenses.

IMPERATIVE
sii (tu)   sia (Lei)   siamo (noi)   siate (voi)   siano (Loro)

PLUPERFECT	**PAST ANTERIOR**
ero stato	fui stato / a

FUTURE · **FUTURE PERFECT**

sarò · sarò stato / a

PRESENT CONDITIONAL · **CONDITIONAL PERFECT**

sarei · sarei stato / a

PRESENT SUBJUNCTIVE · **PERFECT SUBJUNCTIVE**

sia · sia stato / a
sia
sia
siamo
siate
siano

IMPERFECT SUBJUNCTIVE · **PLUPERFECT SUBJUNCTIVE**

fossi · fossi stato / a
fossi
fosse
fossimo
foste
fossero

Oggi è difficile trovare lavoro.	Nowadays *it is* difficult to find work.
—**Cosa c'è?**	—What *is* the matter?
—**Sono disoccupata.**	—*I am* unemployed.
—**Sarà più facile in un'altra città?**	—*Might it be* easier in another town?
—**Non credo che sia così facile.**	—I do not think *it is* so easy.
—**Sei sempre così pessimista?**	—*Are you* always such a pessimist?

PRESENT GERUND	PAST PARTICIPLE
evadendo	**evaso**

PRESENT INDICATIVE	PRESENT PERFECT
evado	sono evaso / a

PRESENT PROGRESSIVE	IMPERFECT PROGRESSIVE
sto evadendo	stavo evadendo

IMPERFECT	PAST DEFINITE
evadevo	**evasi**
	evadesti
	evase
	evademmo
	evadeste
	evasero

Similar verb

invadere   invade

Note: The main irregular features of the verb are

- the past participle
- the past definite tense

IMPERATIVE
evadi (tu)   evada (Lei)   evadiamo (noi)   evadete (voi)   evadano (Loro)

PLUPERFECT ero evaso	**PAST ANTERIOR** fui evaso / a
FUTURE evaderò	**FUTURE PERFECT** sarò evaso / a
PRESENT CONDITIONAL evaderei	**CONDITIONAL PERFECT** sarei evaso / a
PRESENT SUBJUNCTIVE evada	**PERFECT SUBJUNCTIVE** sia evaso / a
IMPERFECT SUBJUNCTIVE evadessi	**PLUPERFECT SUBJUNCTIVE** fossi evaso / a

Ho paura che l'uomo sia già evaso dalla prigione.	I am afraid the man *might have* already *escaped* from the prison / jail.
Purtroppo i ladri evasero.	Unfortunately the robbers *escaped*.
Le erbacce invasero il mio giardino.	My garden *was overrun* with weeds.
Il fiume invase i campi.	The river *flooded* the fields.
Hanno invaso il campo.	They *invaded* the field / pitch.
L'imperatore invase il paese.	The emperor *invaded* the country.

PRESENT GERUND	PAST PARTICIPLE
fondendo	**fuso**

PRESENT INDICATIVE	PRESENT PERFECT
fondo	ho fuso

PRESENT PROGRESSIVE	IMPERFECT PROGRESSIVE
sto fondendo	stavo fondendo

IMPERFECT	PAST DEFINITE
fondevo	**fusi**
	fondesti
	fuse
	fondemmo
	fondeste
	fusero

Similar verbs

diffondere	give out, broadcast, diffuse
infondere	instill
profondere	squander
***profondersi in**	be profuse in

Note: The main irregular features of the verb are

- the past definite tense
- the past participle

IMPERATIVE
fondi (tu)   fonda (Lei)   fondiamo (noi)   fondete (voi)   fondano (Loro)

PLUPERFECT avevo fuso	**PAST ANTERIOR** ebbi fuso
FUTURE fonderò	**FUTURE PERFECT** avrò fuso
PRESENT CONDITIONAL fonderei	**CONDITIONAL PERFECT** avrei fuso
PRESENT SUBJUNCTIVE fonda	**PERFECT SUBJUNCTIVE** abbia fuso
IMPERFECT SUBJUNCTIVE fondessi	**PLUPERFECT SUBJUNCTIVE** avessi fuso

Il vetraio ha fuso il vetro nella fornace.	The glassmaker *melted* the glass in the furnace.
L'artista fuse i due colori.	The artist *blended* the two colors / colours.
La notizia è stata diffusa per radio.	The news *was broadcast* on the radio.
Claudio ha infuso il coraggio a Luigi.	Claudio *instilled* Luigi with courage.
Antonio profuse il denaro in divertimenti.	Antonio *squandered* the money on entertainment.
La signora si profondeva sempre in lodi.	The lady *was* always *lavish* in her praise.

PRESENT GERUND	PAST PARTICIPLE
giacendo	**giaciuto**

PRESENT INDICATIVE	PRESENT PERFECT
giaccio	sono giaciuto / a
giaci	
giace	
giacciamo / giaciamo	
giacete	
giacciono	

PRESENT PROGRESSIVE	IMPERFECT PROGRESSIVE
sto giacendo	stavo giacendo

IMPERFECT	PAST DEFINITE
giacevo	**giacqui**
	giacesti
	giacque
	giacemmo
	giaceste
	giacquero

Note: The main irregular features of the verb are

- the present indicative and subjunctive tenses
- the past definite tense
- the insertion of the **-i** in the past participle

IMPERATIVE

giaci (tu)	**giaccia** (Lei)	**giacciamo** / giaciamo (noi)
giacete (voi)	**giacciano** (Loro)	

PLUPERFECT
ero giaciuto / a

PAST ANTERIOR
fui giaciuto / a

FUTURE
giacerò

FUTURE PERFECT
sarò giaciuto / a

PRESENT CONDITIONAL
giacerei

CONDITIONAL PERFECT
sarei giaciuto / a

PRESENT SUBJUNCTIVE
giaccia

PERFECT SUBJUNCTIVE
sia giaciuto / a

IMPERFECT SUBJUNCTIVE
giacessi

PLUPERFECT SUBJUNCTIVE
fossi giaciuto / a

— **Giacque sulla spiaggia.**
— *He lay* on the beach.

— **Giacevano sull'erba quando siamo arrivati.**
— *They were lying* in the grass when we arrived.

— **Giacerei al sole tutta la giornata!**
— *I would lie* in the sun all day long!

PRESENT GERUND giungendo	**PAST PARTICIPLE** **giunto**
PRESENT INDICATIVE giungo	**PRESENT PERFECT** sono giunto / a
PRESENT PROGRESSIVE sto giungendo	**IMPERFECT PROGRESSIVE** stavo giungendo
IMPERFECT giungevo	**PAST DEFINITE** **giunsi** giungesti **giunse** giungemmo giungeste **giunsero**

Similar verbs

† **aggiungere**	add
† **congiungere**	join, match
† **disgiungere**	separate
† **raggiungere**	catch up with, reach, attain
† **soggiungere**	add

verbs marked † can take **essere** when used intransitively or **avere** when used transitively

Note: The main irregular features of the verb are

- the past definite tense
- the past participle

IMPERATIVE
giungi (tu)   giunga (Lei)   giungiamo (noi)   giungete (voi)   giungano (Loro)

PLUPERFECT
ero giunto / a

PAST ANTERIOR
fui giunto / a

FUTURE
giungerò

FUTURE PERFECT
sarò giunto / a

PRESENT CONDITIONAL
giungerei

CONDITIONAL PERFECT
sarei giunto / a

PRESENT SUBJUNCTIVE
giunga

PERFECT SUBJUNCTIVE
sia giunto / a

IMPERFECT SUBJUNCTIVE
giungessi

PLUPERFECT SUBJUNCTIVE
fossi giunto / a

Giunsi in Italia all'inizio di giugno.	I *arrived* in Italy at the beginning of June.
Nessun suono giungeva al mio orecchio.	No sound *reached* my ears.
Dopo aver parlato a lungo del problema, siamo giunti alla conclusione che non valeva la pena querelare.	After talking about the problem at length, *we reached* the conclusion that it wasn't worth our suing.
Il nonno è giunto all'età di novant'anni.	Grandad *has reached* the age of ninety.
Va' avanti, ti raggiungo presto.	Go on ahead, *I'll catch up* soon.
Il prezzo raggiunge i tre mille euro.	The price *comes to* three thousand euro.
Congiunsero le mani per pregare.	*They joined* their hands to pray.

PRESENT GERUND leggendo	**PAST PARTICIPLE** **letto**

PRESENT INDICATIVE leggo	**PRESENT PERFECT** ho letto

PRESENT PROGRESSIVE
sto leggendo

IMPERFECT PROGRESSIVE
stavo leggendo

IMPERFECT
leggevo

PAST DEFINITE
lessi
leggesti
lesse
leggemmo
leggeste
lessero

Similar verb

eleggere   elect

Note: The main irregular features of the verb are

  • the past definite tense
  • the past participle

IMPERATIVE
leggi (tu)   legga (Lei)   leggiamo (noi)   leggete (voi)   leggano (Loro)

PLUPERFECT avevo letto	**PAST ANTERIOR** ebbi letto
FUTURE leggerò	**FUTURE PERFECT** avrò letto
PRESENT CONDITIONAL leggerei	**CONDITIONAL PERFECT** avrei letto
PRESENT SUBJUNCTIVE legga	**PERFECT SUBJUNCTIVE** abbia letto
IMPERFECT SUBJUNCTIVE leggessi	**PLUPERFECT SUBJUNCTIVE** avessi letto

Lo leggo nei tuoi occhi.	*I can read* it in your eyes.
Legga attentamente questa lettera.	*Read* this letter carefully.
La lesse a voce alta.	*He read* it out aloud.
Sa leggere la musica a prima vista.	He knows how to *sight-read* music.
Ho letto fra le righe.	*I read* between the lines.
Quando non riuscivo a dormire, leggevo.	When I could not sleep, *I used to read*.
È stato eletto ieri.	He was *elected* yesterday.

PRESENT GERUND	PAST PARTICIPLE
mettendo	**messo**

PRESENT INDICATIVE	PRESENT PERFECT
metto	ho messo

PRESENT PROGRESSIVE	IMPERFECT PROGRESSIVE
sto mettendo	stavo mettendo

IMPERFECT	PAST DEFINITE
mettevo	**misi**
	mettesti
	mise
	mettemmo
	metteste
	misero

Similar verbs

ammettere	admit	**permettere**	permit
commettere	commit	**promettere**	promise
compromettere	compromise	**rimettere**	replace
emettere	emit	**scommettere**	bet
frammettere	interpose, insert	**smettere**	stop
immettere	admit, let in	**trasmettere**	transmit
omettere	omit		

Note: The main irregular features of the verb are

   • the past definite tense
   • the past participle

Abbiamo messo il riscaldamento centrale.	*We put in* central heating.
Mise il fazzoletto in tasca.	*He put* the handkerchief in his pocket.

IMPERATIVE
metti (tu)　　metta (Lei)　　mettiamo (noi)　　mettete (voi)　　mettano (Loro)

PLUPERFECT avevo messo	**PAST ANTERIOR** ebbi messo
FUTURE metterò	**FUTURE PERFECT** avrò messo
PRESENT CONDITIONAL metterei	**CONDITIONAL PERFECT** avrei messo
PRESENT SUBJUNCTIVE metta	**PERFECT SUBJUNCTIVE** abbia messo
IMPERFECT SUBJUNCTIVE mettessi	**PLUPERFECT SUBJUNCTIVE** avessi messo

Dubito che abbia messo da parte quei soldi.	I doubt whether *he has put* that money aside.
Ho messo la tavola all'asta.	*I put* the table up for auction.
Ha messo indietro l'orologio.	*He put* his watch back.
Quanto tempo ci hai messo a farlo?	How long *did it take you* to do it?
Ammettiamo pure che tu abbia ragione.	*Let's suppose* (*admit*) that you are right.
Luigi emise un grido forte.	Luigi *let out* a loud cry.
Mi promise un bel regalo!	*He promised* me a beautiful present.
Ho smesso di fumare!	*I've stopped* smoking!
Scommetto che non lo sa!	*I bet* he does not know it!
Trasmettevo alla radio ogni domenica pomeriggio.	*I used to broadcast* on the radio every Sunday afternoon.

PRESENT GERUND mordendo	PAST PARTICIPLE **morso**
PRESENT INDICATIVE mordo	PRESENT PERFECT ho morso
PRESENT PROGRESSIVE sto mordendo	IMPERFECT PROGRESSIVE stavo mordendo
IMPERFECT mordevo	PAST DEFINITE **morsi** mordesti **morse** mordemmo mordeste **morsero**

Similar verbs

*mordersi	bite oneself
rimordere	bite back; prick

Note: The main irregular features of the verb are

- the past definite tense
- the past participle

IMPERATIVE
mordi (tu)   morda (Lei)   mordiamo (noi)   mordete (voi)   mordano (Loro)

PLUPERFECT	PAST ANTERIOR
avevo morso	ebbi morso

FUTURE	FUTURE PERFECT
morderò	avrò morso

PRESENT CONDITIONAL	CONDITIONAL PERFECT
morderei	avrei morso

PRESENT SUBJUNCTIVE	PERFECT SUBJUNCTIVE
morda	abbia morso

IMPERFECT SUBJUNCTIVE	PLUPERFECT SUBJUNCTIVE
mordessi	avessi morso

Il cane mi ha morso il braccio.	The dog *bit* my arm.
Pulci e zanzare mordono.	Fleas and mosquitoes *bite*.
Sentiva un vento gelido mordergli il viso.	*He felt* an icy wind on his face.
Morsero la polvere.	*They bit* the dust.
Mi sono morsa la lingua.	*I bit* my tongue.
Mi sarei morsa la lingua.	*I could have* kicked myself.
Gli rimorse la coscienza.	His conscience *pricked* him.

PRESENT GERUND	PAST PARTICIPLE
morendo	**morto**

PRESENT INDICATIVE
muoio
muori
muore
moriamo
morite
muoiono

PRESENT PERFECT
sono morto / a

PRESENT PROGRESSIVE
sto morendo

IMPERFECT PROGRESSIVE
stavo morendo

IMPERFECT
morivo

PAST DEFINITE
morii

Note: The main irregular features are

  • the present indicative and subjunctive tenses
  • the past participle

IMPERATIVE
muori (tu)   **muoia** (Lei)   moriamo (noi)   morite (voi)   **muoiano** (Loro)

PLUPERFECT ero morto / a	**PAST ANTERIOR** fui morto / a
FUTURE morrò / morirò	**FUTURE PERFECT** sarò morto / a
PRESENT CONDITIONAL morrei / morirei	**CONDITIONAL PERFECT** sarei morto / a
PRESENT SUBJUNCTIVE **muoia** **muoia** **muoia** moriamo moriate **muoiano**	**PERFECT SUBJUNCTIVE** sia morto / a
IMPERFECT SUBJUNCTIVE morissi	**PLUPERFECT SUBJUNCTIVE** fossi morto / a

—**Muoio dal caldo!**
—**Dubito che tu muoia dal caldo!**

Dopo una giornata di lavoro, sono stanca morta!

— *I'm dying* from the heat.
—I doubt that *you'll die* from the heat.

After a day's work, I am *dead* tired.

PRESENT GERUND	PAST PARTICIPLE
nascendo	**nato**

PRESENT INDICATIVE
nasco

PRESENT PERFECT
sono nato / a

PRESENT PROGRESSIVE
sto nascendo

IMPERFECT PROGRESSIVE
stavo nascendo

IMPERFECT
nascevo

PAST DEFINITE
nacqui
nascesti
nacque
nascemmo
nasceste
nacquero

Similar verb

rinascere   be born again

Note: The main irregular features of the verb are

- the past definite tense
- the past participle

IMPERATIVE
nasci (tu)   nasca (Lei)   nasciamo (noi)   nascete (voi)   nascano (Loro)

PLUPERFECT ero nato / a	**PAST ANTERIOR** fui nato / a
FUTURE nascerò	**FUTURE PERFECT** sarò nato / a
PRESENT CONDITIONAL nascerei	**CONDITIONAL PERFECT** sarei nato / a
PRESENT SUBJUNCTIVE nasca	**PERFECT SUBJUNCTIVE** sia nato / a
IMPERFECT SUBJUNCTIVE nascessi	**PLUPERFECT SUBJUNCTIVE** fossi nato / a

La bambina è nata stamattina.	The baby girl *was born* this morning.
Il morto era nato ottantatré anni fa.	The dead man *was born* eighty-three years ago.
Boccaccio nacque secoli fa.	Boccaccio *was born* centuries ago.
Deve ancora nascere chi saprà risolvere tali problemi.	The man who can solve such problems is yet *to be born*.
Mi sento rinascere.	I feel like a new person (*reborn*).
Quando lo rividi, mi rinacque l'odio.	When I saw him, my feelings of hatred *began again*.
Il Po nasce dal Monviso.	The river Po *has its source* on Monviso.

163

PRESENT GERUND	PAST PARTICIPLE
parendo	**parso**

PRESENT INDICATIVE	PRESENT PERFECT
paio	sono parso / a
pari	
pare	
paiamo	
parete	
paiono	

PRESENT PROGRESSIVE	IMPERFECT PROGRESSIVE
sto parendo	stavo parendo

IMPERFECT	PAST DEFINITE
parevo	**parvi**
	paresti
	parve
	paremmo
	pareste
	parvero

Note: The verb **parere** is mostly used impersonally and is consequently rare except for the third persons.

The main irregular features of the verb are

- the present indicative and subjunctive tenses
- the future stem
- the past definite tense
- the past participle

There are also some similarities with the verb **apparire** [▸ 23].

IMPERATIVE
(There is none.)

PLUPERFECT	**PAST ANTERIOR**
ero parso / a	fui parso / a
FUTURE	**FUTURE PERFECT**
parrò	sarò parso / a
PRESENT CONDITIONAL	**CONDITIONAL PERFECT**
parrei	sarei parso / a
PRESENT SUBJUNCTIVE	**PERFECT SUBJUNCTIVE**
paia	sia parso / a
paia	
paia	
paiamo	
pariate	
paiano	
IMPERFECT SUBJUNCTIVE	**PLUPERFECT SUBJUNCTIVE**
paressi	fossi parso / a

Mi pare importante.	It *seems* important to me.
Non mi pareva semplice.	It *did* not *seem* easy to me.
Gli paiono grandi.	*They seem* big to him.
Ti parevano stretti?	*Did you think* they were narrow?

PRESENT GERUND	PAST PARTICIPLE
perdendo	**perso** / perduto

PRESENT INDICATIVE	PRESENT PERFECT
perdo	ho perso

PRESENT PROGRESSIVE	IMPERFECT PROGRESSIVE
sto perdendo	stavo perdendo

IMPERFECT	PAST DEFINITE
perdevo	**persi** / perdei / perdetti
	perdesti
	perse / perdé / perdette
	perdemmo
	perdeste
	persero / perderono / perdettero

Similar verb

*__perdersi__   get lost

Note: The main irregular features of the verb are

- the past definite tense
- the past participle (although it is possible to use the regular past participle)

IMPERATIVE
perdi (tu)   perda (Lei)   perdiamo (noi)   perdete (voi)   perdano (Loro)

PLUPERFECT avevo perso	**PAST ANTERIOR** ebbi perso
FUTURE perderò	**FUTURE PERFECT** avrò perso
PRESENT CONDITIONAL perderei	**CONDITIONAL PERFECT** avrei perso
PRESENT SUBJUNCTIVE perda	**PERFECT SUBJUNCTIVE** abbia perso
IMPERFECT SUBJUNCTIVE perdessi	**PLUPERFECT SUBJUNCTIVE** avessi perso

Ho perso la penna.	*I lost* the pen.
L'ho persa ieri.	*I lost* it (the pen) yesterday.
Gianna ha perso un figlio.	Gianna *has lost* a son (through death).
L'anno scorso ha perso un anno perché era ammalata.	Last year *she fell* a year behind because she was sick.
Antonio ha perso il treno.	Antonio *has missed* the train.
Questo secchio perde acqua.	This bucket *is leaking* water.
Mi sono perso a Firenze.	*I got lost* in Florence.
È inutile spiegarmi queste cose, mi ci perdo.	It's no use explaining these things to me, *I can't make head or tail of* them.

PRESENT GERUND persuadendo	**PAST PARTICIPLE** **persuaso**

PRESENT INDICATIVE
persuado

PRESENT PERFECT
ho persuaso

PRESENT PROGRESSIVE
sto persuadendo

IMPERFECT PROGRESSIVE
stavo persuadendo

IMPERFECT
persuadevo

PAST DEFINITE
persuasi
persuadesti
persuase
persuademmo
persuadeste
persuasero

Similar verb

dissuadere   dissuade

Note: The main irregular features of the verb are

- the past definite tense
- the past participle

IMPERATIVE
persuadi (tu)   persuada (Lei)   persuadiamo (noi)
persuadete (voi)   persuadano (Loro)

PLUPERFECT avevo persuaso	**PAST ANTERIOR** ebbi persuaso
FUTURE persuaderò	**FUTURE PERFECT** avrò persuaso
PRESENT CONDITIONAL persuaderei	**CONDITIONAL PERFECT** avrei persuaso
PRESENT SUBJUNCTIVE persuada	**PERFECT SUBJUNCTIVE** abbia persuaso
IMPERFECT SUBJUNCTIVE persuadessi	**PLUPERFECT SUBJUNCTIVE** avessi persuaso

Ho avuto difficoltà a persuaderla.	I had difficulty in *persuading* her.
Finii per persuaderla a farlo.	I finally *persuaded* her to do it.
La persuasi che aveva torto.	I *persuaded* her that she was wrong.
L'ho persuaso dell'innocenza di Gianni.	I *convinced* him of Gianni's innocence.
Dissuadila dal venire!	*Dissuade* her from coming!
Nulla la dissuaderà dal provare ancora una volta.	Nothing *will dissuade* her from trying one more time.

PRESENT GERUND	PAST PARTICIPLE
piacendo	**piaciuto**

PRESENT INDICATIVE	PRESENT PERFECT
piaccio	sono piaciuto / a
piaci	
piace	**è piaciuto / a**
piacciamo / piaciamo	
piacete	
piacciono	**sono piaciuti / e**

PRESENT PROGRESSIVE	IMPERFECT PROGRESSIVE
sto piacendo	stavo piacendo

IMPERFECT	PAST DEFINITE
piacevo	**piacqui**
	piacesti
	piacque
	piacemmo
	piaceste
	piacquero

Similar verbs

*compiacere	please
*dispiacere	displease

Note: The verb **piacere** is mostly used impersonally and is consequently mainly found in the third person singular or plural. The main irregular features of the verb are

- the present indicative and subjunctive tenses
- the past definite tense
- the addition of the **i** in the past participle

IMPERATIVE
piaci (tu)   **piaccia** (Lei)   piaciamo (noi)   piacete (voi)   **piacciano** (Loro)

PLUPERFECT	**PAST ANTERIOR**
ero piaciuto / a	fui piaciuto / a
FUTURE	**FUTURE PERFECT**
piacerò	sarò piaciuto / a
PRESENT CONDITIONAL	**CONDITIONAL PERFECT**
piacerei	sarei piaciuto / a

PRESENT SUBJUNCTIVE   **PERFECT SUBJUNCTIVE**
piaccia   sia piaciuto / a
piaccia
piaccia
piacciamo / piaciamo
piacciate / piaciate
piacciano

IMPERFECT SUBJUNCTIVE   **PLUPERFECT SUBJUNCTIVE**
piacessi   fossi piaciuto / a

—Ti piace la pasta?   — *Do you like* pasta?

—Si, molto, e mi piacciono   — Yes, a lot, and *I* particularly *like*
soprattutto gli spaghetti.   spaghetti.

—Piacciono anche a Giovanni?   — *Does* Giovanni *like* it
                                         (spaghetti) too?

—Beh, penso che non gli   — Well, I don't think *he dislikes*
dispiacciano.   it (spaghetti).

—So che gli piacciono di più i   —I know *he prefers* tortellini.
tortellini.

Mi dispiace, ma non posso   *I am sorry*, but I cannot come this
venire stasera.   evening.

L'ho compiaciuto nei suoi   *I humored* his whims.
capricci.

PRESENT GERUND piangendo	**PAST PARTICIPLE** **pianto**

PRESENT INDICATIVE piango	**PRESENT PERFECT** ho pianto

PRESENT PROGRESSIVE
sto piangendo

IMPERFECT PROGRESSIVE
stavo piangendo

IMPERFECT
piangevo

PAST DEFINITE
piansi
piangesti
pianse
piangemmo
piangeste
piansero

Similar verbs

compiangere   pity, sympathize
rimpiangere   regret

Note: The main irregular features of the verb are

- the past definite tense
- the past participle

IMPERATIVE
piangi (tu)   pianga (Lei)   piangiamo (noi)   piangete (voi)   piangano (Loro)

PLUPERFECT
avevo pianto

PAST ANTERIOR
ebbi pianto

FUTURE
piangerò

FUTURE PERFECT
avrò pianto

PRESENT CONDITIONAL
piangerei

CONDITIONAL PERFECT
avrei pianto

PRESENT SUBJUNCTIVE
pianga

PERFECT SUBJUNCTIVE
abbia pianto

IMPERFECT SUBJUNCTIVE
piangessi

PLUPERFECT SUBJUNCTIVE
avessi pianto

Luisa pianse dal dolore.	Luisa *cried* with pain.
Mi piangono gli occhi per il fumo.	My eyes *are watering* because of the smoke.
Rimpiango di non esserci andata.	*I regret* not having gone.
Compiango il tuo dolore.	*I sympathize* with you in your grief.
Piansi di rabbia.	*I cried* with anger.
Piange la giovinezza perduta.	*He weeps* for his lost youth.
Beati quelli che piangono.	Blessed are those that *mourn*.
Chi è causa del suo mal, pianga se stesso. (Proverb)	You have made your bed, now lie in it. *(Proverb)*

PRESENT GERUND	PAST PARTICIPLE
piovendo	piovuto

PRESENT INDICATIVE
piove
piovono

PRESENT PERFECT
ha piovuto / è piovuto / a
hanno piovuto / sono piovuti / e

PRESENT PROGRESSIVE
sta piovendo
stanno piovendo

IMPERFECT PROGRESSIVE
stava piovendo
stavano piovendo

IMPERFECT
pioveva
piovevano

PAST DEFINITE
piovvi
piovesti
piovve
piovemmo
pioveste
piovvero

Note: **piovere** and all impersonal verbs associated with weather terms take either **avere** or **essere** almost indifferently. In addition, **piovere** takes **essere** when it is used figuratively to mean 'to pour in' or 'to turn up unexpectedly.' It is irregular only in the past definite tense.

PLUPERFECT
aveva piovuto / era piovuto / a
avevano piovuto / erano piovuti / e

PAST ANTERIOR
ebbe piovuto / fu piovuto / a
ebbero piovuto / furono piovuti / e

FUTURE
pioverà
pioveranno

FUTURE PERFECT
avrà piovuto / sarà piovuto / a
avranno piovuto / saranno piovuti / e

PRESENT CONDITIONAL
pioverebbe
pioverebbero

CONDITIONAL PERFECT
avrebbe piovuto / sarebbe piovuto / a
avrebbero piovuto / sarebbero piovuti / e

PRESENT SUBJUNCTIVE
piova

PERFECT SUBJUNCTIVE
abbia piovuto / sia piovuto / a

IMPERFECT SUBJUNCTIVE
piovesse

PLUPERFECT SUBJUNCTIVE
aresse piovuto / fosse piovuto / a

Ha piovuto. / È piovuto.	*It has rained.*
Piovve a catinelle.	*It rained* buckets.
Non ci piove sopra.	There's no doubt about it.
Le piovvero inviti da ogni parte.	Invitations *showered* upon her from all sides.
La luce pioveva nella stanza dalla finestra aperta.	The light *poured into* the room through the open window.
Lettere gli piovevano da ogni lato.	Letters *poured in* for him from all sides.

PRESENT GERUND	PAST PARTICIPLE
ponendo	**posto**

PRESENT INDICATIVE	PRESENT PERFECT
pongo	ho posto
poni	
pone	
poniamo	
ponete	
pongono	

PRESENT PROGRESSIVE	IMPERFECT PROGRESSIVE
sto ponendo	stavo ponendo

IMPERFECT	PAST DEFINITE
ponevo	**posi**
	ponesti
	pose
	ponemmo
	poneste
	posero

Similar verbs

There are many compounds of **porre**, which follow this pattern.

apporre	affix	**opporre**	oppose
comporre	compose; dial (number)	**posporre**	postpone
decomporre	decompose	**preporre**	place / put
disporre	dispose		before; prefer
esporre	expose	**presupporre**	presuppose
frapporre	insert	**proporre**	propose
imporre	impose	**riporre**	put again
interporre	interpose	**supporre**	suppose

Note: The main irregular features of these verbs are

- the present indicative and subjunctive tenses
- the past definite tense
- the past participle
- the future stem

IMPERATIVE
poni (tu)   ponga (Lei)   poniamo (noi)   ponete (voi)   pongano (Loro)

PLUPERFECT	**PAST ANTERIOR**
avevo posto	ebbi posto
FUTURE	**FUTURE PERFECT**
porrò	avrò posto
PRESENT CONDITIONAL	**CONDITIONAL PERFECT**
porrei	avrei posto
PRESENT SUBJUNCTIVE	**PERFECT SUBJUNCTIVE**
ponga	abbia posto
ponga	
ponga	
poniamo	
poniate	
pongano	
IMPERFECT SUBJUNCTIVE	**PLUPERFECT SUBJUNCTIVE**
ponessi	avessi posto

— **Allora cosa proponi tu?**	— So what do you *propose?*
— **Porrei la sedia qui ed il divano lì.**	— *I would put* the chair here and the sofa there.
— **No, non mi piace così. Perchè non poniamo la sedia accanto al divano?**	— No, I don't like it like that. Why don't *we put* the chair next to the sofa?
— **Suppongo che devo spostare anche la televisione?**	— *I suppose* I'll have to move the television as well?
Spensierata, composi il numero.	Without thinking, *I dialed* the number.
Ha esposto delle camicie in vetrina.	*He displayed* some shirts in the window.
Esporrò le mie idee dopodomani.	*I will explain* my ideas the day after tomorrow.

PRESENT GERUND	PAST PARTICIPLE
potendo	potuto

PRESENT INDICATIVE	PRESENT PERFECT
posso	ho potuto / sono potuto / a
puoi	
può	
possiamo	
potete	
possono	

PRESENT PROGRESSIVE	IMPERFECT PROGRESSIVE
sto potendo	stavo potendo

IMPERFECT	PAST DEFINITE
potevo	potei

PLUPERFECT	PAST ANTERIOR
avevo potuto / ero potuto / a	ebbi potuto / fui potuto / a

Note: The verb **potere** is a frequently used modal verb. It is important to distinguish between **potere** and **sapere**, both of which can translate the English word 'can.' The verb **potere** denotes physical capability rather than skill.

The main irregular features of the verb are

- the present indicative and subjunctive tenses
- the past definite tense
- the future stem

The imperative is never used.

IMPERATIVE
(There is none.)

FUTURE potrò	**FUTURE PERFECT** avrò potuto / sarò potuto / a
PRESENT CONDITIONAL potrei	**CONDITIONAL PERFECT** avrei potuto / sarei potuto / a
PRESENT SUBJUNCTIVE possa possa possa possiamo possiate possano	**PERFECT SUBJUNCTIVE** abbia potuto / sia potuto / a
IMPERFECT SUBJUNCTIVE potessi	**PLUPERFECT SUBJUNCTIVE** avessi potuto / fossi potuto / a

— **Mi dispiace, non posso andare in città.**	— I'm sorry, *I can*'t go into town.
— **Ma mi hai detto che potevi venire!**	— But you said *you could* come!
— **Sì, è vero, ma ho tanto da fare. Non ne posso più.**	— Yes, it's true, but I have so much to do. *I am* completely *exhausted.*
— **Nemmeno Carlo è potuto venire.**	— Not even Carlo *has been able to* come.
— **Avresti potuto dirmelo prima!**	— *You could have* told me before now.

Note: In the last two examples the auxiliary used depends on the auxiliary normally used by the dependent infinitive, not **potere.** Thus, in **è potuto / a venire** the auxiliary is **essere** because **venire** takes **essere;** and in the final sentence **avere** is used because **dire** takes **avere.**

PRESENT GERUND	PAST PARTICIPLE
prendendo	**preso**

PRESENT INDICATIVE	PRESENT PERFECT
prendo	ho preso

PRESENT PROGRESSIVE	IMPERFECT PROGRESSIVE
sto prendendo	stavo prendendo

IMPERFECT	PAST DEFINITE
prendevo	**presi**
	prendesti
	prese
	prendemmo
	prendeste
	presero

Similar verbs

apprendere	learn	**intraprendere**	undertake
comprendere	understand, consist of	**sorprendere**	surprise

Note: The main irregular features of the verb are

- the past definite tense
- the past participle.

Hanno preso il ladro.	*They caught* the thief.
Prendo lezioni d'italiano.	*I take* Italian lessons.
Lo presi per il collo.	*I took* him by the scruff of his neck.
Fu preso dalla paura.	*He was seized* by fear.
Devi andare a prendere la zia.	You've got to go and *get* auntie.
Ho preso un appartamento in affitto.	*I rented* an apartment.
Stefano ha preso un raffreddore.	Stephen *has caught* a cold.
Tu mi sorprendi spesso!	You often *surprise* me!

IMPERATIVE
prendi (tu)   prenda (Lei)   prendiamo (noi)   prendete (voi)   prendano (Loro)

PLUPERFECT	**PAST ANTERIOR**
avevo preso	ebbi preso
FUTURE	**FUTURE PERFECT**
prenderò	avrò preso
PRESENT CONDITIONAL	**CONDITIONAL PERFECT**
prenderei	avrei preso
PRESENT SUBJUNCTIVE	**PERFECT SUBJUNCTIVE**
prenda	abbia preso
IMPERFECT SUBJUNCTIVE	**PLUPERFECT SUBJUNCTIVE**
prendessi	avessi preso

Comprese il suo errore.	*He understood* what he had done wrong.
La casa comprende un salotto, due camere, un bagno e una cucina.	The house *consists of* a lounge, two bedrooms, a bathroom, and a kitchen.
Gianni l'ha sorpreso mentre fumava.	Gianni *caught* him smoking.
Il ragazzo le prese da suo padre.	The boy *was smacked* by his father.
Prende sempre brutti voti.	*He* always *gets* bad grades.
Non ha appreso nulla a scuola.	He *has* not *learned* anything at school.
Quanto prendi al mese?	How much *do you earn* a month?
Per chi mi prendi?	Whom *do you take* me for?
Che ti prende?	What's *the matter* with you?
Non prendertela!	Don't *worry about it.*
Se l'ha presa a cuore.	He *has taken* it to heart.

PRESENT GERUND	PAST PARTICIPLE
proteggendo	**protetto**

PRESENT INDICATIVE	PRESENT PERFECT
proteggo	ho protetto

PRESENT PROGRESSIVE	IMPERFECT PROGRESSIVE
sto proteggendo	stavo proteggendo

IMPERFECT	PAST DEFINITE
proteggevo	**protessi**
	proteggesti
	protesse
	proteggemmo
	proteggeste
	protessero

Note: The main irregular features of the verb are

- the past definite tense
- the past participle

IMPERATIVE

proteggi (tu)	protegga (Lei)	proteggiamo (noi)
proteggete (voi)	proteggano (Loro)	

PLUPERFECT	**PAST ANTERIOR**
avevo protetto	ebbi protetto
FUTURE	**FUTURE PERFECT**
proteggerò	avrò protetto
PRESENT CONDITIONAL	**CONDITIONAL PERFECT**
proteggerei	avrei protetto
PRESENT SUBJUNCTIVE	**PERFECT SUBJUNCTIVE**
protegga	abbia protetto
IMPERFECT SUBJUNCTIVE	**PLUPERFECT SUBJUNCTIVE**
proteggessi	avessi protetto

Quest'ombrello ti proteggerà dalla pioggia.	This umbrella *will protect* you from the rain.
Il cane protesse la casa.	The dog *protected* the house.
Un angelo protegge il bambino.	An angel *is protecting* the baby.
Che Dio ti protegga!	May God *protect* you!
La fortuna protegge gli audaci.	Fortune *favors* the brave.

PRESENT GERUND	PAST PARTICIPLE
pungendo	**punto**

PRESENT INDICATIVE	PRESENT PERFECT
pungo	ho punto

PRESENT PROGRESSIVE	IMPERFECT PROGRESSIVE
sto pungendo	stavo pungendo

IMPERFECT	PAST DEFINITE
pungevo	**punsi**
	pungesti
	punse
	pungemmo
	pungeste
	punsero

Similar verbs

fungere	act as
mungere	milk
ungere	oil, grease, lubricate, anoint

Note: The main irregular features of the verb are

- the past definite tense
- the past participle

IMPERATIVE
pungi (tu)   punga (Lei)   pungiamo (noi)   pungete (voi)   pungano (Loro)

PLUPERFECT avevo punto	**PAST ANTERIOR** ebbi punto
FUTURE pungerò	**FUTURE PERFECT** avrò punto
PRESENT CONDITIONAL pungerei	**CONDITIONAL PERFECT** avrei punto
PRESENT SUBJUNCTIVE punga	**PERFECT SUBJUNCTIVE** abbia punto
IMPERFECT SUBJUNCTIVE pungessi	**PLUPERFECT SUBJUNCTIVE** avessi punto

Le rose pungono.	Roses *prick*.
Le vespe pungono.	Wasps *sting*.
Mi punsi la mano.	*I pricked* my hand.
Gli punge il desiderio di vederla.	*He was spurred on* by the wish to see her.
Il freddo mi pungeva il viso.	The cold *stung* my face.
Fu punto dal rimorso.	*He was pricked* with remorse.
Mi punse la coscienza.	My conscience *pricked* me.
Munse la vacca.	*He milked* the cow.
Unsero le ruote.	*They oiled* the wheels.
Fu unto re.	*He was anointed* king.
L'uomo funse da capo.	The man *acted as* leader.

PRESENT GERUND radendo	**PAST PARTICIPLE** **raso**

PRESENT INDICATIVE rado	**PRESENT PERFECT** ho raso
PRESENT PROGRESSIVE sto radendo	**IMPERFECT PROGRESSIVE** stavo radendo
IMPERFECT radevo	**PAST DEFINITE** **rasi** radesti **rase** rademmo radeste **rasero**

Similar verb

*radersi   shave oneself

Note: The main irregular features of the verb are

  • the past definite tense
  • the past participle

IMPERATIVE
radi (tu)   rada (Lei)   radiamo (noi)   radete (voi)   radano (Loro)

PLUPERFECT avevo raso	**PAST ANTERIOR** ebbi raso
FUTURE raderò	**FUTURE PERFECT** avrò raso
PRESENT CONDITIONAL raderei	**CONDITIONAL PERFECT** avrei raso
PRESENT SUBJUNCTIVE rada	**PERFECT SUBJUNCTIVE** abbia raso
IMPERFECT SUBJUNCTIVE radessi	**PLUPERFECT SUBJUNCTIVE** avessi raso

Mi ha raso male.	*He shaved* me badly.
La città fu rasa al suolo.	The city *was razed* to the ground.
Rase la superficie dell'acqua.	*It skimmed* the surface of the water.
Mi rado ogni mattina.	*I shave* every morning.

PRESENT GERUND	PAST PARTICIPLE
reggendo	**retto**

PRESENT INDICATIVE	PRESENT PERFECT
reggo	ho retto

PRESENT PROGRESSIVE	IMPERFECT PROGRESSIVE
sto reggendo	stavo reggendo

IMPERFECT	PAST DEFINITE
reggevo	**ressi**
	reggesti
	resse
	reggemmo
	reggeste
	ressero

Similar verbs

correggere   correct
sorreggere   support, hold up

Note: The main irregular features of the verb are

- the past definite tense
- the past participle

IMPERATIVE
reggi (tu)   regga (Lei)   reggiamo (noi)   reggete (voi)   reggano (Loro)

PLUPERFECT avevo retto	**PAST ANTERIOR** ebbi retto
FUTURE reggerò	**FUTURE PERFECT** avrò retto
PRESENT CONDITIONAL reggerei	**CONDITIONAL PERFECT** avrei retto
PRESENT SUBJUNCTIVE regga	**PERFECT SUBJUNCTIVE** abbia retto
IMPERFECT SUBJUNCTIVE reggessi	**PLUPERFECT SUBJUNCTIVE** avessi retto

Regge il governo.	*He is the head of* the government.
Le gambe non mi reggono.	I *cannot stand* on my feet.
Quella corda non lo reggerà.	That rope *will* not *hold* him.
La mensola non reggerà quei libri.	The shelf *will* not *support* those books.
Non reggo il vino.	I *cannot take* wine.
Questo materiale regge il fuoco.	This material *is fireproof.*
Non reggo più.	I *cannot go on.*
Bisogna correggere quel bambino.	That child *should be corrected.*
Hai corretto i compiti?	*Have you corrected* the homework?
Correggerò il tuo caffè col cognac.	*I'll lace* your coffee with brandy.
I genitori hanno sorretto il bambino.	The parents *supported / held up* the child.

PRESENT GERUND rendendo	**PAST PARTICIPLE** **reso**

PRESENT INDICATIVE rendo	**PRESENT PERFECT** ho reso

PRESENT PROGRESSIVE sto rendendo	**IMPERFECT PROGRESSIVE** stavo rendendo

IMPERFECT rendevo	**PAST DEFINITE** **resi** rendesti **rese** rendemmo rendeste **resero**

Similar verbs

*arrendersi	surrender
*rendersi conto di	realize

Note: The main irregular features of the verb are

- the past definite tense
- the past participle

IMPERATIVE
rendi (tu)   renda (Lei)   rendiamo (noi)   rendete (voi)   rendano (Loro)

PLUPERFECT	**PAST ANTERIOR**
avevo reso	ebbi reso

FUTURE
renderò

FUTURE PERFECT
avrò reso

PRESENT CONDITIONAL
renderei

CONDITIONAL PERFECT
avrei reso

PRESENT SUBJUNCTIVE
renda

PERFECT SUBJUNCTIVE
abbia reso

IMPERFECT SUBJUNCTIVE
rendessi

PLUPERFECT SUBJUNCTIVE
avessi reso

Mi ha reso il libro ieri.	He *gave* me the book *back* yesterday.
Rendimi la penna che ti ho prestata.	*Give* me *back* the pen that I lent you.
Questo lavoro non rende molto.	This job *is* not well *paid.*
L'amore rende felici.	Love *makes* you happy.
Questa notizia lo rese incapace di parlare.	This piece of news *left* him speechless.
È difficile rendere il senso dell'originale in una traduzione.	It is difficult to *render* the sense of the original in a translation.
Non mi sono reso conto di ciò che è successo.	I *did* not *realize* what happened.
I soldati si sono arresi.	The soldiers *surrendered.*

PRESENT GERUND	PAST PARTICIPLE
ridendo	**riso**

PRESENT INDICATIVE	PRESENT PERFECT
rido	ho riso

PRESENT PROGRESSIVE	IMPERFECT PROGRESSIVE
sto ridendo	stavo ridendo

IMPERFECT	PAST DEFINITE
ridevo	**risi**
	ridesti
	rise
	ridemmo
	rideste
	risero

Similar verbs

deridere   deride, ridicule
sorridere   smile

Note: The main irregular features of the verb are

- the past definite tense
- the past participle

IMPERATIVE
ridi (tu)   rida (Lei)   ridiamo (noi)   ridete (voi)   ridano (Loro)

PLUPERFECT avevo riso	**PAST ANTERIOR** ebbi riso
FUTURE riderò	**FUTURE PERFECT** avrò riso
PRESENT CONDITIONAL riderei	**CONDITIONAL PERFECT** avrei riso
PRESENT SUBJUNCTIVE rida	**PERFECT SUBJUNCTIVE** abbia riso
IMPERFECT SUBJUNCTIVE ridessi	**PLUPERFECT SUBJUNCTIVE** avessi riso

---

Non c'è da ridere!	It's not a laughing matter!
Non ci vedo niente da ridere.	I can't see anything *to laugh about*.
Ma non farmi ridere!	But don't make me *laugh!*
Quella bambina sorride sempre.	That girl *is* always *smiling*.
Gianni mi sorrise.	Gianni *smiled* at me.
La fortuna gli sorride.	Good fortune *smiles* on him.
L'hanno deriso.	*They ridiculed* him.
Risero alle sue spalle.	*They laughed* behind his back.
I suoi occhi risero di gioia.	Her eyes *sparkled* with happiness.
Ride bene chi ride ultimo. **(Proverbio)**	*He* who *laughs* last *laughs* best. (*Proverb*)
La fortuna gli ride.	Good luck *smiles* at him.
Chi ride il venerdì, piange la domenica.	*Laugh* today, for tomorrow you may cry.

PRESENT GERUND	PAST PARTICIPLE
rimanendo	**rimasto**

PRESENT INDICATIVE	PRESENT PERFECT
rimango	sono rimasto / a
rimani	
rimane	
rimaniamo	
rimanete	
rimangono	

PRESENT PROGRESSIVE	IMPERFECT PROGRESSIVE
sto rimanendo	stavo rimanendo

IMPERFECT	PAST DEFINITE
rimanevo	**rimasi**
	rimanesti
	rimase
	rimanemmo
	rimaneste
	rimasero

Note: The main irregular features of the verb are

- the present indicative and subjunctive tenses
- the past definite tense
- the past participle
- the future stem

IMPERATIVE
rimani (tu)   **rimanga** (Lei)   rimaniamo (noi)   rimanete (voi)   rimangano (Loro)

PLUPERFECT ero rimasto / a	**PAST ANTERIOR** fui rimasto / a
FUTURE rimarrò	**FUTURE PERFECT** sarò rimasto / a
PRESENT CONDITIONAL **rimarrei**	**CONDITIONAL PERFECT** sarei rimasto / a
PRESENT SUBJUNCTIVE **rimanga** **rimanga** **rimanga** rimaniamo rimaniate **rimangano**	**PERFECT SUBJUNCTIVE** sia rimasto / a
IMPERFECT SUBJUNCTIVE rimanessi	**PLUPERFECT SUBJUNCTIVE** fossi rimasto / a

---

—**Quanto tempo rimani in Italia?**	—How long *are you staying* in Italy?
—**Rimango due settimane.**	—*I am staying* two weeks.
—**Che ti rimane da fare?**	—What *have you left* to do?
—**Mi rimane soltanto la conclusione del tema.**	—*I have* only the essay's conclusion *left* to do.
—**Dubito che tu rimanga fino alla festa allora.**	—I doubt that *you are staying* until the party then.

PRESENT GERUND risolvendo	PAST PARTICIPLE **risolto**

PRESENT INDICATIVE risolvo	PRESENT PERFECT ho risolto

PRESENT PROGRESSIVE sto risolvendo	IMPERFECT PROGRESSIVE stavo risolvendo

IMPERFECT risolvevo	PAST DEFINITE **risolsi** / risolvei / risolvetti risolvesti **risolse** risolvemmo risolveste **risolsero**

Similar verbs

assolvere   absolve, acquit
dissolvere   dissolve
***risolversi di**   decide, make up one's mind

Note: The main irregular features of the verb are

   • the past definite tense
   • the past participle

IMPERATIVE
risolvi (tu)   risolva (Lei)   risolviamo (noi)   risolvete (voi)   risolvano (Loro)

PLUPERFECT avevo risolto	**PAST ANTERIOR** ebbi risolto
FUTURE risolverò	**FUTURE PERFECT** avrò risolto
PRESENT CONDITIONAL risolverei	**CONDITIONAL PERFECT** avrei risolto
PRESENT SUBJUNCTIVE risolva	**PERFECT SUBJUNCTIVE** abbia risolto
IMPERFECT SUBJUNCTIVE risolvessi	**PLUPERFECT SUBJUNCTIVE** avessi risolto

Risolse di farlo lui stesso.	*He resolved* to do it himself.
Hai risolto l'equazione?	*Have you solved* the equation?
Dubito che quel problema sia stato risolto.	I doubt whether that problem *has been resolved.*
Si risolse di andare via.	*He made up his mind* to go away.
Il ladro fu assolto.	The thief *was acquitted.*

PRESENT GERUND	PAST PARTICIPLE
rispondendo	**risposto**

PRESENT INDICATIVE	PRESENT PERFECT
rispondo	ho risposto

PRESENT PROGRESSIVE
sto rispondendo

IMPERFECT PROGRESSIVE
stavo rispondendo

IMPERFECT
rispondevo

PAST DEFINITE
risposi
rispondesti
rispose
rispondemmo
rispondeste
risposero

Similar verbs

corrispondere	correspond
nascondere	hide
*nascondersi	hide (oneself)

Note: The main irregular features of the verb are

- the past definite tense
- the past participle

IMPERATIVE

rispondi (tu)	risponda (Lei)	rispondiamo (noi)
rispondete (voi)	rispondano (Loro)	

PLUPERFECT
avevo risposto

PAST ANTERIOR
ebbi risposto

FUTURE
risponderò

FUTURE PERFECT
avrò risposto

PRESENT CONDITIONAL
risponderei

CONDITIONAL PERFECT
avrei risposto

PRESENT SUBJUNCTIVE
risponda

PERFECT SUBJUNCTIVE
abbia risposto

IMPERFECT SUBJUNCTIVE
rispondessi

PLUPERFECT SUBJUNCTIVE
avessi risposto

Ha risposto subito alla mia proposta.	*He replied* immediately to my proposal.
Risposi per iscritto.	*I replied* in writing.
Gianna rispose con un cenno del capo.	Gianna *replied* with a nod of the head.
Io non rispondo delle azioni di mio fratello.	*I cannot be held responsible* for the actions of my brother.
Questo motore non risponde.	This engine *is* not *responding*.
Nascose la sua identitá.	*He hid* his identity.
Nadia e Giulia si sono nascoste nel giardino.	Nadia and Giulia *hid* in the garden.
La descrizione nel pieghevole non corrispondeva alla realtà.	The description in the brochure *did* not *correspond* to reality / give a true picture.

PRESENT GERUND	PAST PARTICIPLE
rompendo	**rotto**

PRESENT INDICATIVE	PRESENT PERFECT
rompo	ho rotto

PRESENT PROGRESSIVE	IMPERFECT PROGRESSIVE
sto rompendo	stavo rompendo

IMPERFECT	PAST DEFINITE
rompevo	**ruppi**
	rompesti
	ruppe
	rompemmo
	rompeste
	ruppero

Similar verbs

corrompere	corrupt
interrompere	interrupt
irrompere	break into
prorompere	burst out
*rompersi	break up

Note: The main irregular features of the verb are

- the past definite tense
- the past participle

IMPERATIVE
rompi (tu)   rompa (Lei)   rompiamo (noi)   rompete (voi)   rompano (Loro)

PLUPERFECT
avevo rotto

PAST ANTERIOR
ebbi rotto

FUTURE
romperò

FUTURE PERFECT
avrò rotto

PRESENT CONDITIONAL
romperei

CONDITIONAL PERFECT
avrei rotto

PRESENT SUBJUNCTIVE
rompa

PERFECT SUBJUNCTIVE
abbia rotto

IMPERFECT SUBJUNCTIVE
rompessi

PLUPERFECT SUBJUNCTIVE
avessi rotto

Ho rotto un vaso ieri.	*I broke* a vase yesterday.
Hai rotto la tua promessa!	*You have broken* your promise!
Vorrei romperla con quel ragazzo.	I would like *to break up* with that boy.
La nave si ruppe sulle rocce.	The ship *broke up* on the rocks.
Hai corrotto tutto!	*You have corrupted* everything!
Interruppe la nostra conversazione.	*He interrupted* our conversation.
Ho interrotto il viaggio a Firenze.	*I called off* my trip to Florence.
La corrente è stata interrotta per un'ora.	The electricity was *cut off* for an hour.
I ladri irruppero nella casa.	The thieves *broke into* the house.
La folla irruppe nello stadio.	The crowd *broke into* the stadium.

PRESENT GERUND	**PAST PARTICIPLE**
salendo	salito

PRESENT INDICATIVE	**PRESENT PERFECT**
salgo	ho salito / sono salito / a
sali	
sale	
saliamo	
salite	
salgono	

PRESENT PROGRESSIVE	**IMPERFECT PROGRESSIVE**
sto salendo	stavo salendo

IMPERFECT	**PAST DEFINITE**
salivo	salii

Similar verb

† **assalire**   attack, seize, overcome

Note: The main irregular features of the verb are

• the present indicative and subjunctive tenses
• it takes **avere** when used transitively and **essere** when used intransitively

IMPERATIVE
sali (tu)   **salga** (Lei)   saliamo (noi)   salite (voi)   salgano (Loro)

PLUPERFECT avevo salito / ero salito / a	**PAST ANTERIOR** ebbi salito / fui salito / a
FUTURE salirò	**FUTURE PERFECT** avrò salito / sarò salito / a
PRESENT CONDITIONAL salirei	**CONDITIONAL PERFECT** avrei salito / sarei salito / a
PRESENT SUBJUNCTIVE **salga** **salga** **salga** saliamo saliate **salgano**	**PERFECT SUBJUNCTIVE** abbia salito / sia salito / a
IMPERFECT SUBJUNCTIVE salissi	**PLUPERFECT SUBJUNCTIVE** avessi salito / fossi salito / a

—**Saliamo fino a quel punto lì?**	— *Shall we go up* to that point there?
—**Io non salgo più!**	— I'*m* not *going up* any further.
—**Che peccato che tu non salga lassù — c'è un panorama bellissimo da quel punto.**	— What a shame that *you are* not *going up* there — there is a beautiful view from that point.
Fu assalita dai dubbi.	*She was assailed* by doubts.
Fummo assaliti dal temporale.	*We were caught* in the storm.

PRESENT GERUND	**PAST PARTICIPLE**
sapendo	saputo

PRESENT INDICATIVE	**PRESENT PERFECT**
so	ho saputo
sai	
sa	
sappiamo	
sapete	
sanno	

PRESENT PROGRESSIVE	**IMPERFECT PROGRESSIVE**
sto sapendo	stavo sapendo

IMPERFECT	**PAST DEFINITE**
sapevo	**seppi**
	sapesti
	seppe
	sapemmo
	sapeste
	seppero

Note: The verb **sapere** is frequently used as a modal verb. It is important to distinguish between **potere** [▶65] and **sapere,** both of which can translate the English word 'can.' The verb **sapere** denotes skill rather than physical capability.

It is also important to distinguish between the verbs **conoscere** [▶34] and **sapere,** which can both be translated as 'to know' in English. **Conoscere** means to know a person or a place, whereas **sapere** means to know a fact or to know how to do something.

The main irregular features of the verb **sapere** are

- the present indicative and subjunctive tenses
- the past definite tense
- the future stem

IMPERATIVE
sappi (tu)   **sappia** (Lei)   **sappiamo** (noi)   **sappiate** (voi)   **sappiano** (Loro)

PLUPERFECT	PAST ANTERIOR
avevo saputo	ebbi saputo

FUTURE	FUTURE PERFECT
saprò	avrò saputo

PRESENT CONDITIONAL	CONDITIONAL PERFECT
saprei	avrei saputo

PRESENT SUBJUNCTIVE	PERFECT SUBJUNCTIVE
sappia	abbia saputo
sappia	
sappia	
sappiamo	
sappiate	
sappiano	

IMPERFECT SUBJUNCTIVE	PLUPERFECT SUBJUNCTIVE
sapessi	avessi saputo

—So suonare il flauto adesso.

—Non saprei da dove cominciare!

—Conosci la mia maestra?

—No, non la conosco, ma so dove abita.

—Pare che sappia suonare molto bene.

—*I know* how to play the flute now.

—*I would*n't *know* where to begin!

—Do you know my teacher?

—No, I don't know her, but *I know* where she lives.

—It seems that she *knows* how to play very well.

PRESENT GERUND	PAST PARTICIPLE
scendendo	**sceso**

PRESENT INDICATIVE	PRESENT PERFECT
scendo	ho sceso / sono sceso / a

PRESENT PROGRESSIVE	IMPERFECT PROGRESSIVE
sto scendendo	stavo scendendo

IMPERFECT	PAST DEFINITE
scendevo	**scesi**
	scendesti
	scese
	scendemmo
	scendeste
	scesero

Similar verbs

† **accondiscendere**	consent
† **ascendere**	ascend
† **discendere**	descend

† Like **scendere,** these verbs can take either **avere** or **essere,** depending on whether they are used transitively or intransitively.

Note: The main irregular features of the verb are

- the past definite tense
- the past participle

Sono sceso / a.	*I went downstairs.*
Scese le scale correndo.	*He came running downstairs.*
Sono scesi dal tram.	*They got off the tram.*
La montagna scende verso il mare.	*The mountain slopes down towards the sea.*

IMPERATIVE
scendi (tu)   scenda (Lei)   scendiamo (noi)   scendete (voi)   scendano (Loro)

PLUPERFECT	**PAST ANTERIOR**
avevo sceso / ero sceso / a	ebbi sceso / fui sceso / a
FUTURE	**FUTURE PERFECT**
scenderò	avrò sceso / sarò sceso / a
PRESENT CONDITIONAL	**CONDITIONAL PERFECT**
scenderei	avrei sceso / sarei sceso / a
PRESENT SUBJUNCTIVE	**PERFECT SUBJUNCTIVE**
scenda	abbia sceso / sia sceso / a
IMPERFECT SUBJUNCTIVE	**PLUPERFECT SUBJUNCTIVE**
scendessi	avessi sceso / fossi sceso / a

La temperatura è scesa oggi.	The temperature *has gone down* today.
Perché non scendiamo al bar a prendere un caffè?	Why *don*'t *we go* to the bar for a coffee?
I capelli le scendevano alle spalle.	Her hair *fell over* her shoulders.
Accondiscese a una riduzione di prezzo.	*He consented* to a reduction in price.
Ascese al trono.	*He ascended* to the throne.
I cristiani credono che dopo la Risurrezione Gesú sia asceso al cielo.	Christians believe that after his Resurrection, Jesus *ascended to* heaven.
Discesi le scale.	*I went* downstairs.
Il fiume discende verso il mare.	The river *flows down* to the sea.

PRESENT GERUND scorgendo	PAST PARTICIPLE **scorto**
PRESENT INDICATIVE scorgo	PRESENT PERFECT ho scorto
PRESENT PROGRESSIVE sto scorgendo	IMPERFECT PROGRESSIVE stavo scorgendo
IMPERFECT scorgevo	PAST DEFINITE **scorsi** scorgesti **scorse** scorgemmo scorgeste **scorsero**

Similar verbs

*accorgersi	notice
porgere	hand, give, hold out
*risorgere	rise again, revive
*sorgere	rise
*sporgere	project, stick out, jut out
*sporgersi	lean out

Note: The main irregular features of the verb are

• the past definite tense
• the past participle

In lontananza scorgevo una figura di uomo avvicinarsi.	In the distance *I noticed* the shape of a man approach.
Se ne andò senza farsi scorgere.	He went away without *being noticed.*
Non vuole farsi scorgere da lui.	She does not want him *to notice* her.

IRREGULAR VERBS   scorgere 80

IMPERATIVE
scorgi (tu)   scorga (Lei)   scorgiamo (noi)   scorgete (voi)   scorgano (Loro)

PLUPERFECT avevo scorto	**PAST ANTERIOR** ebbi scorto
FUTURE scorgerò	**FUTURE PERFECT** avrò scorto
PRESENT CONDITIONAL scorgerei	**CONDITIONAL PERFECT** avrei scorto
PRESENT SUBJUNCTIVE scorga	**PERFECT SUBJUNCTIVE** abbia scorto
IMPERFECT SUBJUNCTIVE scorgessi	**PLUPERFECT SUBJUNCTIVE** avessi scorto

Non me ne sono nemmeno accorto!	*I did*n't even *notice!*
Non si era accorta che pioveva.	She *didn't notice* it was raining.
Poi sorse una grande discussione.	Then a great discussion *arose*.
Le montagne sorgono davanti a me.	The mountains *are looming* in front of me.
Ho visto sorgere il sole.	I saw the sun *rise*.
La nebbia sorse dal lago.	The fog *rose* from the lake.
Le sue speranze risorsero.	His hopes *revived*.
È pericoloso sporgersi dal finestrino.	It is dangerous *to lean out* of the window.

PRESENT GERUND	PAST PARTICIPLE
scrivendo	**scritto**

PRESENT INDICATIVE	PRESENT PERFECT
scrivo	ho scritto

PRESENT PROGRESSIVE	IMPERFECT PROGRESSIVE
sto scrivendo	stavo scrivendo

IMPERFECT	PAST DEFINITE
scrivevo	**scrissi**
	scrivesti
	scrisse
	scrivemmo
	scriveste
	scrissero

Similar verbs

descrivere	describe
iscrivere	enroll, register
*iscriversi	enroll (oneself)

Note: The main irregular features of the verb are

- the past definite tense
- the past participle

IMPERATIVE
scrivi (tu)　scriva (Lei)　scriviamo (noi)　scrivete (voi)　scrivano (Loro)

PLUPERFECT avevo scritto	**PAST ANTERIOR** ebbi scritto
FUTURE scriverò	**FUTURE PERFECT** avrò scritto
PRESENT CONDITIONAL scriverei	**CONDITIONAL PERFECT** avrei scritto
PRESENT SUBJUNCTIVE scriva	**PERFECT SUBJUNCTIVE** abbia scritto
IMPERFECT SUBJUNCTIVE scrivessi	**PLUPERFECT SUBJUNCTIVE** avessi scritto

Come si scrive questa parola?	How *do you spell* this word?
Sa scrivere la musica.	He knows how *to write* music.
Gli ho scritto due righe.	*I wrote* him a note (two lines).
Scrissi a casa non appena fui arrivata a Roma.	*I wrote* home as soon as I arrived in Rome.
Ti iscrivo al club?	*Shall I enroll* you (as a member) in the club?
Mi sono iscritto all'università.	*I enrolled* at the university.
Descrisse la scena in montagna.	*He described* the scene in the mountains.
Vorrei descrivere un'ampia curva.	I would like *to describe* a wide curve.

PRESENT GERUND	PAST PARTICIPLE
scotendo	**scosso**

PRESENT INDICATIVE	PRESENT PERFECT
scuoto	ho scosso
scuoti	
scuote	
scotiamo	
scotete	
scuotono	

PRESENT PROGRESSIVE	IMPERFECT PROGRESSIVE
sto scuotendo	stavo scuotendo

IMPERFECT	PAST DEFINITE
scotevo	**scossi**
	scotesti
	scosse
	scotemmo
	scoteste
	scossero

Similar verbs

percuotere	beat, strike
ripercuotere	beat again
*ripercuotersi	reverberate, affect
riscuotere	collect, cash

Note: The main irregular features of the verb are

  • the past definite tense
  • the past participle

IMPERATIVE
scuoti (tu)   scuota (Lei)   scotiamo (noi)   scotete (voi)   scuotano (Loro)

PLUPERFECT
avevo scosso

PAST ANTERIOR
ebbi scosso

FUTURE
scoterò

FUTURE PERFECT
avrò scosso

PRESENT CONDITIONAL
scoterei

CONDITIONAL PERFECT
avrei scosso

PRESENT SUBJUNCTIVE
scuota

PERFECT SUBJUNCTIVE
abbia scosso

IMPERFECT SUBJUNCTIVE
scotessi

PLUPERFECT SUBJUNCTIVE
avessi scosso

Scosse l'albero.	*He shook* the tree.
Scuote la testa.	*He shakes* his head.
Fu scossa dalla notizia.	*She was shaken* by the news.
Ho riscosso l'assegno.	*I cashed* the check.
La sua influenza si ripercosse su tutti i colleghi.	His influence *reverberated* on all his colleagues.
Lo percosse a morte.	*He struck* him dead.

PRESENT GERUND	PAST PARTICIPLE
solendo	**solito**

PRESENT INDICATIVE
soglio
suoli
suole
sogliamo
solete
sogliono

IMPERFECT	PAST DEFINITE
solevo	solei
solevi	solesti
soleva	
solevamo	
solevate	
solevano	

Note: The main irregular features of the verb are

• the present indicative
• the past participle
• **solere** is a 'defective verb' (**verbo difettivo**), which means that some forms of it exist but not others. The other forms either never existed or have fallen out of use. In their place, one uses corresponding tenses of verbal expressions **essere solito** and **avere l'abitudine / la consuetudine.**

PRESENT SUBJUNCTIVE
soglia
soglia
soglia
sogliamo
sogliate
sogliano

IMPERFECT SUBJUNCTIVE
solessi
solessi
solesse
solessimo
soleste
solessero

Soleva alzarsi tardi ogni giorno.	*He used to* get up late every day.
Oggi lavora di più di quanto soleva fare due anni fa.	Nowadays he works more than *he used to* two years ago.
Suole alzarsi di buon'ora.	He usually gets up early.
Ogni sera al tramonto del sole le ragazze solevano andare a fare una passeggiata.	Every evening at sunset the girls *used to* go for a walk.
La domenica siamo soliti pranzare all'una.	On Sundays *we are used to* having dinner at one.
Come si suol dire, 'Meglio tardi che mai'!	As they say, 'Better late than never'!
Ci sogliamo ritrovare a casa dei genitori ogni domenica.	*We are used to* meeting at the parents' house every Sunday.

PRESENT GERUND	PAST PARTICIPLE
spargendo	**sparso**

PRESENT INDICATIVE	PRESENT PERFECT
spargo	ho sparso

PRESENT PROGRESSIVE	IMPERFECT PROGRESSIVE
sto spargendo	stavo spargendo

IMPERFECT	PAST DEFINITE
spargevo	**sparsi**
	spargesti
	sparse
	spargemmo
	spargeste
	sparsero

Similar verbs

aspergere	sprinkle
***emergere**	emerge
immergere	immerse
sommergere	submerge

Note: The main irregular features of the verb are

- the past definite tense
- the past participle

IMPERATIVE
spargi (tu)   sparga (Lei)   spargiamo (noi)   spargete (voi)   spargano (Loro)

PLUPERFECT
avevo sparso

PAST ANTERIOR
ebbi sparso

FUTURE
spargerò

FUTURE PERFECT
avrò sparso

PRESENT CONDITIONAL
spargerei

CONDITIONAL PERFECT
avrei sparso

PRESENT SUBJUNCTIVE
sparga

PERFECT SUBJUNCTIVE
abbia sparso

IMPERFECT SUBJUNCTIVE
spargessi

PLUPERFECT SUBJUNCTIVE
avessi sparso

Sparse fiori sulla tomba.	*He scattered* flowers on the grave.
Ho sparso zucchero sulla torta.	*I sprinkled* sugar on the cake.
Il lume spargeva una luce fioca.	The lamp *shed* a dim light.
Sparge una notizia ai quattro venti!	He always tells everyone!
Il prete aspergerà l'acqua sul bambino.	The priest *will sprinkle* water on the baby.
Le onde avevano sommerso la barca.	The waves *had submerged* the boat.
L'ho immerso in acqua.	*I immersed* it in water.
Una sirena è emersa dall'acqua.	A mermaid *emerged* from the water.

PRESENT GERUND	PAST PARTICIPLE
spegnendo	**spento**

PRESENT INDICATIVE	PRESENT PERFECT
spengo	ho spento
spegni	
spegne	
spegniamo	
spegnete	
spengono	

PRESENT PROGRESSIVE	IMPERFECT PROGRESSIVE
sto spegnendo	stavo spegnendo

IMPERFECT	PAST DEFINITE
spegnevo	**spensi**
	spegnesti
	spense
	spegnemmo
	spegneste
	spensero

Note: The main irregular features of the verb are

- the present indicative and subjunctive tenses
- the past definite tense
- the past participle

IMPERATIVE
spegni (tu) **spenga** (Lei) spegniamo (noi) spegnete (voi) spengano (Loro)

PLUPERFECT
avevo spento

PAST ANTERIOR
ebbi spento

FUTURE
spegnerò

FUTURE PERFECT
avrò spento

PRESENT CONDITIONAL
spegnerei

CONDITIONAL PERFECT
avrei spento

PRESENT SUBJUNCTIVE
spenga
spenga
spenga
spegniamo
spegniate
spengano

PERFECT SUBJUNCTIVE
abbia spento

IMPERFECT SUBJUNCTIVE
spegnessi

PLUPERFECT SUBJUNCTIVE
avessi spento

Gianna spense la luce nella sala.

Gianna *turned off* the light in the room.

Spenta la luce, cominciò ad avere paura.

When the light *went off,* she began to be afraid.

«Ho paura che il fantasma spenga ogni luce nella casa», disse.

"I am afraid that the ghost *will turn off* every light in the house," she said.

PRESENT GERUND	PAST PARTICIPLE
spingendo	**spinto**

PRESENT INDICATIVE	PRESENT PERFECT
spingo	ho spinto

PRESENT PROGRESSIVE	IMPERFECT PROGRESSIVE
sto spingendo	stavo spingendo

IMPERFECT	PAST DEFINITE
spingevo	**spinsi**
	spingesti
	spinse
	spingemmo
	spingeste
	spinsero

Similar verbs

dipingere	paint
fingere	pretend
respingere	push back
sospingere	push, drive

Note: The main irregular features of the verb are

- the past definite tense
- the past participle

IMPERATIVE
spingi (tu)   spinga (Lei)   spingiamo (noi)   spingete (voi)   spingano (Loro)

PLUPERFECT avevo spinto	**PAST ANTERIOR** ebbi spinto
FUTURE spingerò	**FUTURE PERFECT** avrò spinto
PRESENT CONDITIONAL spingerei	**CONDITIONAL PERFECT** avrei spinto
PRESENT SUBJUNCTIVE spinga	**PERFECT SUBJUNCTIVE** abbia spinto
IMPERFECT SUBJUNCTIVE spingessi	**PLUPERFECT SUBJUNCTIVE** avessi spinto

Spingete!	*Push!*
Che cosa ti ha spinto a partire così presto?	What *has driven* you to leave so early?
Mio padre mi spinge a studiare di più.	My father *is urging* me to study harder.
Spinse Luigi dentro.	*He pushed* Luigi inside.
Spinse l'amore fino al ridicolo.	*She carried* her love to ridiculous extremes.
Hai spinto quello scherzo oltre i limiti.	*You have pushed* that joke too far.
Respinsero la folla.	*They pushed back* the crowd.
La fame la sospinse a rubare.	Hunger *drove* her to steal.
Finsi di essere addormentata.	*I pretended* I was asleep.
L'anno scorso dipinsi sette quadri, mentre quest'anno ne ho dipinto appena due.	Last year *I painted* seven pictures, whereas this year I barely painted two.

PRESENT GERUND	**PAST PARTICIPLE**
stando	stato

PRESENT INDICATIVE	**PRESENT PERFECT**
sto	sono stato / a
stai	
sta	
stiamo	
state	
stanno	

IMPERFECT	**PAST DEFINITE**
stavo	**stetti**
	stesti
	stette
	stemmo
	steste
	stettero

Note: The verb **stare** often takes over the duties of **essere,** and indeed the verb **essere** *borrows* the past participle of **stare.**

The main irregular features of the verb are

- the present indicative and subjunctive tenses
- the imperfect subjunctive tense
- the past definite tense
- the future stem

IMPERATIVE
sta / sta' / stai (tu)   **stia** (Lei)   stiamo (noi)   state (voi)   stiano (Loro)

PLUPERFECT ero stato	**PAST ANTERIOR** fui stato / a
FUTURE **starò**	**FUTURE PERFECT** sarò stato / a
PRESENT CONDITIONAL **starei**	**CONDITIONAL PERFECT** sarei stato / a
PRESENT SUBJUNCTIVE **stia** **stia** **stia** stiamo stiate **stiano**	**PERFECT SUBJUNCTIVE** sia stato / a
IMPERFECT SUBJUNCTIVE **stessi** **stessi** **stesse** **stessimo** **steste** **stessero**	**PLUPERFECT SUBJUNCTIVE** fossi stato / a

— **Come stai oggi?**	— How *are you* today?
— **Sto un po meglio, grazie.**	— *I am* a little better, thank you.
Stettero tre giorni a Roma e due in provincia.	*They stayed* three days in Rome and two in the country.
Stavo per andarmene quando arrivò Maurizio.	I was about to leave when Maurizio arrived.

PRESENT GERUND	PAST PARTICIPLE
stringendo	**stretto**

PRESENT INDICATIVE	PRESENT PERFECT
stringo	ho stretto

PRESENT PROGRESSIVE	IMPERFECT PROGRESSIVE
sto stringendo	stavo stringendo

IMPERFECT	PAST DEFINITE
stringevo	**strinsi**
	stringesti
	strinse
	stringemmo
	stringeste
	strinsero

Similar verbs

costringere	force
restringere	narrow, tighten

Note: The main irregular features of the verb are

- the past definite tense
- the past participle

IMPERATIVE
stringi (tu)   stringa (Lei)   stringiamo (noi)   stringete (voi)   stringano (Loro)

PLUPERFECT avevo stretto	**PAST ANTERIOR** ebbi stretto
FUTURE stringerò	**FUTURE PERFECT** avrò stretto
PRESENT CONDITIONAL stringerei	**CONDITIONAL PERFECT** avrei stretto
PRESENT SUBJUNCTIVE stringa	**PERFECT SUBJUNCTIVE** abbia stretto
IMPERFECT SUBJUNCTIVE stringessi	**PLUPERFECT SUBJUNCTIVE** avessi stretto

Mi strinse la mano.	He *shook* my hand.
Strinsi mia figlia tra le braccia.	*I hugged* my daughter.
Ha stretto la moneta in mano.	*He gripped* the coin in his hand.
Devo stringere la cinghia.	I must *tighten* my belt.
Mi hanno costretto ad andarmene.	*They forced* me out.
Mi ha costretto a venire stasera.	*He made* me come this evening.
Ho fatto restringere il vestito.	I have had the dress *taken in*.

PRESENT GERUND	PAST PARTICIPLE
struggendo	**strutto**

PRESENT INDICATIVE	PRESENT PERFECT
struggo	ho strutto

PRESENT PROGRESSIVE
sto struggendo

IMPERFECT PROGRESSIVE
stavo struggendo

IMPERFECT
struggevo

PAST DEFINITE
strussi
struggesti
strusse
struggemmo
struggeste
strussero

Similar verb

distruggere   destroy

Note: The main irregular features of the verb are

- the past definite tense
- the past participle

IMPERATIVE
struggi (tu)   strugga (Lei)   struggiamo (noi)   struggete (voi)   struggano (Loro)

PLUPERFECT
avevo strutto

PAST ANTERIOR
ebbi strutto

FUTURE
struggerò

FUTURE PERFECT
avrò strutto

PRESENT CONDITIONAL
struggerei

CONDITIONAL PERFECT
avrei strutto

PRESENT SUBJUNCTIVE
strugga

PERFECT SUBJUNCTIVE
abbia strutto

IMPERFECT SUBJUNCTIVE
struggessi

PLUPERFECT SUBJUNCTIVE
avessi strutto

Strussi la cera.	*I melted* the wax.
La malattia lo strugge.	*He is wasting away* because of the illness / sickness.
Distrussero la casa.	*They destroyed* the house.
Fu distrutto dal dolore alla gamba.	*He was overcome* with the pain in his leg.
Il vino l'ha distrutto.	Wine *has been his ruin.*
I bombardamenti distrussero tutta la zona.	The bombardments *destroyed* the entire region.

PRESENT GERUND	PAST PARTICIPLE
tacendo	taciuto

PRESENT INDICATIVE	PRESENT PERFECT
taccio	ho taciuto
taci	
tace	
taciamo	
tacete	
tacciono	

PRESENT PROGRESSIVE	IMPERFECT PROGRESSIVE
sto tacendo	stavo tacendo

IMPERFECT	PAST DEFINITE
tacevo	**tacqui**
	tacesti
	tacque
	tacemmo
	taceste
	tacquero

Note: The main irregular features of the verb are

- the present indicative and subjunctive tenses
- the past definite tense
- the additional **i** in the past participle

IMPERATIVE
taci (tu)   **taccia** (Lei)   **tacciamo** (noi)   tacete (voi)   **tacciano** (Loro)

PLUPERFECT	**PAST ANTERIOR**
avevo taciuto	ebbi taciuto
FUTURE	**FUTURE PERFECT**
tacerò	avrò taciuto
PRESENT CONDITIONAL	**CONDITIONAL PERFECT**
tacerei	avrei taciuto
PRESENT SUBJUNCTIVE	**PERFECT SUBJUNCTIVE**
taccia	abbia taciuto
taccia	
taccia	
taciamo	
taciate	
tacciano	
IMPERFECT SUBJUNCTIVE	**PLUPERFECT SUBJUNCTIVE**
tacessi	avessi taciuto

Il padre tacque.	The father *fell silent.*
I ragazzi non tacquero, però.	The children *were* not *silent,* however.
«Tacete», disse la mamma.	"*Be quiet,*" said their mother.
I bambini tacevano ed ascoltavano la maestra.	The children *were silent,* and they listened to the teacher.

PRESENT GERUND tendendo	**PAST PARTICIPLE** **teso**

PRESENT INDICATIVE tendo	**PRESENT PERFECT** ho teso

PRESENT PROGRESSIVE sto tendendo	**IMPERFECT PROGRESSIVE** stavo tendendo

IMPERFECT tendevo	**PAST DEFINITE** **tesi** tendesti **tese** tendemmo tendeste **tesero**

Similar verbs

attendere	wait
contendere	contend
distendere	stretch
estendere	extend
intendere	intend, understand
pretendere	claim
sottintendere	hint at
stendere	spread, stretch out

Note: The main irregular features of the verb are

- the past definite tense
- the past participle

Mi tese la mano.	*He stretched out* his hand.
Il cane ha teso gli orecchi.	The dog *pricked up* its ears.
Ho teso la corda.	*I pulled* the rope tight.
Ha teso le corde del violino.	*He tightened* the strings of the violin.

IMPERATIVE
tendi (tu)   tenda (Lei)   tendiamo (noi)   tendete (voi)   tendano (Loro)

PLUPERFECT avevo teso	**PAST ANTERIOR** ebbi teso
FUTURE tenderò	**FUTURE PERFECT** avrò teso
PRESENT CONDITIONAL tenderei	**CONDITIONAL PERFECT** avrei teso
PRESENT SUBJUNCTIVE tenda	**PERFECT SUBJUNCTIVE** abbia teso
IMPERFECT SUBJUNCTIVE tendessi	**PLUPERFECT SUBJUNCTIVE** avessi teso

Tende ad ingrassare.	*She tends* to get fat.
Che colore è? Tende al rosso.	What color / colour is it? A reddish color / colour.
Pretende di essere un grande artista.	*He pretends* to be a great artist.
Pretese di aver ragione.	*He claimed* to be right.
Attendiamo una pronta risposta.	*We are waiting* for a prompt reply.
Nessuno gli contese i suoi diritti.	No one *contested* his rights.
Distesi la mano per aiutare la ragazza.	*I stretched out* my hand to help the girl.
Che cosa intendi fare?	What *do you intend* to do?
Sottintende la verità.	*He is hinting* at the truth.
Giuliana stese il bucato sull'erba.	Giuliana *laid out* the washing on the grass.
Mi ha steso la mano.	*He streched out* his hand to me.

PRESENT GERUND	PAST PARTICIPLE
tenendo	tenuto

PRESENT INDICATIVE	PRESENT PERFECT
tengo	ho tenuto
tieni	
tiene	
teniamo	
tenete	
tengono	

PRESENT PROGRESSIVE	IMPERFECT PROGRESSIVE
sto tenendo	stavo tenendo

IMPERFECT	PAST DEFINITE
tenevo	**tenni**
	tenesti
	tenne
	tenemmo
	teneste
	tennero

Similar verbs

appartenere	belong	**ottenere**	obtain
***astenersi**	abstain	**ritenere**	retain
contenere	contain	**sostenere**	support
detenere	detain, stop	**trattenere**	restrain, detain
mantenere	maintain		

Note: The main irregular features of the verb are

- the present indicative and subjunctive tenses
- the past definite tense
- the future stem

Non riesco più a tenere la casa. È troppo lavoro.	I can no longer *keep* the house. It's too much work.
La terrò per un altro anno, e poi la vendo.	*I will keep* it for one more year, and then I'll sell it.

IMPERATIVE
tieni (tu)   **tenga** (Lei)   teniamo (noi)   tenete (voi)   tengano (Loro)

PLUPERFECT
avevo tenuto

PAST ANTERIOR
ebbi tenuto

FUTURE
terrò

FUTURE PERFECT
avrò tenuto

PRESENT CONDITIONAL
terrei

CONDITIONAL PERFECT
avrei tenuto

PRESENT SUBJUNCTIVE
tenga
tenga
tenga
teniamo
teniate
tengano

PERFECT SUBJUNCTIVE
abbia tenuto

IMPERFECT SUBJUNCTIVE
tenessi

PLUPERFECT SUBJUNCTIVE
avessi tenuto

—**A chi appartiene quel cane?**
—**L'ho ottenuto l'anno scorso.**

—Whom *does* that dog *belong* to?
—*I got* it last year.

Questa bevanda contiene alcool.

This drink *contains* alcohol.

Dovrei astenermi dall'alcool.

I should *abstain* from drinking alcohol.

Mantengo sempre buone relazioni con Giovanni.

I always *maintain* a good relationship with Giovanni.

Il muro è sostenuto da lunghi pali.

The wall *is supported* by long poles.

Sostenne la sua innocenza.

He maintained his innocence.

Fu trattenuto a scuola.

He was kept in at school.

PRESENT GERUND	**PAST PARTICIPLE**
tingendo	**tinto**

PRESENT INDICATIVE	**PRESENT PERFECT**
tingo	ho tinto

PRESENT PROGRESSIVE

sto tingendo

IMPERFECT PROGRESSIVE

stavo tingendo

IMPERFECT

tingevo

PAST DEFINITE

tinsi
tingesti
tinse
tingemmo
tingeste
tinsero

Similar verbs

attingere	draw up, draw out
dipingere	paint, portray

Note: The main irregular features of the verb are

- the past definite tense
- the past participle

IMPERATIVE
tingi (tu)   tinga (Lei)   tingiamo (noi)   tingete (voi)   tingano (Loro)

PLUPERFECT avevo tinto	**PAST ANTERIOR** ebbi tinto
FUTURE tingerò	**FUTURE PERFECT** avrò tinto
PRESENT CONDITIONAL tingerei	**CONDITIONAL PERFECT** avrei tinto
PRESENT SUBJUNCTIVE tinga	**PERFECT SUBJUNCTIVE** abbia tinto
IMPERFECT SUBJUNCTIVE tingessi	**PLUPERFECT SUBJUNCTIVE** avessi tinto

— Hai tinto i capelli?	— *Have you dyed* your hair?
— No, ma ho tinto questo vestito di nero!	— No, but *I have dyed* this dress black.
Il sole tingeva le montagne di rosa.	The sun *tinged* the mountains with a rosy glow.
Attinse l'acqua dal pozzo.	*He drew out* water from the well.
Ha dipinto il ritratto ad olio.	*He painted* the picture in oils.

PRESENT GERUND	PAST PARTICIPLE
torcendo	**torto**

PRESENT INDICATIVE	PRESENT PERFECT
torco	ho torto

PRESENT PROGRESSIVE	IMPERFECT PROGRESSIVE
sto torcendo	stavo torcendo

IMPERFECT	PAST DEFINITE
torcevo	**torsi**
	torcesti
	torse
	torcemmo
	torceste
	torsero

Similar verbs

contorcere	contort, distort
*contorcersi	writhe, twist
*torcersi	twist, writhe
storcere	twist, wrench

Note: The main irregular features of the verb are

- the past definite tense
- the past participle

IMPERATIVE
torci (tu)   torca (Lei)   torciamo (noi)   torcete (voi)   torcano (Loro)

PLUPERFECT	**PAST ANTERIOR**
avevo torto	ebbi torto
FUTURE	**FUTURE PERFECT**
torcerò	avrò torto
PRESENT CONDITIONAL	**CONDITIONAL PERFECT**
torcerei	avrei torto
PRESENT SUBJUNCTIVE	**PERFECT SUBJUNCTIVE**
torca	abbia torto
IMPERFECT SUBJUNCTIVE	**PLUPERFECT SUBJUNCTIVE**
torcessi	avessi torto

Vorrei torcere il collo a quel ragazzo.	I'd like *to wring* that boy's neck!
Torse i panni.	*He wrung out* the washing.
Torceva il naso.	*He was turning up* his nose.
Anna ha torto i fili.	Anna *twisted* the threads.
Si torceva dal dolore.	*He was writhing* in pain.
Tieni la fune diritta, non storcer la.	Hold the rope straight, *don*'t *twist* it.

PRESENT GERUND	PAST PARTICIPLE
traducendo	**tradotto**

PRESENT INDICATIVE	PRESENT PERFECT
traduco	ho tradotto
traduci	
traduce	
traduciamo	
traducete	
traducono	

PRESENT PROGRESSIVE	IMPERFECT PROGRESSIVE
sto traducendo	stavo traducendo

IMPERFECT	PAST DEFINITE
traducevo	**tradussi**
	traducesti
	tradusse
	traducemmo
	traduceste
	tradussero

Similar verbs

addurre	convey	**introdurre**	introduce
condurre	conduct, lead, drive	**produrre**	produce
		ridurre	reduce
dedurre	deduce	**riprodurre**	reproduce
indurre	induce, induct	**sedurre**	seduce

Note: The main irregular features of the verb are

- the irregular present tense stem
- the irregular future stem
- the past definite tense
- the past participle

Ho tradotto il suo ultimo libro.   *I translated* his last book.

IMPERATIVE
traduci (tu)　traduca (Lei)　traduciamo (noi)　traducete (voi)　traducano (Loro)

PLUPERFECT	PAST ANTERIOR
avevo tradotto	ebbi tradotto

FUTURE	FUTURE PERFECT
tradurrò	avrò tradotto

PRESENT CONDITIONAL	CONDITIONAL PERFECT
tradurrei	avrei tradotto

PRESENT SUBJUNCTIVE	PERFECT SUBJUNCTIVE
traduca	abbia tradotto

IMPERFECT SUBJUNCTIVE	PLUPERFECT SUBJUNCTIVE
traducessi	avessi tradotto

Dubito che l'opera sia stata tradotta in inglese.	I doubt that the work *was translated* into English.
Mi condusse al teatro.	*He took* me to the theater / theatre.
Condussero una vita miserabile.	*They led* a miserable life.
Tutte le strade conducono a Roma.	All roads *lead* to Rome.
Mi introdusse allo studio della lingua italiana.	*He introduced* me to the study of the Italian language.
Quest'albero non ha prodotto mai frutta.	This tree *has* never *produced* any fruit.
Ridusse la velocità all'angolo della strada.	*He reduced* his speed at the corner of the road.

PRESENT GERUND	PAST PARTICIPLE
traendo	**tratto**

PRESENT INDICATIVE	PRESENT PERFECT
traggo	ho tratto
trai	
trae	
traiamo	
traete	
traggono	

PRESENT PROGRESSIVE	IMPERFECT PROGRESSIVE
sto traendo	stavo traendo

IMPERFECT	PAST DEFINITE
traevo	**trassi**
	traesti
	trasse
	traemmo
	traeste
	trassero

Similar verbs

attrarre	attract
contrarre	contract
distrarre	distract
estrarre	extract
sottrarre	subtract
***sottrarsi**	get out of; shirk

Note: The main irregular features of these verbs are

- the present indicative and subjunctive tenses
- the future stem
- the past definite tense
- the past participle

IMPERATIVE
trai (tu)   **tragga** (Lei)   traiamo (noi)   traete (voi)   **traggano** (Loro)

PLUPERFECT	**PAST ANTERIOR**
avevo tratto	ebbi tratto
FUTURE	**FUTURE PERFECT**
trarrò	avrò tratto
PRESENT CONDITIONAL	**CONDITIONAL PERFECT**
trarrei	avrel tratto
PRESENT SUBJUNCTIVE	**PERFECT SUBJUNCTIVE**
tragga	abbia tratto
tragga	
tragga	
traiamo	
traiate	
traggano	
IMPERFECT SUBJUNCTIVE	**PLUPERFECT SUBJUNCTIVE**
traessi	avessi tratto

Non ne traggo nessun piacere.	*I do*n't *get* any pleasure from it.
Trae origine da una nobile famiglia.	*He traces* his origins back to a noble family.
La minima cosa lo distraeva.	The slightest thing *distracted* him.
Mi sento attratto verso quella ragazza.	I feel *attracted* to that girl.
Sottrai quattro da dieci.	*Subtract* four from ten.
Lo sottrassero alla morte.	*They rescued* him from death.
Luigi si sottrasse al proprio dovere.	Luigi *shirked* his duty.
Contrasse una malattia dolorosa.	*He contracted* a painful illness / sickness.

PRESENT GERUND	PAST PARTICIPLE
uccidendo	**ucciso**

PRESENT INDICATIVE	PRESENT PERFECT
uccido	ho ucciso

PRESENT PROGRESSIVE	IMPERFECT PROGRESSIVE
sto uccidendo	stavo uccidendo

IMPERFECT	PAST DEFINITE
uccidevo	**uccisi**
	uccidesti
	uccise
	uccidemmo
	uccideste
	uccisero

Similar verb

*uccidersi   kill oneself, commit suicide

Note: The main irregular features of this verb are:

- the past definite tense
- the past participle

IMPERATIVE
uccidi (tu)   uccida (Lei)   uccidiamo (noi)   uccidete (voi)   uccidano (Loro)

PLUPERFECT avevo ucciso	**PAST ANTERIOR** ebbi ucciso
FUTURE ucciderò	**FUTURE PERFECT** avrò ucciso
PRESENT CONDITIONAL ucciderei	**CONDITIONAL PERFECT** avrei ucciso
PRESENT SUBJUNCTIVE uccida	**PERFECT SUBJUNCTIVE** abbia ucciso
IMPERFECT SUBJUNCTIVE uccidessi	**PLUPERFECT SUBJUNCTIVE** avessi ucciso

Ha ucciso un lupo.	*He killed* a wolf.
Uccise l'uomo, sparandogli alla testa.	*He shot* the man through the head.
Fu ucciso in un incidente stradale.	*He was killed* in a road accident.
Si uccise per disperazione.	*He killed himself* out of despair.

PRESENT GERUND	PAST PARTICIPLE
udendo	udito

PRESENT INDICATIVE	PRESENT PERFECT
odo	ho udito
odi	
ode	
udiamo	
udite	
odono	

PRESENT PROGRESSIVE	IMPERFECT PROGRESSIVE
sto udendo	stavo udendo

IMPERFECT	PAST DEFINITE
udivo	udii

Note: The main irregular features of the verb are
   • the present indicative and subjunctive tenses

IMPERATIVE
odi (tu)   **oda** (Lei)   udiamo (noi)   udite (voi)   **odano** (Loro)

PLUPERFECT	**PAST ANTERIOR**
avevo udito	ebbi udito
FUTURE	**FUTURE PERFECT**
udirò / udrò	avrò udito
PRESENT CONDITIONAL	**CONDITIONAL PERFECT**
udirei / udrei	avrei udito
PRESENT SUBJUNCTIVE	**PERFECT SUBJUNCTIVE**
oda	abbia udito
oda	
oda	
udiamo	
udiate	
odano	
IMPERFECT SUBJUNCTIVE	**PLUPERFECT SUBJUNCTIVE**
udissi	avessi udito

—L'hai mai udito cantare?
—Non ancora, ma l'udirò forse domani.

Spero che Dio oda le mie preghiere!

—*Have you* ever *heard* him sing?
—Not yet, but *I shall* perhaps *hear* him tomorrow.

I hope God *will listen to* my prayers.

PRESENT GERUND	**PAST PARTICIPLE**
uscendo	uscito

PRESENT INDICATIVE	**PRESENT PERFECT**
esco	sono uscito / a
esci	
esce	
usciamo	
uscite	
escono	

PRESENT PROGRESSIVE	**IMPERFECT PROGRESSIVE**
sto uscendo	stavo uscendo

IMPERFECT	**PAST DEFINITE**
uscivo	uscii

Similar verb

*riuscire   succeed

Note: The main irregular features of the verb are
   • the present indicative and subjunctive tenses

IMPERATIVE
esci (tu)   **esca** (Lei)   usciamo (noi)   uscite (voi)   **escano** (Loro)

PLUPERFECT	**PAST ANTERIOR**
ero uscito	fui uscito / a
FUTURE	**FUTURE PERFECT**
uscirò	sarò uscito / a
PRESENT CONDITIONAL	**CONDITIONAL PERFECT**
uscirei	sarei uscito / a
PRESENT SUBJUNCTIVE	**PERFECT SUBJUNCTIVE**
esca	sia uscito / a
esca	
esca	
usciamo	
usciate	
escano	
IMPERFECT SUBJUNCTIVE	**PLUPERFECT SUBJUNCTIVE**
uscissi	fossi uscito / a

— **A che ora usciamo stasera?**	— What time *are we going out* tonight?
— **Beh, io esco alle sette, ma Mario non esce fino alle sette e mezzo.**	— Well, *I'm going out* at 7:00, but Mario *is* not *going out* till 7:30.
— **E Carlo?**	— And what about Carlo?
— **Non credo che esca stasera.**	— I don't think *he's going out* tonight.
— **Non sei riuscito a telefonargli?**	— *Did you* not *manage* to call him?
— **Sì, ci sono riuscito, ma era uscito con Antonia.**	— Yes, *I did manage to;* but *he had gone out* with Antonia.

PRESENT GERUND valendo	PAST PARTICIPLE **valso**
PRESENT INDICATIVE **valgo** vali vale valiamo valete **valgono**	**PRESENT PERFECT** sono valso / a
PRESENT PROGRESSIVE sto valendo	**IMPERFECT PROGRESSIVE** stavo valendo
IMPERFECT valevo	**PAST DEFINITE** **valsi** valesti **valse** valemmo valeste **valsero**

Similar verb

*prevalere   prevail

Note: The main irregular features of the verb are

- the present indicative and subjunctive tenses
- the past definite tense
- the past participle
- the future stem

IMPERATIVE
vali (tu) **valga** (Lei) valiamo (noi) valete (voi) **valgano** (Loro)

PLUPERFECT ero valso / a	**PAST ANTERIOR** fui valso / a
FUTURE **varrò**	**FUTURE PERFECT** sarò valso / a
PRESENT CONDITIONAL **varrei**	**CONDITIONAL PERFECT** sarei valso / a
PRESENT SUBJUNCTIVE **valga** **valga** **valga** valiamo valiate **valgano**	**PERFECT SUBJUNCTIVE** sia valso / a
IMPERFECT SUBJUNCTIVE valessi	**PLUPERFECT SUBJUNCTIVE** fossi valso / a

—**Quanto valgono queste due statue?**	— How much *are* these two statues *worth*?
—**Non credo che valgano molto.**	— I do not think *they are worth* a lot.
—**Quella più grande vale forse duecento.**	— The larger one is perhaps *worth* two hundred.
Questo biglietto vale per 24 ore.	This ticket *is valid* for 24 hours.
Litigarsi per una cosa tale, non ne vale la pena.	Fighting for something of the sort *is* not *worth it.*
Dicono cose che non valgono a nulla.	They are talking nonsense.

101 vedere see

PRESENT GERUND vedendo	**PAST PARTICIPLE** **visto** / veduto

PRESENT INDICATIVE vedo	**PRESENT PERFECT** ho visto
PRESENT PROGRESSIVE sto vedendo	**IMPERFECT PROGRESSIVE** stavo vedendo
IMPERFECT vedevo	**PAST DEFINITE** **vidi** vedesti **vide** vedemmo vedeste **videro**

Similar verbs

*****avvedersi**	perceive
prevedere	foresee
provvedere	provide
rivedere	see again
travedere	be wrong

Note: The main irregular features of the verb are

- the past definite tense
- the past participle (although the regular past participle is also accepted)
- the future stem

IMPERATIVE
vedi (tu)   veda (Lei)   vediamo (noi)   vedete (voi)   vedano (Loro)

PLUPERFECT avevo visto	**PAST ANTERIOR** ebbi visto
FUTURE **vedrò**	**FUTURE PERFECT** avrò visto
PRESENT CONDITIONAL **vedrei**	**CONDITIONAL PERFECT** avrei visto
PRESENT SUBJUNCTIVE veda	**PERFECT SUBJUNCTIVE** abbia visto
IMPERFECT SUBJUNCTIVE vedessi	**PLUPERFECT SUBJUNCTIVE** avessi visto

— **Vedi quell'uomo laggiù?**	— *Do you see* that man down there?
— **Sì, l'ho visto anche ieri. Chi è?**	— Yes, *I saw* him yesterday as well. Who is he?
— **Non lo so. Mai visto prima!**	— I don't know, *I have* never *seen* him before today.
— **Credi che lui ci abbia visti?**	— Do you think *he has seen* us?
Tu travedi, se credi che lui sia colpevole.	You *are making a mistake* if you think he is guilty.
Non l'ho mai più rivista.	*I never saw* her *again.*
Avresti dovuto prevederlo.	You should have *foreseen* it.
Ti ferì senza avvedersene.	He hurt your feelings without *realizing.*
L'ho sempre provveduto di tutto.	*I have* always *provided* him with everything.

PRESENT GERUND	PAST PARTICIPLE
venendo	**venuto**

PRESENT INDICATIVE	PRESENT PERFECT
vengo	sono venuto / a
vieni	
viene	
veniamo	
venite	
vengono	

PRESENT PROGRESSIVE	IMPERFECT PROGRESSIVE
sto venendo	stavo venendo

IMPERFECT	PAST DEFINITE
venivo	**venni**
	venisti
	venne
	venimmo
	veniste
	vennero

Similar verbs

***avvenire**	happen	***provenire**	proceed from,
***convenire**	agree, gather		come from
	together	† **rinvenire**	find, discover;
***divenire**	become		recover; come to
***intervenire**	intervene	***sopravvenire**	arrive; happen
***pervenire**	reach, arrive	***sovvenire**	aid
		***svenire**	faint

Note: The main irregular features of the verb are

- the present indicative and subjunctive tenses
- the past definite tense
- the past participle
- the future stem

IMPERATIVE
vieni (tu)   **venga** (Lei)   veniamo (noi)   venite (voi)   vengano (Loro)

PLUPERFECT	**PAST ANTERIOR**
ero venuto / a	fui venuto / a
FUTURE	**FUTURE PERFECT**
verrò	sarò venuto / a
PRESENT CONDITIONAL	**CONDITIONAL PERFECT**
verrei	sarei venuto / a
PRESENT SUBJUNCTIVE	**PERFECT SUBJUNCTIVE**
venga	sia venuto / a
venga	
venga	
veniamo	
veniate	
vengano	
IMPERFECT SUBJUNCTIVE	**PLUPERFECT SUBJUNCTIVE**
venissi	fossi venuto / a

Digli che venga subito.	Tell him *to come* at once.
Ha detto che verrà domani.	He said *he will come* tomorrow.
Avevo paura che non venisse oggi.	I was afraid that *he might* not *come* today.
Ci conviene partire subito.	*We had better* leave immediately.
Il prezzo è convenuto.	The price *is agreed upon.*
Non credo che provenga da una buona famiglia.	I don't think *he comes* from a good family.
Svenne per la fame.	*He fainted* from hunger.
Antonella ha rinvenuto un libro raro.	Antonella *found* a rare book.
La maestra intervenne quando vide i due ragazzi bisticciarsi.	The teacher *intervened* when she saw the two boys fighting.

PRESENT GERUND	PAST PARTICIPLE
vincendo	**vinto**

PRESENT INDICATIVE	PRESENT PERFECT
vinco	ho vinto

PRESENT PROGRESSIVE	MPERFECT CONTINUOUS
sto vincendo	stavo vincendo

IMPERFECT	PAST DEFINITE
vincevo	**vinsi**
	vincesti
	vinse
	vincemmo
	vinceste
	vinsero

Similar verbs

avvincere   bind, tie up
convincere   convince

Note: The main irregular features of the verb are

- the past definite tense
- the past participle

IMPERATIVE
vinci (tu)   vinca (Lei)   vinciarno (noi)   vincete (voi)   vincano (Loro)

PLUPERFECT	**PAST ANTERIOR**
avevo vinto	ebbi vinto

FUTURE	**FUTURE PERFECT**
vincerò	avrò vinto

PRESENT CONDITIONAL	**CONDITIONAL PERFECT**
vincerei	avrei vinto

PRESENT SUBJUNCTIVE	**PERFECT SUBJUNCTIVE**
vinca	abbia vinto

IMPERFECT SUBJUNCTIVE	**PLUPERFECT SUBJUNCTIVE**
vincessi	avessi vinto

La sua bellezza mi vinse.	I *was won over* by her beauty.
Hai vinto un premio?	*Did you win* a prize?
Il partito ha vinto.	The (political) party *has won.*
Vinsi di stretta misura.	I *won* by a short margin.
Il ladro avvinse l'uomo.	The robber *tied up* the man.
Mi sono lasciato vincere dalla tentazione.	I *yielded* to temptation.
Fu vinto dall'ira.	*He was overcome* by rage.
L'hai convinto?	*Did you convince* him?

PRESENT GERUND	PAST PARTICIPLE
vivendo	**vissuto**

PRESENT INDICATIVE	PRESENT PERFECT
vivo	ho vissuto / sono vissuto / a

PRESENT PROGRESSIVE	IMPERFECT PROGRESSIVE
sto vivendo	stavo vivendo

IMPERFECT	PAST DEFINITE
vivevo	**vissi**
	vivesti
	visse
	vivemmo
	viveste
	vissero

Similar verbs

† **rivivere**   live again, relive
† **sopravvivere**   survive; outlive; live on

These verbs, like **vivere** take **avere** when used transitively and **essere** when used intransitively.

Note: The main irregular features of the verb are

- the past definite tense
- the past participle

IMPERATIVE
vivi (tu)   viva (Lei)   viviamo (noi)   vivete (voi)   vivano (Loro)

PLUPERFECT avevo vissuto / ero vissuto/a	**PAST ANTERIOR** ebbi vissuto / fui vissuto/a
FUTURE vivrò	**FUTURE PERFECT** avrò vissuto / sarò vissuto/a
PRESENT CONDITIONAL vivrei	**CONDITIONAL PERFECT** avrei vissuto / sarei vissuto/a
PRESENT SUBJUNCTIVE viva	**PERFECT SUBJUNCTIVE** abbia vissuto / sia vissuto/a
IMPERFECT SUBJUNCTIVE vivessi	**PLUPERFECT SUBJUNCTIVE** avessi vissuto / fossi vissuto/a

Vive in città da tre anni.	*He has been living* in town for three years.
Visse bene del proprio lavoro.	*He lived* well from his own work.
Hai di che vivere?	Do you have enough *to live on?*
Antonio sa vivere.	Antonio knows how *to live!*
Come si vive così si muore. (Proverbio)	As *we live* so shall we die. (*Proverb*)
Vorrei rivivere quei momenti.	I would like *to relive* those moments.
Mi sento rivivere.	I feel like a new person.
Ha sopravvisuto un terribile incidente stradale.	*He survived* a terrible road accident.

PRESENT GERUND	PAST PARTICIPLE
volendo	voluto

PRESENT INDICATIVE	PRESENT PERFECT
voglio	ho voluto / sono voluto / a
vuoi	
vuole	
vogliamo	
volete	
vogliono	

PRESENT PROGRESSIVE	IMPERFECT PROGRESSIVE
sto volendo	stavo volendo

IMPERFECT	PAST DEFINITE
volevo	**volli**
	volesti
	volle
	volemmo
	voleste
	vollero

Note: The verb **volere** is frequently used as a modal verb, before the infinitive of another verb. It takes **avere** or **essere** according to which one the dependent infinitive takes, although, in speech, **avere** is more common when wishing / wanting is stressed.

The main irregular features of the verb are

• the present indicative and subjunctive tenses
• the past definite tense
• the future stem

IMPERATIVE
vogli (tu) **voglia** (Lei) vogliamo (noi) **vogliate** (voi) **vogliano** (Loro)

PLUPERFECT avevo voluto / ero voluto / a	**PAST ANTERIOR** ebbi voluto / fui voluto / a
FUTURE **vorrò**	**FUTURE PERFECT** avrò voluto / sarò voluto / a
PRESENT CONDITIONAL **vorrei**	**CONDITIONAL PERFECT** avrei voluto / sarei voluto / a
PRESENT SUBJUNCTIVE **voglia** **voglia** **voglia** **vogliamo** **vogliate** **vogliano**	**PERFECT SUBJUNCTIVE** abbia voluto / sia voluto / a
IMPERFECT SUBJUNCTIVE volessi	**PLUPERFECT SUBJUNCTIVE** avessi voluto / fossi voluto / a

Non capisco ciò che vuoi dire.	I don't understand what *you mean.*
Voglio rimanere qui in Italia.	*I want to* stay in Italy.
Non vorrei malintesi.	*I would* not *want* any misunderstandings.
Ci vuole almeno un'ora per andare da Anna.	*It takes* at least an hour to get to Anna's house.
Vorresti accompagnarmi?	*Would you like* to come with me?
Avevo voluto mangiare in quel ristorante.	*I had wanted to* eat in that restaurant.
La mamma non volle che partissimo.	My mother *did* not *want* us to leave.

PRESENT GERUND	PAST PARTICIPLE
volgendo	**volto**

PRESENT INDICATIVE	PRESENT PERFECT
volgo	ho volto

PRESENT PROGRESSIVE	IMPERFECT PROGRESSIVE
sto volgendo	stavo volgendo

IMPERFECT	PAST DEFINITE
volgevo	**volsi**
	volgesti
	volse
	volgemmo
	volgeste
	volsero

Similar verbs

avvolgere	wrap up
coinvolgere	involve
involgere	wrap
ravvolgere	wrap up
rivolgere	turn
sconvolgere	upset
svolgere	unfold

Note: The main irregular features of the verb are

- the past definite tense
- the past participle

IMPERATIVE
volgi (tu)   volga (Lei)   volgiamo (noi)   volgete (voi)   volgano (Loro)

PLUPERFECT avevo volto	**PAST ANTERIOR** ebbi volto
FUTURE volgerò	**FUTURE PERFECT** avrò volto
PRESENT CONDITIONAL volgerei	**CONDITIONAL PERFECT** avrei volto
PRESENT SUBJUNCTIVE volga	**PERFECT SUBJUNCTIVE** abbia volto
IMPERFECT SUBJUNCTIVE volgessi	**PLUPERFECT SUBJUNCTIVE** avessi volto

Quando arrivi al semaforo, volgi a destra.	When you get to the red light, *turn* right.
Volse i passi verso la casa.	*He turned* his steps towards home.
Volsi la scenetta a mio vantaggio.	*I turned* the scene to my advantage.
Volgo la vicenda nella mente.	*I am turning over* the event in my mind.
Il tempo volge al brutto.	The weather *is making a turn* for the worse.
Avvolse il regalo nella carta.	*He wrapped up* the present in paper.
Ho ravvolto il vaso in molta carta.	*I have wrapped* the vase in a lot of paper.
Sconvolsero i suoi piani.	*They upset* his plans.
Si è trovato coinvolto nello scandalo di cui tutti parlano.	He found himself *involved* in the scandal that is the talk of the day.

C
SUBJECT INDEX

SUBJECT INDEX

The references given here relate to the relevant section in *The verb system in Italian*.

D
VERB INDEX

Verb Index

An **[M]** beside a verb indicates that it is one of the Model Verbs.
An * before a verb indicates that this verb takes **essere**.

A † before a verb indicates that this verb can take **essere** or **avere**; usually, **essere** when it is intransitive and **avere** when it is transitive.

If the verb is usually used impersonally, this is indicated by *(Imp.)*

The number beside the verb indicates the model verb pattern(s) it follows.

A

abbagliare *(tr)*	dazzle 13
abbaiare *(intr)*	bark 13
abbandonare *(tr)*	abandon, desert, give up 3
abbassare *(tr)*	depress, turn down (light / window) 3
abbattere *(tr)*	knock over 4
*****abbattersi su**	hit upon 4, 7
abbondare *(intr)*	abound 3
abbotdare *(tr)*	accost 3
abbottonare *(tr)*	button 3
abbozzare *(tr)*	draft, sketch 3
abbracciare *(tr)*	cuddle, embrace 12
*****abbronzarsi** *(intr / refl)*	tan, brown in sun 7
abitare *(tr)*	live, dwell 3
abituare *(tr)*	accustom 3
*****abituarsi a** *(intr / refl)*	become accustomed to, get used to 7
abolire *(tr)*	abolish 6
abortire *(tr / intr)*	miscarry 6
*****abortire** *(intr)*	fail, come to nothing 6
*****accadere** *(intr)*	occur, happen, turn out transpire *(Imp.)* 28
accalcarsi *(intr / refl)*	huddle 7, 11
accarezzare *(tr)*	caress, stroke 3
accecare *(tr)*	blind 11
*****accedere** *(intr)*	access; approach; comply with 33
accelerare *(tr / intr)*	speed up, accelerate 3
accendere *(tr)*	turn on, light, ignite, strike (match) 17 **[M]**
*****accendersi** *(intr)*	go on (of lighting), light up 17, 7

accennare a *(intr)*	refer to, mention 3
accennare di sì *(intr)*	nod 3
accentuare *(tr)*	emphasize 3
accertare *(tr)*	assess 3
accettare di *(tr)*	accept 3
acchiappare *(tr)*	catch 3
accludere *(tr)*	enclose, attach 20
*accoccolarsi *(intr / refl)*	squat, crouch 7
accogliere *(tr)*	welcome 31
accomodare *(tr)*	arrange 3
accomodarsi *(intr / refl)*	come in; sit down 7
accompagnare *(tr)*	accompany, take (for a walk) 3
*accondiscendere a *(intr)*	consent 79
acconsentire a *(intr)*	accept, agree to 5
*accontentarsi di *(intr / refl)*	make do with 7
accoppiare *(tr)*	couple 13
*accoppiarsi *(intr / refl)*	mate 13, 7
accorciare *(tr)*	shorten 12
*accorciarsi *(intr / refl)*	become shorter, draw in 12, 7
accordare *(tr)*	grant, concede, tune, string (instrument) 3
*accordarsi *(intr / refl)*	agree 7
*accorgersi di *(intr / refl)*	notice, take note 80, 7
accorrere *(intr)*	run, rush 35
accrescere *(tr)*	increase 36
accumulare *(tr)*	accumulate, hoard 3
accusare di *(tr)*	accuse (of), charge (criminal) 3
accusare ricevuta di	acknowledge receipt of 3
acquistare *(tr)*	acquire, get 3
adattare *(tr)*	adapt 3
adattare a *(intr)*	adapt to 3
addebitare *(tr)*	charge to account, debit 3
addizionare *(tr)*	count up 3
addolcire *(tr)*	sweeten 6
*addormentarsi *(intr / refl)*	fall asleep 7
addurre *(tr)*	convey 95
adempire *(tr)*	implement, perform (a function) 6
aderire a *(intr)*	adhere to 6
adorare *(tr)*	adore, worship 3
adottare *(tr)*	adopt 3
aerare *(tr)*	air a room 3
affascinare *(tr)*	charm, fascinate 3
affermare *(tr)*	affirm, assert 3
afferrare *(tr)*	grasp, snatch, tackle 3
afferrare strettamente *(tr)*	grip 3
affettare *(tr)*	affect, feign, simulate 3
*affezionarsi a *(intr / refl)*	become fond of, take a liking to 7
affidare *(tr)*	entrust 3
*affidarsi a *(intr / refl)*	rely on, trust in 7

VERB INDEX

affiggere *(tr)*	post / put (up), attach; fix 18 **[M]**
affilare *(tr)*	sharpen 3
affittare *(tr)*	hire, rent house, lease out 3
affliggere *(tr)*	suffer from, afflict 19 **[M]**
†affogare *(tr / intr)*	drown 2, 11
affollare *(intr)*	crowd 3
affrettare *(tr)*	hurry 3
*affrettarsi a *(intr / refl)*	hurry (to) 7
affrontare *(tr)*	confront, stand up to, face 3
agganciare (tr)	hook 12
aggiogare (tr)	yoke 11
aggiornare *(tr)*	adjourn, postpone, write up (diary) 3
*aggiornarsi *(intr / refl)*	get up to date 7
aggiungere *(tr)*	add, say further, append, add 52
aggiustare *(tr)*	adjust, patch 3
agire *(intr)*	act, do 6
agire per *(intr)*	act for 6
agire seguendo i consigli	act on advice 6
agire su	act on, work on 6
agitare *(tr)*	ruffle, stir, shake, stir, move 3
*agitarsi *(intr / refl)*	bustle 7
aiutare *(tr)*	aid, assist, help 3
albeggiare *(intr)*	dawn 12
alienare *(tr)*	alienate 3
alimentare *(tr)*	feed 3
allacciare *(tr)*	fasten (seatbelt) 12
allargare *(tr)*	broaden, enlarge, widen 11
allarmare *(tr)*	alarm 3
allattare *(tr)*	nurse (baby), suckle 3
alleggerire *(tr)*	lighten 6
*allenarsi *(intr / refl)*	exercise 7
allentare *(tr)*	slacken 3
allevare *(tr)*	raise, rear 3
alleviare *(tr)*	alleviate, relieve (pain, anxiety) 13
allineare *(tr)*	align 3
*allinearsi *(intr / refl)*	line up 7
alloggiare *(tr)*	house 12
alloggiare in *(intr)*	stay (as guest) 12
allontanare *(tr)*	push away 3
*allontanarsi da *(intr / refl)*	get away from 7
alludere a *(intr)*	allude at, hint at 20 **[M]**
allungare *(tr)*	draw out, become longer, stretch out 11
alterare *(tr)*	alter 3
alternare *(tr)*	alternate 3
alzare *(tr)*	elevate, put up (price), raise, lift 3
alzare *(tr)* la voce	speak up 3
alzare gli occhi *(tr)*	look up 3

*alzarsi *(intr / refl)*	get up, stand, rise to feet 7
amalgamare *(tr)*	amalgamate 3
amare *(tr)*	love 3
ammaccare *(tr)*	bruise 11
*ammalarsi *(intr / refl)*	become ill, fall ill 7
ammettere di *(tr)*	admit, grant to be true, allow 54
ammiccare a qlcu. *(intr)*	wink 11
amministrare *(tr)*	administer, run, manage 3
ammirare *(tr)*	admire 3
ammobiliare *(tr)*	furnish, equip 13
†ammontare a *(intr / tr)*	number, amount to 3
ammorbidire *(tr)*	soften 6
ammucchiare *(tr)*	heap, pile up 13
*ammucchiarsi *(intr / refl)*	pile up 13, 7
ammuffire *(intr)*	go moldy 6
amplificare *(tr)*	amplify 11
amputare *(tr)*	amputate 3
analizzare *(tr)*	analyze 3
ancorare *(tr)*	anchor, moor 3
*andare *(intr)*	go, ride (in car) 21 **[M]**
*andare a fare le spese *(intr)*	shop 21
*andare a prendere *(intr)*	go for (e.g., doctor), fetch 21
*andare a trovare *(tr)*	call on, visit 21
*andare a vapore *(intr)*	steam, move by steam 21
*andare avanti *(intr)*	get on, be fast (clock) 21
*andare bene *(intr)*	fit, be right size, match in color 21
*andare bene a *(intr)*	suit 21
*andare d'accordo con *(intr)*	get along with 21
*andare da *(intr)*	see (doctor) 21
*andare in autobus *(intr)*	bus 21
*andare in bicicletta *(intr)*	bike 21
*andare in fretta *(intr)*	speed 21
*andare in pensione *(intr)*	retire 21
*andare meglio *(intr)*	get better 21
*andare pazzo per *(intr)*	rave about 21
*andarsene *(refl / intr)*	go away, clear off 21
anestetizzare *(tr)*	anesthetize 3
animare *(tr)*	animate, brighten up 3
annegare *(tr)*	drown 11
†annerire *(tr)*	blacken 6
annettere *(tr)*	attach, add, annex 22 **[M]**
annichilire *(tr)*	annihilate 6
annodare *(tr)*	knot (rope) 3
annoiare *(tr)*	bore 13
*annoiarsi *(intr / refl)*	be bored 13, 7
annullare *(tr)*	annul, write off, accept loss of 3
*annullarsi *(intr / refl)*	cancel out 7
annunziare *(tr)*	announce 13

*annuvolarsi *(intr / refl)*	cloud over 7
ansimare *(intr)*	pant 3
anticipare *(tr)*	advance payment, anticipate 3
appannarsi *(intr / refl)*	become misty 7
apparecchiare *(tr)*	lay (table) 13
*apparire *(intr)*	appear, seem; make an appearance 23 **[M]**
appartenere *(intr)*	belong 92
*appassire *(intr)*	wilt, dry up 6
*appellarsi a *(intr / refl)*	appeal to the law 7
appendere *(tr)*	hang, suspend 17
appianare *(tr)*	even out 3
appiattire *(tr)*	flatten 6
applaudire *(intr)*	applaud, clap 6
applicare *(tr)*	apply, use 11
applicare *(tr)* le manette a	handcuff 11
*appoggiarsi *(intr / refl)*	lean up against (back) 12, 7
apporre *(tr)*	affix 64
apprendere a *(tr)*	learn (to) 66
*apprestarsi a *(intr / refl)*	get ready to 7
apprezzare *(tr)*	appreciate the value, prize 3
*approfittare di *(intr)*	take advantage of 3
approfondire *(tr)*	deepen 6
appropriare *(tr)*	appropriate 13
*appropriarsi indebitamente di *(intr / refl)*	embezzle 13, 7
approssimare *(tr)*	approximate 3
approvare *(tr)*	approve, endorse, pass (a law) 3
aprire *(tr)*	open 24 **[M]**
aprire con chiave *(tr)*	unlock 24
arare *(tr)*	plough 3
arbitrare *(tr)*	arbitrate, umpire, referee, file (IT) 3
ardere *(tr)*	burn 47
armare *(tr)*	arm 3
armonizzare *(intr)*	harmonize, match 3
aromatizzare *(tr)*	flavor / flavour 3
*arrabbiarsi con *(intr / refl)*	be / get angry, lose one's temper with 13, 7
arrampicare *(tr)*	climb 11
*arrendersi *(intr / refl)*	capitulate 71, 7
arrestare *(tr)*	arrest, stem, check, stop 3
†arricchire *(intr / tr)*	enrich, grow rich 6
arricciare *(tr)*	curl 12
arrischiare *(tr)*	chance, gamble 13
*arrivare a *(intr)*	arrive at, get to 2
*arrossire *(intr)*	blush 6
arrostire *(tr)*	roast 6
arrotondare *(tr)*	approximate, round up (figures) 3
*arrugginirsi *(intr / refl)*	rust 6, 7
arruolare *(tr)*	enroll in 3

*arruolarsi *(intr/refl)*	join up army 7
*ascendere *(intr)*	ascend 79
asciugare *(tr)*	dry, wipe, wipe up 11
ascoltare *(tr)*	listen, listen to 3
aspergere *(tr)*	sprinkle 84
aspettare *(tr)*	expect, hold (telephone), wait 3
*aspettarsi di *(intr/refl)*	anticipate, expect 7
aspirare a *(intr)*	aspire to 3
assalire *(tr)*	attack, seize, overcome 77
assassinare *(tr)*	assassinate, murder 3
assegnare *(tr)*	allocate, assign, award 3
*assentarsi da *(intr/refl)*	absent oneself, be absent 7
assicurare *(tr)*	assure, ensure, insure, secure 3
assimilare *(tr)*	assimilate 3
assistere *(tr)*	assist; attend 25 **[M]**
assistere a *(intr)*	be present, stand by, observe, attend 25
associare *(tr)*	associate 12
assolvere *(tr)*	absolve, acquit 74
assomigliare a *(intr)*	resemble 13
*assopirsi *(intr/refl)*	nod off, doze off 6, 7
assorbire *(tr)*	absorb, soak up 6
assordare *(tr)*	deafen 3
assottigliare *(tr)*	taper, thin down 13
assumere *(tr)*	assume; hire; raise 26 **[M]**
*assumersi *(intr/refl)*	undertake, assume (responsibility) 26, 7
*astenersi da *(intr/refl)*	abstain, refrain from 92, 7
astrarre *(tr)*	abstract 96
atomizzare *(tr)*	atomize 3
attaccare *(tr)*	attach, harness, hang up (telephone) 11
attendere *(tr/intr)*	wait 91
atterrire *(tr)*	terrorize 6
attestare *(tr)*	vouch 3
attingere *(tr)*	draw up, draw out 93
attirare / attrarre *(tr)*	attract, lure 3, 86, 96
attorcigliare *(tr)*	twist 13
attrarre *(tr)*	attract 96
attraversare *(tr)*	come across / over, go across / through 3
attraversare velocemente *(tr)*	shoot (rapids) 3
attribuire *(tr)*	credit with 6
attutire *(tr)*	deaden 6
†aumentare *(intr/tr)*	rise, add to, increase, raise (prices) 3
autorizzare a *(tr)*	authorize, license s.one (to) 3
†avanzare *(intr/tr)*	progress, advance, move / put forward 3
avanzare a fatica *(intr)*	slog away 3

VERB INDEX

*avanzarsi *(intr / refl)*	advance, go forward 7
avere *(tr)*	have 27 **[M]**
avercela con *(tr)*	have it in for 27
avere bisogno di *(tr)*	need, require 27
avere caldo *(tr)*	feel hot 27
avere cura di *(tr)*	take care of 27
avere da *(tr)*	have to 27
avere disponibile *(tr)*	have available 27
avere fiducia in *(tr)*	trust 27
avere freddo *(tr)*	be / feel cold 27
avere il prurito *(tr)*	itch, have an itch 27
avere in mente di *(tr)*	have in mind 27
avere l'aria di *(tr)*	look (like) 27
avere l'intenzione di *(tr)*	think, intend to, be going to 27
avere la diarrea *(tr)*	have diarrhea 27
avere luogo *(tr)*	take place, happen 27
avere mal di mare *(tr)*	be seasick 27
avere paura di *(tr)*	be afraid, regret 27
avere qlc. in contrario a *(tr)*	object to 27
avere ragione *(tr)*	be right 27
avere tendenza ad *(tr)*	tend, be inclined to 27
avere torto *(tr)*	be wrong 27
avere un rapporto sessuale con *(tr)*	have intercourse with 27
avere un ruolo importante *(tr)*	star 27
avere uno strappo muscolare *(tr)*	have a pulled muscle 27
avere vergogna di *(tr)*	be ashamed of 27
avere voglia di *(tr)*	want 27
avvedersi *(refl)*	perceive 101
avvelenare *(tr)*	poison 3
*avvenire *(intr)*	happen *(Imp.)* 102
*avventurarsi *(intr / refl)*	venture 7
avvertire *(tr)*	warn, alert 5
*avviarsi verso *(intr / refl)*	make for, move towards 13, 7
avvicinare *(tr)*	approach 3
*avvicinarsi a *(intr)*	approach, close in 7
avvincere *(tr)*	bind, tie up 103
avvisare *(tr)*	advise, inform, notify 3
avvistare *(tr)*	sight 3
avvitare *(tr)*	screw 3
avvolgere *(tr)*	scroll, wrap 106
avvolgersi *(intr)*	coil up 106, 7
*azzardarsi *(intr / refl)*	dare (to) 7
*azzuffarsi *(intr / refl)*	brawl 7

B

baciare *(tr)*	kiss 13
badare *(intr)*	attend, pay attention 3
badare a *(intr)*	look after, mind 3
badare di *(intr)*	take care to 3
bagnare *(tr)*	bathe, dampen, soak, wet 3

*bagnarsi *(intr / refl)*	bathe 7
balbettare *(tr)*	stammer 3
ballare *(tr)*	dance 3
barattare *(tr)*	barter 3
barcollare *(intr)*	stagger, totter 3
barricare *(tr)*	barricade 11
basare *(tr)*	base (an argument on) 3
*bastare *(intr)*	be enough, be sufficient *(Imp.)* 3
battere *(tr)*	beat, strike, hit, tap, whip 4
battere le palpebre *(tr)*	blink 4
battere violentemente *(tr)*	bang 4
battezzare *(tr)*	baptize 3
beccare *(tr)*	peck (chicken) 11
belare *(intr)*	bleat (animals) 3
bendare *(tr)*	bandage 3
benedire *(tr)*	bless 9
bere *(tr)*	drink 8 **[M]**
*biforcarsi *(intr / refl)*	fork (road), branch off 11, 7
bighellonare *(intr)*	saunter 3
bilanciare *(tr)*	balance, break even, even up 12
biodegradare *(tr)*	biodegrade 6
bisbigliare *(tr)*	whisper 13
*bisognare *(intr)*	need *(Imp.)* 3
bloccare *(tr)*	block, stop 11
bocciare *(tr)*	fail someone in a test / an exam 12
boicottare *(tr)*	boycott 3
bollare *(tr)*	stamp 3
bollire *(tr)*	boil 5
bollire lentamente *(tr)*	simmer 5
bombardare *(tr)*	bomb, shell, bombard 3
brevettare *(tr)*	patent 3
brillare *(intr)*	shine, excel 3
brontolare *(intr)*	growl, grumble, nag 3
bruciare *(tr)*	burn 12
brulicare di *(intr)*	crawl with (insects) 11
bussare *(tr)*	knock 3
buttare via *(tr)*	throw away 3
C cacciare *(tr)*	hunt, chase, drive away, cause to go 12
cacciare di frodo *(tr)*	poach 12
*cadere *(intr)*	fall (motion) 28 **[M]**
calare *(tr)*	lower 3
calare *(tr)*	set, go down 3
calciare *(tr)*	kick 12
calcolare *(tr)*	calculate, work out, plan 3
calmare *(tr)*	calm, allay, quieten 3
*calmarsi *(intr / refl)*	calm down 7
calunniare *(tr)*	slander 13

cinguettare *(intr)*	twitter 3
cintare *(tr)*	fence 3
circolare *(tr)*	circulate, pass round 3
circondare con *(tr)*	encircle, enclose, surround 3
circondare con una siepe *(tr)*	hedge (round) 3
citare *(tr)*	quote 3
civettare *(intr)*	flirt 3
classificare *(tr)*	grade, rank, sort, label, classify 11
coabitare *(intr)*	cohabit 3
coesistere *(intr)*	coexist 25
cogliere *(tr)*	gather 31 **[M]**
coincidere *(intr)*	coincide 39
coinvolgere *(tr)*	involve in 106
colare *(intr / tr)*	leak, strain 3
collaborare *(tr)*	collaborate 3
collocare *(tr)*	place 11
colorare *(tr)*	color in 3
colpire *(tr)*	impress, knock against, shock, smack, strike, hit 6
colpire a morte *(tr)*	shoot dead 6
colpire violentemente *(tr)*	bash 6
coltivare *(tr)*	farm, garden, rear (crops), till (soil) 3
comandare *(intr / tr)*	command, boss about, order 3
combattere *(tr)*	fight, wrestle 4
†cominciare a *(tr)*	begin, get started, initiate, begin, start, commence, take up (pastime) 12
commemorare *(tr)*	commemorate 3
commentare *(tr)*	comment 3
commerciare in *(intr)*	deal in, trade in 12
commettere *(tr)*	commit 54
commuovere *(tr)*	move, affect emotionally 15
commutare *(tr)*	commute 3
comp(e)rare *(tr)*	purchase, buy 1
*comparire *(intr)*	appear 6
compatire *(tr)*	pity 6
*compiacere *(intr)*	please 61
compiangere *(tr)*	pity, sympathize 62
compiere / compire *(tr)*	finish, achieve 6
compilare *(tr)*	compile 3
completare *(tr)*	complete 3
complicare *(tr)*	complicate 11
complimentare *(tr)*	compliment 3
comporre *(tr)*	compose music; dial 64
comporre un indice *(tr)*	index 64
comporre il numero *(tr)*	dial telephone number 64
*comportarsi *(intr / refl)*	behave (animals / humans) 7
comprare *(tr)*	buy, purchase 1 **[M]**

consolare *(tr)*	console 3
consolidare *(tr)*	consolidate 3
consultare *(tr)*	consult 3
consumare *(tr)*	consume, erode, spend, use up 3
contaminare *(tr)*	contaminate 3
contare *(tr)*	count, number 3
contare su *(intr)*	bank upon, reckon on 3
contemplare *(tr)*	survey, contemplate 3
contendere *(tr/intr)*	contend 91
contenere *(tr)*	contain, store 92
continuare a *(intr)*	carry on, keep going, go on 3
contorcere *(tr)*	twist, contort 94
contrabbandare *(tr)*	smuggle 38
contraddire *(tr)*	contradict 9
contraffare *(tr)*	counterfeit 10
contrarre *(tr)*	contract 96
contrastare *(tr)*	contrast 3
contravvenire *(tr)*	contravene 102
contribuire a *(tr)*	contribute to 6
controllare *(tr)*	check verify, inspect, monitor, service 3
†convenire *(tr/intr)*	agree, gather together *(Imp.)* 102
conversare *(intr)*	converse with 3
convertire *(tr)*	convert 5
convincere a *(tr)*	convict, convince s.one (to) 103
convocare *(tr)*	summon 11
cooperare **(intr)**	cooperate 3
coordinare *(tr)*	coordinate 3
copiare *(tr)*	copy, write out 13
coprire *(tr)*	cap, cover 24
*coricarsi *(intr/refl)*	go to bed, lie down 7
coronare *(tr)*	crown 3
correggere *(tr)*	correct 70
†correre a *(tr/intr)*	run, race (to) 35 **[M]**
corrispondere *(intr)*	correspond with 75
corrodere *(tr)*	corrode 47
corrompere *(tr)*	corrupt 76
corrugare *(tr)*	wrinkle 11
corteggiare *(tr)*	court, woo 12
cospirare *(intr)*	conspire against 3
*costare *(intr)*	cost *(Imp.)* 3
costeggiare *(tr)*	skirt 12
costernare *(tr)*	dismay 3
costituire *(tr)*	constitute 6
costringere a *(tr)*	force, compel (to), constrain, pin down 88
costruire *(tr)*	build, construct, erect 6
costruire un ponte su *(intr)*	bridge (a river) 6
covare *(tr)*	brood over, hatch 3

VERB INDEX

creare *(tr)*	create 3
credere di *(tr)*	believe 4
credere a / in *(intr)*	believe in 4
cremare *(tr)*	cremate 3
*crepare *(intr)*	break 3
†crescere *(tr / intr)*	grow, grow up 36 **[M]**
cristallizzare *(tr)*	crystalize 3
criticare *(tr)*	criticize 11
crocifiggere *(tr)*	crucify 18
croliare *(tr)*	collapse 3
cronometrare *(tr)*	time (race) 3
cucire *(tr)*	sew, stitch 5
cucire con graffette *(tr)*	staple 5
cultivare *(tr)*	cultivate 3
cuocere *(tr)*	cook 37 **[M]**
cuocere a stufato *(tr)*	braise 37
cuocere a vapore *(tr)*	steam, cook by steam 37
cuocere ai ferri **(tr)**	grill 37
cuocere al forno *(tr)*	bake 37
curare *(tr)*	care for, tend, nurse, look after, treat (patient), edit 3
curvare *(tr)*	bend, curve 3
*curvarsi *(intr)*	stoop 7

D

danneggiare *(tr)*	damage 12
dannare *(tr)*	damn 3
dare *(tr)*	give 38 **[M]**
dare (un esame) *(tr)*	take (an examination) 38
dare (frutti) *(tr)*	bear (fruit) 38
dare il benvenuto a *(intr)*	welcome 38
dare a nolo *(tr)*	hire / rent out 38
dare alla luce *(tr)*	give birth 38
dare del Lei a qlcu. *(tr)*	use 'Lei' form 38
dare del tu a qlcu. *(tr)*	use 'tu' form 38
dare del voi a qlcu. *(tr)*	use 'voi' form 38
dare forma a *(tr)*	shape 38
dare il colpo di grazia a *(tr)*	finish off 38
dare su *(intr)*	open onto (doors) 38
dare sui nervi *(intr)*	get on the nerves of 38
dare un nome a *(tr)*	name 38
dare un pugno a *(tr)*	punch (with fist) 38
dare un'occhiata a *(tr)*	glance at 38
dare via *(tr)*	give away 38
*darsi a *(intr / refl)*	take to, adopt as habit 38, 7
*darsi delle arie *(intr / refl)*	show off, boast 38, 7
decidere di *(tr)*	decide (to), make up one's mind, settle 39 **[M]**
decidere su *(intr)*	decide upon 39
*decidersi a *(intr / refl)*	make up one's mind (to) 39, 7

decifrare *(tr)*	decode 3
declinare *(tr)*	disclaim (responsibility) 3
decollare *(tr)*	take off (plane) 3
decomporre *(tr)*	decompose 64
decorare *(tr)*	decorate 3
***descrescere** *(intr)*	decrease, go down 36
decretare *(tr)*	decree 3
dedicare *(tr)*	dedicate, devote to 11
***dedicarsi a** *(intr/refl)*	devote oneself to 11, 7
dedurre *(tr)*	deduce, deduct, infer 95
definire *(tr)*	define 6
defraudare *(tr)*	defraud 3
degradare *(tr)*	degrade 3
delegare *(tr)*	delegate 11
deliberare *(tr/intr)*	deliberate 3
delineare *(tr)*	outline, sketch out (plans) 3
deludere *(tr)*	disappoint, take in, delude, let down 30, 20
demolire *(tr)*	demolish 6
denudare *(tr)*	bare 3
denunciare *(tr)*	denounce 12
***deperire** *(intr)*	decay, waste away 6
depositare *(tr)*	deposit 3
depositare in una banca *(tr)*	bank (money) 3
deprimere *(tr)*	depress, make sad 32
deridere *(tr)*	deride, ridicule 72
***derivare da** *(intr)*	be derived from, spring, result from 3
derubare *(tr)*	rob 3
descrivere *(tr)*	describe 81
desiderare *(tr)*	desire, long for, want, wish 3
designare *(tr)*	style, design 3
desumere *(tr)*	deduce, assume, infer; gather 26
detenere *(tr)*	detain, stop 92
deteriorare *(tr)*	deteroriate 3
determinare *(tr)*	determine 3
detestare *(tr)*	detest 3
dettare *(tr)*	dictate 3
devastare *(tr)*	devastate 3
deviare *(tr)*	deviate, divert, turn aside 13
devolvere *(intr)*	transfer 4, 25
diagnosticare *(tr)*	diagnose 11
dibattere *(tr)*	debate 4
dichiarare di *(tr)*	declare, state 3
difendere da *(tr)*	defend from 17
differenziare *(tr)*	differentiate 13
differire *(intr)*	differ 6
diffidare di *(intr)*	distrust 3
diffondere *(tr)*	broadcast 50

digerire *(tr)*	digest 6
digiunare *(intr)*	fast, not eat 3
diluire *(tr)*	dilute, water down 6
***dimagrire** *(intr)*	get thin, slim, eat less 6
dimenticare di *(tr)*	forget (to), leave behind 11 **[M]**
***dimenticarsi di** *(intr / refl)*	forget 11, 7
***dimettersi** *(intr / refl)*	resign 54, 7
†**diminuire** *(intr / tr)*	decrease, dwindle, diminish, lessen 6
dimostrare *(tr)*	demonstrate, show / prove (innocence) 3
***dipendere da** *(intr)*	depend on 17
dipingere *(tr)*	depict, paint 86, 93
dire di *(tr)*	say, utter remark, tell (to), order 9 **[M]**
dirigere *(tr)*	direct, conduct (music), control, guide 40 **[M]**
***dirigersi verso** *(intr / refl)*	make one's way towards 40, 7
disapprovare *(tr)*	disapprove 3
disarmare *(tr)*	disarm 3
discendere *(tr / intr)*	descend 79
dischiudere *(tr)*	disclose; open 30
disciogliere *(tr)*	dissolve 31
discorrere di *(intr)*	discuss, talk about 35
discutere *(tr)*	discuss, argue, debate, dispute 41 **[M]**
discutere di *(intr)*	talk about 41
disdegnare *(tr)*	scorn 3
disegnare *(tr)*	draw (a picture) 3
diseredare *(tr)*	disinherit 3
disfare *(tr)*	undo, untie, unpack 10
***disfarsi di** *(intr / refl)*	dispose of 10, 7
disgiungere *(tr)*	separate 52
disilludere *(tr)*	disillusion 20
disinfettare *(tr)*	disinfect 3
disintegrare *(tr)*	disintegrate 3
disorganizzare *(tr)*	disorganize 3
dispensare *(tr)*	exempt from 3
disperare *(intr)*	despair 3
disperdere *(intr)*	disperse 59
***dispiacere** *(intr)*	be sorry (for), displease 61
disporre *(tr)*	dispose 64
disprezzare *(tr)*	scorn 3
***dissetarsi** *(intr / refl)*	quench (one's thirst) 7
dissodare *(tr)*	dig up 3
dissolvere *(tr)*	dissolve 74
dissuadere *(tr)*	dissuade 60
distendere *(tr)*	stretch 91
distinguere *(tr)*	distinguish, discern, make out 42 **[M]**

distogliere *(tr)*	distract 31
distorcere *(tr)*	distort 94
distrarre *(tr)*	distract 96
distribuire *(tr)*	deal (cards), distribute, give out, hand out / round, share out 6
districare *(tr)*	disentangle 11
distruggere *(tr)*	destroy 89
disturbare *(tr)*	disturb, trouble, upset 3
disubbidire a *(intr)*	disobey 6
divagare *(intr)*	ramble on 11
***divenire** *(intr)*	become 102
***diventare** *(intr)*	become, turn into 3
***diventare grigio** *(intr)*	go grey (hair) 3
***diventare peggio** *(intr)*	get worse 3
divergere *(intr)*	diverge 84
divertire *(tr)*	amuse 5
***divertirsi a** *(intr / refl)*	amuse / enjoy oneself, have fun (doing) 5, 7
dividere *(tr)*	divide, part, separate, split (cost) 43 **[M]**
dividere a metà *(tr)*	halve 43
divorare *(tr)*	devour 3
divorziare (tr / intr)	divorce, get divorced 13
***divorziarsi** *(intr / refl)*	get divorced 13, 7
***dolere** *(intr)*	ache, hurt 44 **[M]**
domandare *(tr)* **qlco. a qlcu.**	ask someone for something 3
domandare di *(intr)*	ask to 3
***domandarsi** *(intr / refl)*	wonder, ask oneself 7
domare *(tr)*	tame 3
dominare *(tr)*	master 3
dominare dall'alto *(tr)*	overlook 3
donare *(tr)*	donate 3
dondolare *(tr)*	rock, swing 3
dormire *(intr)*	sleep 5 **[M]**
dormire troppo a lungo *(intr)*	oversleep 5
dosare *(tr)*	dose 3
†dovere *(intr)*	have to, must, be obliged to, ought to, should; owe 45 **[M]**
†dovere fare qlco. *(intr)*	be obliged to do sth. 45
drogare *(tr)*	dope, drug 11
drogarsi *(intr / refl)*	become addicted, take drugs 11, 7
dubitare *(tr)*	doubt 3
duplicare *(tr)*	duplicate 11
durare *(intr)*	go on, last 3
E **eccitare** *(tr)*	excite, stir, work up (interest) 3
echeggiare *(intr)*	echo 12
editare *(tr)*	edit (IT) 3
educare *(tr)*	educate, train, bring up (children) 11

281

elaborare *(tr)*	process (data) 3
eleggere *(tr)*	elect 53
elencare *(tr)*	list 11
elettrificare *(tr)*	electrify 11
***elevarsi** *(intr / refl)*	soar (prices) 7
eliminare *(tr)*	delete, eliminate 3
eludere *(tr)*	elude, evade 20
emendare *(tr)*	amend 3
***emergere** *(intr)*	emerge from 84
emettere *(tr)*	send out, emit, utter, pass (sentence) 54
emettere *(tr)* vapore	steam, give out vapor / vapour 54
***emigrare** *(intr)*	emigrate, migrate 3
emulsionare *(tr)*	emulsify 3
***entrare in** *(intr)*	enter, come in; get in; come on (stage) 2 **[M]**
***entrare di nascosto in** *(intr)*	steal in 2
***entrare per caso in** *(intr)*	drop in 2
***entusiasmarsi per** *(intr / refl)*	be enthusiastic about 7
equipaggiare *(tr)*	equip 12
***equivalere** *(intr)*	amount to 100
ereditare *(tr)*	succeed, inherit 3
erigere *(tr)*	erect 40
errare *(intr)*	wander, walk aimlessly 3
eruttare *(intr)*	erupt 3
esagerare *(tr)*	exaggerate 3
esalare *(intr)*	exhale 3
esaminare *(tr)*	study, examine carefully 3
esaurire *(tr)*	drain, exhaust, run out of 6
***esaurirsi** *(intr)*	break down (person) 6, 7
esclamare *(tr)*	exclaim 3
escludere *(tr)*	disqualify, except, exclude 30, 20
eseguire *(tr)*	carry out perform, execute 6
esercitare *(tr)*	drill (exercise) 3
esibire *(tr)*	exhibit 6
esigere *(tr)*	require 4, 25
esiliare *(tr)*	banish 13
***esistere** *(intr)*	exist 25
esitare a *(intr)*	hesitate (to), pause 3
esonerare *(tr)*	exonerate 3
espellere *(tr)*	expel 46 **[M]**
***esplodere** *(intr)*	explode 47 **[M]**
esplorare *(tr)*	explore 3
esporre *(tr)*	expose 64
esportare *(tr)*	export 3
esprimere *(tr)*	say, express (opinion) 32
***essere** *(intr)*	be 48 **[M]**
***essere afoso** *(intr)*	be heavy / sultry 48
***essere a dieta** *(tr)*	diet 48

*essere avanti *(intr)*	be fast (clock) 48
*essere contento *(intr)*	be pleased 48
*essere contro *(intr)*	be against 48
*essere d'accordo con *(intr)*	be in agreement, agree (with) 48
*essere di fronte a *(intr)*	face, be opposite 48
*essere disoccupato *(intr)*	be unemployed 48
*essere diverso *(intr)*	be different 48
*essere dovuto a *(intr)*	be due to 48
*essere frequentato da spettri *(intr)*	be haunted 48
*essere fuori *(intr)*	be out 48
*essere (im)paziente *(intr)*	be (im)patient 48
*essere imparentato *(intr)*	be related (family) 48
*essere in concorrenza con *(intr)*	compete with 48
*essere in disaccordo *(intr)*	disagree 48
*essere in periodo di prosperità *(intr)*	be in a boom 48
*essere in ritardo *(intr)*	be delayed, be late 48
*essere indietro *(intr)*	be slow (clock) 48
*essere inguaiato *(intr)*	be stuck 48
*essere mite *(intr)*	be mild 48
*essere ne di *(intr)*	become of 48
*essere necessario *(intr)*	need, be necessary 48
*essere nuvoloso *(intr)*	be cloudy 48
*essere occupato *(intr)*	be busy 48
*essere per *(intr)*	be for, support 48
*essere pieno di	abound with, be full of 48
*essere promosso *(intr)*	go up (in school) 48
*essere responsabile per *(intr)*	be liable / responsible for 48
*essere ricco di *(intr)*	be abundant, abound in 48
*essere seduto *(intr)*	sit, be seated 48
*essere sonnambulo *(intr)*	walk in one's sleep 48
*essere stitico *(intr)*	be constipated 48
*essere sul punto di *(intr)*	be about to 48
*essere umido *(intr)*	be humid / damp 48
*essere valido *(intr)*	be valid 48
*estendersi *(intr / refl)*	expand, branch out 91, 7
estinguere *(tr)*	extinguish 42
estrarre *(tr)*	extract 96
evacuare *(tr)*	evacuate 3
*evadere *(intr)*	evade, escape 49 **[M]**
†evaporare *(tr / intr)*	evaporate, vaporize 3
evidenziare *(tr)*	highlight 13
evitare *(tr)*	avoid, bypass 3
evitare di fare qlco.	avoid doing something 3
evocare *(tr)*	evoke 11
*evolversi *(intr / refl)*	evolve, develop 4,25

F

fabbricare *(tr)*	manufacture 11
facilitare *(tr)*	facilitate 3

VERB INDEX

falciare *(tr)*	mow (grass) 12
*fallire *(intr)*	fail 6
falsificare *(tr)*	fake 11
farcire *(tr)*	stuff (turkey) 6
fare *(tr)*	do, make, add up to, study (subject), cause to be, serve, perform duties, take (photo / bath / shower) 10 **[M]**
fare a meno di *(intr)*	dispense with, do without 10
fare a pezzi *(tr)*	hack to pieces 10
fare amicizia con *(intr)*	make friends with 10
fare attenzione *(intr)*	pay attention, mind (warning) 10
fare bello *(intr)*	be nice / fine 10
fare brutto *(intr)*	be bad / awful 10
fare cadere *(tr)*	drop 10
fare caldo *(intr)*	be hot 10
fare colazione *(tr)*	have breakfast 10
fare da *(intr)*	act as 10
fare da spettatore *(intr)*	look on 10
fare del bene a *(intr)*	benefit, do good to 10
fare del pugilato *(intr)*	box (sport) 10
fare del suo meglio per *(tr)*	do one's best to 10
fare di tutto per *(tr)*	do everything possible to 10
fare dispetti a *(intr)*	tease 10
fare dispetto a *(intr)*	spite, annoy 10
fare entrare *(tr)*	show in (visitor) 10
fare esplodere *(tr)*	blast, set off explosion 10
fare fallire *(tr)*	bankrupt 10
fare fare a qlcu. *(intr)*	get s.one to do sth. 10
fare finta di *(intr)*	pretend 10
fare freddo *(intr)*	be cold 10
fare fresco *(intr)*	be cool / fresh 10
fare fronte a *(intr)*	cope (with) 10
fare giorno *(intr)*	get light 10
fare grazia della vita a qlcu. *(intr)*	spare (life) 10
fare i piatti *(tr)*	wash up 10
fare il jogging *(tr)*	jog 10
fare il nido *(tr)*	nest 10
fare il pieno *(tr)*	fill up (car) 10
fare impazzire *(tr)*	madden 10
fare inciampare *(tr)*	trip 10
fare l'autostop *(tr)*	hitchhike 10
fare l'elemosina *(tr)*	give alms 10
fare l'interprete *(tr)*	act as interpreter 10
fare l'uovo *(tr)*	lay (egg) 10
fare la caricatura di *(intr)*	caricature 10
fare la carta di *(intr)*	chart 10
fare la coda *(tr)*	wait / queue in line 10
fare la conoscenza di *(intr)*	get to know 10

fare la cubatura *(intr)*	cube 10
fare la doccia *(tr)*	shower 10
fare la media di *(intr)*	average 10
fare la permanente *(tr)*	perm 10
fare la pubblicità a *(intr)*	publicize 10
fare le fusa *(tr)*	purr 10
fare le prove di *(intr)*	rehearse 10
fare male *(intr)*	ache 10
fare male a *(intr)*	harm 10
fare marcia indietro *(intr)*	back (car) 10
fare notte *(intr)*	get dark 10
fare pagare *(tr)*	charge (prices) 10
fare pareggio *(intr)*	draw in a match 10
fare parte di una giuria *(intr)*	sit on a jury 10
fare pervenire *(tr)*	send in, submit 10
fare piacere a *(intr)*	please 10
fare prigioniero	take prisoner 10
fare pubblicità *(intr)*	advertise 10
fare ricerche *(tr)*	research 10
fare risatine sciocche *(intr)*	giggle 10
fare saltare *(tr)*	blow up, explode 10
fare saltare *(tr)*	pop 10
fare scattare *(tr)*	clock in 10
fare sedere *(tr)*	seat, sit, cause to sit 10
fare segno a qlcu. *(intr)*	wave to s.one 10
fare soffrire a *(intr)*	pain 10
fare solletico a *(intr)*	tickle 10
fare tacere *(tr)*	silence 10
fare torto a *(intr)*	wrong 10
fare traslochi *(tr)*	remove (furniture) 10
fare tutto il possibile per *(intr)*	do everything possible to 10
fare un bilancio *(tr)*	budget 10
fare un brindisi *(tr)*	toast 10
fare un picnic *(tr)*	picnic 10
fare un salto mortale *(tr)*	somersault 10
fare una collezione di *(tr)*	collect (as a hobby) 10
fare una passeggiata *(tr)*	go for a walk 10
fare una trasfusione a *(tr)*	do a blood transfusion 10
fare uno spuntino *(tr)*	have a snack 10
fare vedere a *(intr)*	show 10
faria franca *(intr)*	get away with 10
farne di tutti i colori a *(intr)*	play up 10
*farsi operare *(intr / refl)*	have an operation 10, 7
*farsi prestare *(intr / refl)*	borrow 10, 7
*farsi vivo *(intr / refl)*	show up, turn up 10, 7
fasciare *(tr)*	swaddle (baby) 12
faticare *(intr)*	labour 11
fatturare *(tr)*	bill 3
favorire *(tr)*	favor / favour, treat well, further 6

ferire *(tr)*	injure, wound 6
fermare *(tr)*	stop, prevent 3
***fermarsi** *(intr/refl)*	stop, stall (engine) 7
fermentare *(intr)*	ferment 3
ferrare *(tr)*	shoe (horse) 3
festeggiare *(tr/intr)*	celebrate, feast 12
ficcare *(tr)*	stick, push sth. pointed 11
***fidanzarsi** *(intr/refl)*	get engaged 7
***fidarsi di** *(intr/refl)*	trust 7
***figurarsi** *(intr/refl)*	imagine 7
filare *(tr)*	spin (wool) 3
filtrare *(tr)*	filter, strain (wine) 3
filtrare attraverso *(intr)*	seep through 3
finanziare *(tr)*	finance 13
fingere di *(tr)*	pretend (to) 86
†finire di *(intr/tr)*	finish, end, end up 6 **[M]**
†finire per *(intr)*	end by, finish by 6
***fiorire** *(intr)*	bloom, flower, flourish 6
firmare *(tr)*	sign (signature) 3
fischiare *(intr/tr)*	whistle 13 **[M]**
fissare *(tr)*	fix, gaze at, stare, stare at 3
fissare con caviglie *(tr)*	peg 3
fissare *(tr)* **un appuntamento**	make a date 3
fiutare rumorosamente *(tr)*	sniff 3
flettere *(tr)*	bend 4, 25
fondare *(tr)*	found 3
fondere *(tr)*	melt, fuse, merge 50 **[M]**
formare *(tr)*	fashion, form 3
formattare *(tr)*	format (IT) 3
fornire *(tr)*	fit out, provide, relay, stock, supply 6
fornire di personale *(tr)*	staff 6
forzare a *(tr)*	force, compel (to) 3
fotocopiare *(tr)*	photocopy, run off, duplicate 13
fotografare *(tr)*	photograph 3
frammettere *(tr)*	interpose, insert 54
frantumare *(tr)*	crush, smash, break 3
***frantumarsi** *(intr/refl)*	shiver 7
frapporre *(tr)*	insert 64
fratturare *(tr)*	fracture 3
fregare *(tr)*	rub, scrub 11
frenare *(tr)*	brake 3
***frenarsi** *(intr/refl)*	control oneself 7
frequentare *(tr)*	attend school, frequent 3
frequentare assiduamente *(tr)*	haunt 3
friggere *(tr)*	fry 19
frizzare *(tr)*	fizz 3
frustrare *(tr)*	foil, frustrate 3
†fuggire *(tr/intr)*	escape, run away, flee 5
fumare *(tr)*	smoke 3

	fungere *(intr)*	act as 68
	funzionare *(intr)*	operate (of machine), work, function 3
G	**galleggiare** *(intr)*	float 12
	garantire *(tr)*	guarantee 6
	†**gelare** *(intr / tr)*	deepfreeze, freeze 3
	gemere *(intr)*	groan, moan 4
	generare *(tr)*	generate 3
	germogliare *(intr)*	sprout 13
	gettare *(tr)*	chuck, fling, pitch, throw, toss 3
	*****ghiacciare** *(intr)*	ice, chill, freeze 12
	*****giacere** *(intr)*	lie 51 **[M]**
	giocare a *(intr)*	play, stake (gambling) 11
	giocare a bocce *(intr)*	play bowls 11
	girare *(intr)*	spin, move round, turn 3
	girare intorno a *(intr)*	circle 3
	girare un film *(tr)*	film, shoot a film / movie 3
	*****girarsi** *(intr / refl)*	turn around 7
	giudicare da *(tr)*	judge by / on 11
	giudicare male *(tr)*	misjudge 11
	*****giungere a** *(intr)*	arrive at, reach 52 **[M]**
	giurare di *(intr)*	swear (to) 3
	giustificare *(tr)*	justify 11
	gocciolare *(tr)*	drip 3
	godere di *(intr)*	enjoy 4
	†**gonfiare** *(intr / tr)*	inflate, swell 3
	*****gonfiarsi di** *(intr / refl)*	bulge with 7
	gorgogliare *(intr)*	bubble 13
	governare *(tr / intr)*	rule, govern 3
	gracchiare *(intr)*	croak 13
	graffiare *(tr)*	scratch 13
	†**grandinare** *(intr)*	hail (weather) 3
	grattare *(tr)*	scrape, scratch 3
	grattugiare *(tr)*	grate (cheese) 12
	gridare *(tr)*	shout, call out, cry out 3
	grugnire *(intr)*	grunt 6
	guadagnare *(tr)*	earn, gain 3
	guardare *(tr)*	look, look at, watch 3
	guardare furtivamente *(tr)*	peep 3
	*****guardarsi da** *(intr / refl)*	beware of 7
	†**guarire** *(intr / tr)*	cure, heal, recover, get better 6
	guastare *(tr)*	spoil (fruit) 3
	guerreggiare *(intr)*	war 12
	guidare *(tr)*	drive, lead, guide 3
	gustare *(tr)*	savour, taste (food) 3
I	**idealizzare** *(tr)*	idealize 3
	identificare *(tr)*	identify 11
	ignorare *(tr)*	be unaware of, not know 3

illudere *(tr)*	deceive, delude, fool 20
illuminare *(tr)*	illuminate 3
illustrare *(tr)*	illustrate 3
imballare *(tr)*	pack, package 3
imbarazzare *(tr)*	embarrass 3
imbarcare *(tr)*	embark, ship 11
*imbarcarsi *(intr / refl)*	board 11, 7
†imbiancare *(intr / tr)*	bleach, turn white 11
imbottigliare *(tr)*	bottle 13
imbucare *(tr)*	post 11
imburrare *(tr)*	butter 3
imitare *(tr)*	mime, imitate 3
immaginare di *(tr)*	imagine, think of 3
*immaginarsi *(intr / refl)*	imagine 7
immergere *(tr)*	immerse, steep (in liquid) 84
immettere *(tr)*	admit, let in 54
immigrare *(tr)*	immigrate 3
immunizzare *(tr)*	immunize 3
*impadronirsi di *(intr / refl)*	seize 6, 7
*impallidire *(intr)*	go white, turn pale 6
imparare a *(tr)*	learn (to) 6
*impazzire *(intr)*	grow mad / crazy 6
impedire di *(tr)*	forbid, stop, hinder, prevent (from) 6
*impegnarsi a *(intr / refl)*	commit oneself, undertake (to) 7
*impennarsi *(intr / refl)*	rear up (horse) 7
impiegare *(tr)*	employ 11
imporre *(tr)*	impose 64
*importare *(intr)*	care about, matter *(Imp.)* 3
importare *(tr)*	import 3
impressionare *(tr)*	strike, impress 3
imprigionare *(tr)*	imprison 3
imprimere *(tr)*	impress, stamp 32
inalare *(tr)*	inhale 3
inargentare *(tr)*	silver, coat with silver 3
inasprire *(tr)*	exasperate 6
incaricare *(tr)*	commission 11
incartare *(tr)*	wrap up (with paper) 3
incassare *(tr)*	cash 3
incatenare *(tr)*	chain (up) 3
incendiare *(tr)*	fire, set fire to 13
inchiodare *(tr)*	nail down 3
*inciampare *(intr)*	stumble 3
incidere su *(tr)*	cut, carve, engrave, incise 39
incitare a *(intr)*	urge to 3
inclinare *(tr)*	incline 3
*inclinarsi *(intr / refl)*	lean 7
includere *(tr)*	comprise, count in, include 20
incollare *(tr)*	stick, glue 3

incolpare *(tr)*	blame 3
*incominciare *(intr)*	begin 12
†incontrare *(intr/tr)*	run/bump into, meet 3
*incontrarsi con *(intr/refl)*	meet 7
incoraggiare a *(tr)*	encourage (to) 12
incorniciare *(tr)*	frame (picture) 12
incorporare *(tr)*	incorporate 3
*incorrere in *(intr)*	incur 35
increspare *(tr)*	ruffle, wrinkle 3
*incrociarsi *(intr/refl)*	cross, intersect 12, 7
incuneare *(tr)*	wedge 3
incutere *(tr)*	strike, rouse 41
indagare su *(intr)*	investigate 11
†indebolire *(intr/tr)*	weaken 6
indicare *(tr)*	show, indicate 11
indicare a dito *(tr)*	point (with finger) 11
indirizzare *(tr)*	address/send a letter 3
*indirizzarsi *(intr/refl)*	apply 7
indossare *(tr)*	put on, wear (clothes) 3
indovinare *(tr)*	guess 3
*indugiarsi *(intr/refl)*	loiter 12, 7
indurire *(tr)*	harden, stiffen 6
*indurirsi *(intr/refl)*	harden 6, 7
infastidire *(tr)*	bother, worry s.one 6
infettare *(tr)*	infect 3
*infettarsi *(intr/refl)*	become infected 7
infiammare *(tr)*	inflame 3
infilare *(tr)*	thread 3
*infilarsi *(intr)*	slip on (clothes) 7
*infischiarsi *(intr/refl)*	care nothing (about sth.) 13, 7
infliggere *(tr)*	inflict 19
influenzare *(tr)*	influence 3
influire su *(intr)*	influence, affect 6
infondere *(tr)*	instill 50
informare *(tr)*	inform 3
*informarsi di/su *(intr/refl)*	get information about, ask about 7
ingannare *(tr)*	bluff, cheat, circumvent, deceive, mislead, trick 3
ingessare *(tr)*	plaster 3
inghiottire *(tr)*	swallow 6
*inginocchiarsi *(intr/refl)*	kneel down 13, 7
ingiuriare qlcu. *(tr)*	call s.one names 13
†ingrassare *(intr/tr)*	fatten put on weight 3
iniettare *(tr)*	inject 3
inizializzare *(tr)*	boot (IT) 3
iniziare a *(tr)*	initiate (s.one) 13
innaffiare *(tr)*	water 13
innalzare *(tr)*	heighten 3
*innamorarsi di *(intr/refl)*	fall in love 7

VERB INDEX

*innervosirsi *(intr / refl)*	get nervous 6, 7
innestare la retromarcia *(tr)*	reverse (car) 3
inoculare *(tr)*	innoculate 3
inoltrare *(tr)*	send on (letters) 3
inoltrare una domanda	apply (for job) 3
inondare *(tr)*	flood, overflow 3
inquinare *(tr)*	pollute 3
insaponare *(tr)*	soap 3
insegnare a *(tr)*	teach (to) 3
inseguire *(tr)*	hound, pursue, track 5
inserire *(tr)*	write in, insert 6
insistere su *(intr)*	insist (on) 25
installare *(tr)*	install 3
insultare *(tr)*	be rude to, insult 3
integrare *(tr)*	integrate 3
intendere *(tr)*	mean, intend (to say) 91, 17
*intendersi di *(intr / refl)*	know about, be an expert on 17, 7
intensificare *(tr)*	intensify 11
interdire *(tr)*	forbid 9
interessare *(tr)*	interest *(Imp.)* 3
*interessarsi (a / di) *(intr / refl)*	take an interest in, care 7
interferire *(intr)*	interfere 6
interporre *(tr)*	interpose 64
interpretare *(tr)*	interpret, read / play (a part) 3
interpretare male *(tr)*	misinterpret 3
interrogare *(tr)*	interrogate, question 11
interrompere *(tr)*	interrupt, switch off 76
*intervenire *(intr)*	intervene, chip in, cut off 102
intervistare *(tr)*	interview 3
intitolare *(tr)*	entitle 3
intraprendere *(tr)*	take on, undertake (journey) 66
intravedere *(tr)*	glimpse 101
introdurre *(tr)*	bring in, introduce 95
*intrudersi *(intr / refl)*	intrude 20, 7
intuire *(tr)*	sense 6
inumidire *(tr)*	moisten 6
invadere *(tr)*	invade 49
*invecchiare *(intr)*	age 13
*invecchiarsi *(intr / refl)*	age, grow old 13, 7
inventare *(tr)*	make up, invent 3
investigare *(tr)*	investigate 11
investire *(tr)*	invest, run down / over (with car) 5
inviare *(tr)*	send 13
invidiare *(tr)*	envy 13
invitare a *(tr)*	ask, invite (to) 3
involgere *(tr)*	wrap 106
inzuccherare *(tr)*	sugar 3
ionizzare *(tr)*	ionize 3
ipotecare *(tr)*	mortgage 11

	irrigare *(tr)*	irrigate 11
	irritare *(tr)*	irritate 3
	irrompere *(tr)*	break into a building 76
	*iscriversi *(intr / refl)*	enroll, register 81, 7
	isolare *(tr)*	isolate, shut off (water, gas) 3
	ispessire *(tr)*	thicken 6
	istruire *(tr)*	instruct 6
	istupidire *(tr)*	stupefy 6
L	*lagnarsi di *(intr / refl)*	complain about 7
	*lamentarsi di *(intr / refl)*	complain about 7
	lampeggiare *(tr)*	flash, flash (lightning) 12
	lanciare *(tr)*	throw (a bomb) 12
	lanciare un razzo *(tr)*	launch, lift off (rocket) 12
	*lanciarsi *(intr / refl)*	dart out 12, 7
	languire *(intr)*	pine 6
	lappare *(intr)*	lap 3
	lasciare *(tr)*	leave, allow to remain 12
	lasciare entrare *(tr)*	allow in, let in, allow to enter 12
	lasciare passare *(tr)*	allow through, let through 12
	lasciare per testamento *(tr)*	bequeath, will 12
	lasciare vuoto *(tr)*	vacate 12
	*lasciarsi cadere *(intr / refl)*	flop down 12, 7
	lavare *(tr)*	wash 3
	lavare a secco *(tr)*	dry-clean 3
	*lavarsi *(intr / refl)*	wash oneself, get washed, wash up 7 **[M]**
	lavorare *(tr)*	work 3
	lavorare a maglia *(tr)*	knit 3
	lavorare come uno schiavo *(tr)*	slave, work hard 3
	lavoricchiare *(intr)*	potter about 13
	leccare *(tr)*	lick 11
	legalizzare *(tr)*	legalize 3
	legare *(tr)*	bind, fasten, tie, band together 11
	legare con corde *(tr)*	string 11
	leggere *(tr)*	read 53 **[M]**
	leggere ad alta voce *(tr)*	read aloud 53
	levigare con carta vetrata *(tr)*	sand down 11
	liberare *(tr)*	free, release, rescue, set free, rid of 3
	*librarsi a volo *(intr / refl)*	soar (of bird) 7
	licenziare *(tr)*	fire (s.one), sack, dismiss 13
	limare *(tr)*	file (wood, metal) 3
	limitare *(tr)*	keep to, limit 3
	*limitarsi a *(intr / refl)*	confine to 7
	liquefare *(tr)*	liquify, melt 10
	liquidare *(tr)*	pay off debts 3
	lisciare *(tr)*	smooth(e) 12
	litigare con *(intr)*	fall out, quarrel 11

VERB INDEX

livellare *(tr)*	level 3
lodare *(tr)*	praise 1, 3 **[M]**
*logorarsi *(intr / refl)*	wear out 7
lottare contro *(intr)*	struggle against 3
lottare per *(intr)*	struggle for, fight for 3
luccicare *(tr)*	gleam 11
lucidare *(tr)*	shine, polish 3
lusingare *(tr)*	flatter 11

M	macchiare *(tr)*	soil, dirty, spot, mark, stain, blur 13
	macchinare *(tr)*	scheme 3
	maceliare *(tr)*	slaughter 3
	macinare *(tr)*	grind, mill 3
	magnetizzare *(tr)*	magnetize 3
	maledire *(tr)*	curse 9
	maltrattare *(tr)*	mistreat, misuse 3
	*mancare *(intr)*	be missing, miss, lack 11
	*mancare di *(intr)*	fail to do sth. 11
	mandare *(tr)*	send 3
	mandare *(tr)* un fax	fax 3
	mandare a chiamare *(tr)*	send for s.one 3
	mandare a prendere *(tr)*	send for sth. 3
	mandare fuori *(tr)*	send s.one out 3
	mandare per posta *(tr)*	mail 3
	maneggiare *(tr)*	handle 12
	mangiare *(tr)*	eat 12 **[M]**
	mantenere *(tr)*	abide by / keep, maintain, support, provide for 92
	mantenere la parola *(tr)*	stick to your word 92
	mantenere le proprie posizioni *(tr)*	hold one's own, stand, maintain position 92
	marcare *(tr)*	mark 11
	marciare *(intr)*	march 12
	marinare *(tr)* la scuola	play truant 3
	martellare *(tr)*	hammer 3
	massacrare *(tr)*	massacre 3
	masticare *(tr)*	chew 11
	*maturare *(intr)*	ripen 3
	mentire *(intr)*	lie, tell a lie 6
	*meravigliarsi di *(intr / refl)*	be amazed, wonder at 13, 7
	meritare di *(tr)*	deserve 3
	mescolare *(tr)*	jumble up, mix, mix up 3
	mettere *(tr)*	put 54 **[M]**
	mettere all'aria *(tr)*	air 54
	mettere alla prova *(tr)*	test 54
	mettere da parte *(tr)*	put aside, put away, store 54
	mettere fuori *(tr)*	catch out 54
	mettere fuori combattimento *(tr)*	knock out 54
	mettere fuori fase *(tr)*	phase out 54

mettere in comunicazione *(tr)*	put through (telephone) 54
mettere in disordine *(tr)*	make a mess of 54
mettere in fase *(tr)*	phase in 54
mettere in garage *(tr)*	garage (car) 54
mettere in moto *(tr)*	start car 54
mettere in ordine *(tr)*	put in order, tidy up 54
mettere in pensione *(tr)*	pension off 54
mettere in relazione a *(intr)*	relate to 54
mettere insieme *(tr)*	bond, put together 54
mettere per iscritto *(tr)*	set down on paper 54
*mettersi a *(intr / refl)*	begin to 54, 7
*mettersi a sedere *(intr / refl)*	sit down 54, 7
*mettersi al *(intr / refl)*	set in (of weather) 54, 7
*mettersi in contatto con *(intr / refl)*	contact 54, 7
*mettersi in piedi *(intr / refl)*	stand up 54, 7
*mettersi in piega *(intr / refl)*	set hair 54, 7
miagolare *(intr)*	mew 3
mietere *(tr)*	harvest, mow (corn), reap 4
†migliorare *(intr / tr)*	improve 3
minacciare di *(tr)*	threaten (to) 12
mirare a *(intr)*	aim at 3
mischiare *(tr)*	blend 13
misurare *(tr)*	survey, measure 3
modellare *(tr)*	model, mold 3
modernizzare *(tr)*	modernize 3
modificare *(tr)*	modify 11
molestare *(tr)*	molest 3
moltiplicare *(tr)*	multiply 11
monopolizzare *(tr)*	monopolize 3
†montare *(intr / tr)*	ride (bike, horse) 3
mordere *(tr)*	bite 55 **[M]**
mordicchiare *(tr)*	nibble 13
*morire *(intr)*	die 56 **[M]**
*morire di fame *(intr)*	starve 56
mormorare *(tr)*	murmur 3
mostrare *(tr)*	show, allow to be seen 3
motivare *(tr)*	motivate 3
mudare *(intr)*	molt / moult 3
muggire *(intr)*	below (animals) 6
multare *(tr)*	fine (law) 3
mungere *(tr)*	milk 68
muovere *(tr)*	move, stir 15 **[M]**
*muoversi *(intr / refl)*	move oneself 15, 7

N

narrare *(tr)*	narrate, relate (a story) 3
*nascere *(intr)*	be born 57 **[M]**
nascondere *(tr)*	conceal, hide, veil 75
naufragare *(intr / tr)*	be shipwrecked, sink, go down, wreck 11

	negare *(tr)*	deny 11
	negoziare *(tr)*	negotiate, bargain 13
	neutralizzare *(tr)*	neutralize 3
	†nevicare *(intr)*	snow 11
	nitrire *(intr)*	neigh 6
	noleggiare *(tr)*	charter (plane), hire / rent (car) 12
	nominare *(tr)*	appoint, name, nominate 3
	notare *(tr)*	note, notice 3
	notificare *(tr)*	inform, notify 11
	nuocere a *(intr)*	be bad for, harm 16 **[M]**
	nuotare *(intr)*	swim 3
	nutrire *(tr)*	nourish 6
O	**obiettare** *(tr)*	object 3
	obbligare a *(tr)*	oblige s.one to 11
	*occorrere *(intr)*	be necessary *(Imp)*. 35
	occupare *(tr)*	occupy, take up (space) 3
	occupare abusivamente *(tr)*	squat, settle illegally 3
	*occuparsi di *(intr / refl)*	deal with, see about / to, organize 7
	odiare *(tr)*	hate, dislike 13
	offendere *(tr)*	disgust, offend 17
	offrire *(tr)* **a qlcu.**	bid hold out, offer, treat s.one, give (present) to s.one 24
	offrire alloggio a *(tr)*	put up, accommodate 24
	offrire di *(intr)*	offer (to) 24
	*offrirsi *(intr / refl)*	volunteer 24, 7
	omettere *(tr)*	leave out, omit 54
	ondeggiare *(intr)*	flicker 12
	operare *(tr)*	operate 3
	opporre *(tr)*	oppose 64
	*opporsi a *(intr / refl)*	oppose, be opposed to 64, 7
	opprimere *(tr)*	weigh down, oppress 32
	orbitare *(tr)*	orbit 3
	ordinare *(tr)*	file (papers), order (food) 3
	organizzare *(tr)*	organize 3
	orinare *(intr)*	urinate 3
	ornare *(tr)*	embellish 3
	osare *(intr)*	dare 3
	oscillare *(intr)*	oscillate, sway, range (in amount) 3
	oscurare *(tr)*	darken 3
	ospitare *(tr)*	accommodate, put up, entertain 3
	osservare *(tr)*	notice, observe, remark 3
	ossidare *(tr)*	oxidize 3
	ostacolare *(tr)*	hold up (traffic), thwart 3
	ottenere *(intr)*	come by, obtain 92
	otturare *(tr)*	fill (a tooth) 3
	oziare *(intr)*	idle about 13
P	**pagare** *(tr)*	pay, pay in 11
	*pagare il conto *(tr)*	check out, pay bill / check 11

palleggiare *(tr)*	dribble (football / soccer) 13
paralizzare *(tr)*	paralyze 3
parcheggiare *(tr)*	park (car) 12
pareggiare *(tr)*	equalize (sport) 12
***parere di** *(intr)*	appear, seem (to) *(Imp)*. 58 **[M]**
parlare di *(tr / intr)*	speak, talk (of) 3 **[M]**
parlare francamente *(intr)*	speak out 3
partecipare a *(intr)*	take part in, participate in 3
parteggiare per *(intr)*	side with, support 12
***partire** *(intr)*	depart, set off, leave 5
***partire per** *(intr)*	leave for 5
†**passare** *(intr / tr)*	spend (time) 3
***passare a** *(intr)*	pass (an exam) 3
passare *(tr)* **l'aspirapolvere**	vacuum 3
passare a prendere *(tr)*	call for 3
passare a una velocità inferiore *(intr)*	change down (gear) 3
passare a una velocità superiore *(intr)*	change up (gear) 3
passare da *(intr)*	call in 3
passare per *(intr)*	pass by, pass through 3
passeggiare *(intr)*	stroll 12
pattinare *(intr)*	skate 3
peccare *(intr)*	sin 11
pedalare *(intr)*	pedal 3
†**peggiorare** *(intr / tr)*	worsen 3
pendere *(intr)*	slope, overhang 4
penetrare *(tr)*	penetrate, pierce 3
penetrare a forza *(tr)*	force one's way 3
pensare *(intr / tr)*	think 3
pensare a *(intr)*	think about 3
pensare di *(intr)*	plan, think of (opinion) 3
***pentirsi di** *(intr / refl)*	regret, repent (of) 5, 7
percepire *(tr)*	detect, perceive 6
percorrere *(tr)*	cover, go along, scour 35
percuotere *(tr)*	beat, strike 82
perdere *(tr)*	lose 59 **[M]**
perdere *(tr)* **l'equilibrio**	throw off balance 59
perdere tempo *(intr)*	mess about 59
***perdersi** *(intr / refl)*	get lost 59, 7
perdonare *(tr)*	forgive, pardon 3
perfezionare *(tr)*	perfect 3
perforare *(tr)*	punch (holes) 3
***perire** *(intr)*	perish 6
permettere *(intr)*	permit, allow, let, enable 54
***permettersi** *(intr / refl)*	be allowed 54, 7
***permettersi il lusso di** *(intr / refl)*	afford 54, 7
perseguire *(tr)*	follow up, pursue, search for 5
persistere *(intr)*	keep at, persist 25
persuadere a *(tr)*	persuade 60 **[M]**

*pervenire *(intr)*	arrive at 102
pesare *(tr)*	weigh 3
pescare *(tr)*	fish 11
pestare *(tr)*	stamp (with foot) 3
pettinare *(tr)*	comb 3
*piacere a *(intr)*	please, like, be fond of, appeal to 61 **[M]**
piagnucolare *(intr)*	snivel, cry 3
piangere *(intr)*	cry 62 **[M]**
piantare *(tr)*	pitch (tent), plant 3
picchiettare *(intr)*	patter (rain) 3
piegare *(tr)*	fold 11
pieghettare *(tr)*	pleat 3
pigliare *(tr)*	take, catch 13
pilotare *(tr)*	pilot 3
piluccare *(tr)*	peck at 11
†piovere *(intr)*	rain *(Imp)*. 63 **[M]**
piovigginare *(intr)*	drizzle 3
polverizzare *(tr)*	powder, pulverize 3
pompare *(tr)*	pump 3
porgere *(tr)*	hand, give, hold out 80
porre *(tr)*	place, put 64 **[M]**
porre in scatola *(tr)*	box in 64
portare *(tr)*	bear, carry, bring; have on, wear 3
portare a *(intr)*	lead to 3
portare il lutto *(tr)*	mourn 3
portare via *(tr)*	carry off, take away 3
posare *(tr)*	lay, place 3
posporre *(tr)*	postpone 64
possedere *(tr)*	possess, have, own 14, 4
potare *(tr)*	prune 3
†potere *(intr)*	can, be able to 65 **[M]**
pranzare *(intr)*	have lunch 3
praticare *(tr)*	practice, put into practice 11
precipitare *(tr)*	precipitate 3
*precipitarsi *(intr / refl)*	rush 7
*precipitarsi fuori *(intr / refl)*	burst out 7
*precipitarsi in *(intr / refl)*	burst in 7
precisare *(tr)*	specify 3
predicare *(tr)*	preach 11
predire *(tr)*	predict 9
preferire *(tr)*	prefer 6
pregare di *(tr)*	pray, beg, ask 11
premere *(tr)*	press (button) 4
prendere *(tr)*	take, catch (train, cold), have, eat 66 **[M]**
prendere a *(intr)*	begin to 66
prendere d'assalto *(tr)*	storm (a building) 66

P

prendere in considerazione *(tr)*	take into account 66
prendere in trappola *(tr)*	trap 66
prendere le difese di *(tr)*	stand up for 66
prendere nota di *(intr)*	minute, take down (in writing) 66
prendere parte a *(intr)*	take part in 66
prendere per *(intr)*	mistake for 66
prendersi la briga di *(intr/refl)*	take the trouble to 66, 7
prendersela con *(intr)*	be upset with 66, 7
prenotare *(tr)*	book, reserve 3
preoccupare *(tr)*	distress 3
*preoccuparsi di / per *(intr/refl)*	worry, get worried about 7
preparare *(tr)*	get ready, prepare 3
preparare il terreno *(tr)*	pave the way 3
*prepararsi a *(intr/refl)*	get prepared for, get ready for 7
preporre *(tr)*	place / put before; prefer 64
prescegliere *(tr)*	choose from 31
prescrivere *(tr)*	prescribe 81
presentare *(tr)*	introduce, present, produce (show) 3
*presentarsi *(intr/refl)*	arise 7
preservare *(tr)*	preserve 3
presiedere *(tr)*	chair meeting 4
prestare *(tr)*	lend 3
presumere *(tr/intr)*	presume, rely 26
presupporre *(tr)*	presuppose 64
pretendere di *(tr)*	claim, profess (to) 91
*prevalere *(intr)*	prevail 100
prevedere *(tr)*	foresee 101
privare *(tr)*	rob 3
privare di *(tr)*	do out of, stop s.one having 3
privatizzare *(tr)*	privatize 3
processare *(tr)*	try in court 3
procrastinare *(tr)*	procrastinate 3
procreare *(tr)*	procreate 3
procurare *(tr)*	get 3
produrre *(tr)*	yield, produce 95
produrre vescichette *(intr)*	blister 95
profittare *(intr)*	profit 3
profittare da *(intr)*	benefit from 3
profondere *(tr)*	squander 50
profondersi in *(intr/refl)*	be profuse in 50
profumare *(tr)*	scent 3
progettare *(tr)*	devise, project 3
programmare *(tr)*	program 3
proibire di *(tr)*	prohibit (from) 6
proiettare *(tr)*	cast 3
prolungare *(tr)*	prolong 11
promettere *(tr)*	promise 54
promettere a qlcu di fare *(intr)*	promise s.one to do sth. 54

promuovere *(tr)*	pass (candidate), promote, upgrade 15
pronunciare *(tr)*	pronounce 12
proporre di *(tr)*	propose (to); table (a bill) 64
prorompere *(intr)*	burst out 76
proseguire *(intr)*	proceed 5
proseguire *(tr)*	prosecute 5
prosperare *(intr)*	prosper, flourish, thrive 3
***prostituirsi** *(intr / refl)*	prostitute oneself 6, 7
proteggere *(tr)*	protect, guard 67 **[M]**
protestare *(tr)*	protest 3
provare *(tr)*	prove, taste, try on / out, sample 3
provare a *(intr)*	try to 3
provare antipatia per *(intr)*	dislike 3
provare piacere nel fare *(tr)*	delight in doing sth. 3
provare pietà di *(intr)*	take pity on 3
***provenire da** *(intr)*	come from, issue from 102
provocare *(tr)*	challenge 11
provocare un corto circuito *(tr)*	short-circuit 11
provvedere a *(intr)*	provide for, see to 101
pubblicare *(tr)*	bring out, publish, issue 11
pugnalare *(tr)*	stab 3
pulire *(tr)*	clean, clear out, clear up rubbish 6
pungere *(tr)*	prick, sting 68 **[M]**
pungolare *(tr)*	prod 3
punire *(tr)*	discipline, punish 6
puntare *(tr)*	pin 3
puntare a *(intr)*	aim at 3
puntellare *(tr)*	shore up 3
purificare *(tr)*	purify 11
***putrefarsi** *(intr / refl)*	rot 10, 7
puzzare di *(intr)*	stink of 3
Q	**qualificare** *(tr)*	qualify 11
	quantificare *(tr)*	quantify 11
	quotare *(tr)*	quote (prices) 3
R	**racchiudere** *(tr)*	contain; imply 30
	raccogliere *(tr)*	pick, pick up, rake up (leaves). summon up (courage) 31
	raccomandare *(tr)*	recommend 3
	raccontare *(tr)*	report, tell, narrate 3
	raddoppiare *(tr)*	double 13
	raddrizzare *(tr)*	straighten 3
	radere *(tr)*	shave; skim; raze 69 **[M]**
	***radersi** *(intr / refl)*	shave oneself 69, 7
	radiografare *(tr)*	X-ray 3
	raffinare *(tr)*	refine 3
	rafforzare *(tr)*	strengthen 3

*raffreddarsi *(intr / refl)*	get / catch cold 7
raggiungere *(tr)*	reach, attain, catch up with 52
ragionare *(intr)*	reason 3
*rallegrarsi *(intr / refl)*	rejoice 7
rallentare *(tr)*	slow down 3
*rammaricarsi di *(intr / refl)*	regret, feel sorry for 11, 7
rapinare *(tr)*	hijack 3
rapire *(tr)*	kidnap 6
rappresentare *(tr)*	represent, stage (a play) 3
*rassegnarsi a *(intr / refl)*	resign oneself to 7
rassomigliare a *(intr)*	take after, resemble 13
rattristate *(tr)*	sadden 3
ravvolgere *(tr)*	wrap up 106
razionare *(tr)*	ration 3
reagire *(intr)*	react 6
realizzare *(tr)*	accomplish, realize, make real 3
*recarsi *(intr / refl)*	go to 11, 7
recidere *(tr)*	cut off, amputate 39
recitare *(tr)*	act in theater, perform (a play) 3
redigere *(tr)*	draw up (document), compile 4, 25B
refrigerare *(tr)*	refrigerate 3
regalare *(tr)*	give as a present 3
reggere *(tr)*	bear; hold; rule; stand 70 **[M]**
registrare *(tr)*	check in, register, record, video, store data 3
regolare *(tr)*	time, regulate 3
remare *(tr)*	row, paddle 3
rendere *(tr)*	give back; render 71 **[M]**
rendere agro *(tr)*	sour 71
rendere conto di *(intr)*	account for 71
rendere duro come l'acciaio *(tr)*	steel, harden 71
rendere ridicolo *(tr)*	ridicule 71
rendere sicuro *(tr)*	make safe 71
*rendersi conto di *(intr)*	realize 71, 7
reprimere *(tr)*	repress 32
resistere a *(intr)*	resist, weather 25
respingere *(tr)*	cast off (a boat), push back, reject, turn down 86
respirare *(tr)*	breathe 3
*restare *(intr)*	stay 3
*restare alzati *(intr)*	wait up 3
*restare in casa *(intr)*	stay in / indoors 3
restaurare *(tr)*	restore 3
restituire *(tr)*	restore, give back 6
restringere *(tr)*	narrow, tighten, shrink 88
rettificare *(tr)*	rectify 11
rianimare *(tr)*	revive 3

VERB INDEX

rinchiudere *(tr)*	shut in, shut up 30
*rincrescere *(intr)*	regret; mind (*Imp.*) 36
rinforzare *(tr)*	reinforce, steady, make firm 3
rinfrescare *(tr)*	cool, freshen, refresh 11
*rinfrescarsi *(intr / refl)*	cool down 11, 7
ringraziare *(tr)*	say thank you for, thank 3
rinnovare *(tr)*	renew, renovate 3
rinunciare a *(intr)*	renounce, give up 12
rinvenire *(tr / intr)*	find, discover; recover; come to 102
rinviare *(tr)*	send back 13
riordinare *(tr)*	groom 3
riorganizzare *(tr)*	reorganize 3
riparare *(tr)*	mend, fix, repair, screen, shade, shelter 3
ripercuotere *(tr)*	beat again 82
ripetere *(tr)*	repeat 4
ripiegare *(tr)*	fold up 11
riporre *(tr)*	put again 64
riportare *(tr)*	bring back, take back 3
riposare *(tr)*	rest 3
*riposarsi *(intr / refl)*	have a rest 7
riprendere *(tr)*	recover, get back 66
riprodurre *(tr)*	reproduce 95
*risalire a *(intr)*	date back 77
riscaldare *(tr)*	heat, warm up 3
rischiare di *(tr)*	risk, be in danger (of) 13
risciacquare *(tr)*	rinse 3
riscuotere *(tr)*	collect, cash (check) 82
risentire *(tr)*	play back, hear again 5
riservare *(tr)*	reserve 3
risolvere *(tr)*	resolve, solve 74 **[M]**
*risolversi di *(intr / refl)*	decide, make up one's mind 74, 7
risonare *(intr)*	resonate, resound 3
risorgere *(intr)*	rise again, revive 80
risparmiare *(tr)*	economize, save, spare 13
rispecchiare *(tr)*	reflect, mirror 13
rispettare *(tr)*	respect 3
risplendere *(intr)*	glow 17
rispondere a *(intr)*	reply, answer, rejoin, equivalent to 75 **[M]**
*risultare con *(intr)*	result in, turn out 3
risuonare *(intr)*	rattle 3
ritardare *(tr)*	delay 3
ritenere di *(tr)*	retain, consider (doing) 92
ritirare *(tr)*	withdraw 3
ritirarsi *(intr / refl)*	drop out, flinch, pull back, stand back 7
*ritornare *(intr)*	come back, go back, get back, hand back, return 3

*ritrarsi *(intr / refl)*	cower 7
riunire *(tr)*	assemble, put / bring together, gather 6
riunire in mazzo *(tr)*	bundle up 6
*riunirsi *(intr / refl)*	reunite, meet / flock together 6, 7
riuscire a *(intr)*	manage to (do), succeed 99
rivedere *(tr)*	see again; revise 101
rivelare *(tr)*	disclose 3
*rivivere *(intr)*	live again, relive 104
*rivolgersi a *(intr / refl)*	refer to, speak to 106, 7
rivoltare *(tr)*	turn inside out 3
*rizzarsi *(intr / refl)*	sit up 3
rodere *(tr)*	gnaw 47
rombare *(intr)*	rumble 3
rompere *(tr)*	break 76 **[M]**
ronzare *(intr)*	buzz 3
rotolare *(intr / tr)*	roll 3
rovesciare *(tr)*	capsize, knock over, spill, upset 12
†rovinare *(intr / tr)*	ruin, spoil, harm, fall to ruin 3
rubare *(tr)*	pinch, steal 3
ruotare *(tr)*	wheel 3
russare *(intr)*	snore 3

S

sacrificare *(tr)*	sacrifice 11
saggiare *(tr)*	sample 12
salare *(tr)*	salt 3
saldare *(tr)*	pay up, settle (bill); weld 3
†salire *(intr / tr)*	go up, climb, mount, come in (of tide) 77 **[M]**
†salire su *(intr / tr)*	get on, board (bus / train) 77
†saltare *(intr / tr)*	hop, jump, leap 3
*saltare (di valvola) *(intr)*	blow fuse 3
salutare *(tr)*	hail, greet, see off, say good-bye 3
salvare *(tr)*	rescue, salvage, save 3
sanguinare *(intr)*	bleed 3
sapere *(intr)*	know (a fact), know how to 78 **[M]**
sapere di *(intr)*	taste of, smack of 78
sarchiare *(tr)*	weed, hoe 13
sbadigliare *(intr)*	yawn, gape 13
*sbagliarsi *(intr)*	be mistaken 13, 7
sbalordire *(tr)*	stupefy 6
sbarcare *(intr)*	land, disembark 11
sbarrare *(tr)*	dam 3
sbattere *(tr)*	slam, whip (eggs) 4
sbloccare *(tr)*	unblock 11
sborsare *(tr)*	pay out, disburse 3
sbottonare *(tr)*	unbutton 3
sbriciolare *(tr)*	crumble 3
*sbrigarsi *(intr / refl)*	hurry up, make haste 11, 7

*scadere *(intr)*	be due, expire (of credit card) 28
scaldare *(tr)*	warm 3
*scalzarsi *(intr / refl)*	take off shoes 7
scambiare per *(tr)*	mistake for 13
scandalizzare *(tr)*	shock, scandalize 3
*scappare via *(intr)*	dash / rush away 3
scarabocchiare *(tr)*	scribble 13
scaricare *(tr)*	discharge, unload, download (IT) 11
scartare *(tr)*	scrap 3
*scatenarsi *(intr / refl)*	storm (anger) 92, 7
scattare *(tr)*	snap (photo), trigger off 3
scaturire *(tr)*	well, well up 6
scavare *(tr)*	channel, dig, hollow out, mine, scoop 3
scavare *(tr)* (un pozzo)	sink (a well) 3
scegliere di *(tr)*	choose (to), pick select 31
†scendere *(intr / tr)*	go / get / come down, descend 79 **[M]**
†scendere da *(intr / tr)*	get off, get down from 79
scheggiare *(tr)*	chip 12
scherzare *(intr)*	joke 3
schiaffeggiare *(tr)*	slap 12
schiantare *(tr)*	crack 3
schiudere *(tr)*	open, disclose 30
schizzare *(tr)*	sketch 3
sciare *(intr)*	ski sports 12
scintillare *(intr)*	sparkle 3
sciogliere *(tr)*	undo, untie; dissolve 31
*sciogliersi *(intr / refl)*	melt away 31, 7
scioperare *(tr)*	strike, go on strike 3
sciupare *(tr)*	waste 3
*scivolare *(intr)*	skid, slide, slip 3
scoccare *(tr)*	shoot (arrow) 11
scodinzolare *(tr)*	wag (tail) 3
scolare *(tr)*	strain (salad) 3
scommettere *(tr)*	bet 54
scommettere su qlco.	back, gamble on sth. 54
*scomparire *(intr)*	fade, disappear, go out of fashion; cut a poor figure 23
*scomporsi *(intr / refl)*	decompose 64, 7
sconfiggere *(tr)*	defeat, smash (a record) 19
scongiurare *(tr)*	conjure 3
scontare *(tr)*	discount 3
scontentare *(tr)*	dissatisfy 3
*scontrarsi *(intr / refl)*	crash 7
sconvolgere *(tr)*	upset (person) 106
scopare *(tr)*	sweep 3
*scoppiare *(intr)*	burst 13
*scoppiare a ridere	burst out laughing 13

VERB INDEX

scoprire *(tr)*	discover, find out, strike (oil) 24
scoraggiare *(tr)*	discourage 12
scorgere *(tr)*	notice, perceive 80 [M]
*scorrere *(intr)*	flow, glide, stream, flow freely 35
scorrere *(tr)*	browse (books) 35
*scorrere lentamente *(intr)*	trickle 35
scottare *(tr)*	scorch 3
screditare *(tr)*	disparage 3
scricchiolare *(intr)*	crackle 3
scrivere *(tr)*	write, spell, word-process 81 [M]
scrivere un programma *(tr)*	program (IT) 81
scrivere a macchina *(tr)*	type 81
scrollare *(tr)*	shrug 3
scrutare *(tr)*	look through, scan 3
scuoiare *(tr)*	skin 13
scuotere *(tr)*	shake 82 [M]
scusare *(tr)*	excuse, apologize 3
*scusarsi *(intr / refl)*	apologize, say sorry 7
seccare *(tr)*	annoy, pester 11
*seccarsi *(intr / refl)*	get annoyed 11, 7
sedere *(tr)*	sit (in Parliament, Congress, etc.) 14
*sedersi *(intr / refl)*	sit down 14 [M]
sedurre *(tr)*	entice, seduce 95
segnalare *(tr)*	signal 3
segnare *(tr)*	score (sports), sign, check off, mark 3
*segnarsi *(intr / refl)*	cross oneself 7
seguire *(tr)*	follow 5
sellare *(tr)*	saddle 3
*sembrare *(intr)*	appear, seem *(Imp.)* 3
*sembrare di *(intr)*	look, seem, sound (like) 3
seminare *(tr)*	sow (seed) 3
sentire *(intr)*	feel, hear, smell 5
*sentirsi di *(intr / refl)*	feel (well / unwell) 5, 7
sentirsi girare la testa *(intr / refl)*	feel dizzy 5, 7
separare (da) *(tr)*	separate (from) 3
seppellire *(tr)*	bury 6, 25B
servire *(tr)*	serve, wait on, bowl (cricket) 5
*servire da *(intr)*	serve as 5
*servire per *(intr)*	be used for 5
*servirsi di *(intr / refl)*	help oneself, use 5, 7
setacciare *(tr)*	sieve 12
*sfasciarsi contro *(intr / refl)*	smash into 12, 7
sfidare a *(intr)*	challenge to, defy to 3
sfigurare *(tr)*	deform 3
sfiorare *(tr)*	brush against, graze, sweep past 3
sfogare *(tr)*	vent (anger) 11
sfogliare *(tr)*	leaf through 13
*sforzarsi di *(intr / refl)*	try hard (to) 7

sfrecciare via *(intr)*	shoot off quickly 12
sfregiare *(tr)*	deface 12
sganciare *(tr)*	unhook, uncouple 12
sgattaiolare *(intr)*	slip away 3
sgelare *(tr)*	defrost, thaw 3
sgobbare *(tr / intr)*	swot (for exam) 3
sgonfiare *(tr)*	deflate 13
sgranare *(tr)*	shell (peas etc.) 3
sgranocchiare *(tr)*	crunch 13
sgridare *(tr)*	scold 3
sgusciare *(intr)*	slip 12
sgusciare *(tr)*	shell, hull 12
sibilare *(tr)*	hiss 3
sigillare *(tr)*	seal 3
significare *(intr)*	denote, mean, signify, represent 11
singhiozzare *(intr)*	sob 3
sintetizzare *(tr)*	synthesize 3
sintonizzare *(tr)*	tune in 3
slacciare *(tr)*	unfasten 12
slegare *(tr)*	loosen 11
slogare *(tr)*	dislocate 11
smaltire *(tr)* la sbornia	sober up 6
smantellare *(tr)*	dismantle 3
*smarrirsi *(intr / refl)*	get lost, wander, go astray 6, 7
smentire *(tr)*	deny 6
smettere di *(intr)*	stop (doing sth.) 54
smuovere *(tr)*	shift; dissuade 15
socchiudere *(tr)* gli occhi	half close; squint 30
soccorrere *(tr)*	aid, assist 35
soddisfare *(tr)*	fulfill, satisfy 11
soffiare *(tr)*	blow, blow up (balloon) 13
soffocare *(tr)*	choke, suffocate 11
soffriggere *(intr / tr)*	fry lightly 19
soffrire *(tr)*	suffer, be in pain 5, 24
soggiungere *(tr)*	add 52
sognare di *(intr)*	dream (of) 3
sognare ad occhi aperti *(intr)*	daydream 3
*solere *(tr)*	be used / accustomed to 83 **[M]**
solidificare *(tr)*	solidify 11
sollevare *(tr)*	heave, hoist, lift (receiver) 3
sollevare con cricco *(tr)*	jack (car) 3
*sollevarsi *(intr / refl)*	rise, rebel 7
sommergere *(tr)*	submerge 84
sopportare *(tr)*	bear, tolerate, put up with, endure 3
sopprimere *(tr)*	abolish; eliminate; suppress 32
*sopraggiungere *(intr)*	arrive 52
sopravvenire *(intr)*	arrive; happen 102

*sopravvivere a *(intr)*	survive, outlive; live on 104
*sorgere *(intr)*	rise (of sun) 80
sorpassare *(tr)*	overtake 3
sorprendere *(tr)*	surprise 66
soreggere *(tr)*	support, hold up 70
sorridere *(intr)*	smile 72
sorseggiare *(tr)*	sip 12
sorvegliare *(tr)*	supervise 13
sorvolare *(tr)*	hover 3
sospendere *(tr)*	suspend 17
sospettare *(tr)* qcu. di	suspect s.one of 3
sospingere *(tr)*	push, urge 86
sospirare *(intr)*	sigh 3
sostenere *(tr)*	allege, maintain, keep up, prop, stand by, support, uphold, back up 92
sostituire *(tr)*	replace, stand in for 6
sottintendere *(tr)*	hint at 91
sottolineare *(tr)*	stress, underline 3
sottomettere *(tr)*	subject 54
*sottomettersi a *(intr / refl)*	submit to 54, 7
*sottoporsi a *(intr / refl)*	undergo 64, 7
sottoscrivere *(tr)*	undersign, underwrite 81
sottoscrivere a *(intr)*	subscribe 81
*sottostare *(intr)*	submit 87
sottovalutare *(tr)*	undervalue 3
sottrarre *(tr)*	subtract 96
sottrarsi *(refl)*	avoid 96
sovraccaricare *(tr)*	overload 11
sovrintendere a *(intr)*	supervise 91
*sovvenire *(intr)*	aid 102
sovvenzionare *(tr)*	subsidize 3
spaccare *(tr)*	chop, hew, split (wood) 11
spalancare *(tr)*	open wide (door) 11
spandere *(tr / intr)*	spread, spill 25B
sparare *(tr)*	shoot, shoot a goal 3
sparare a *(intr)*	shoot at 3
sparecchiare *(tr)*	clear away 13
spargere *(tr)*	scatter, spread, sprinkle 84 **[M]**
*sparire *(intr)*	pass away, die, vanish 6
spaventare *(tr)*	frighten, scare, startle, terrify 3
*spaventarsi di *(intr / refl)*	be alarmed / startled at 7
spazzare *(tr)*	sweep (chimney) 3
spazzolare *(tr)*	brush 3
*specializzarsi in *(intr / refl)*	specialize 7
specificare *(tr)*	specify 11
speculare *(tr / intr)*	speculate 3
spedire *(tr)*	send, dispatch 6
spegnere *(tr)*	turn off, extinguish, put out 85 **[M]**

spegnersi *(intr/refl)*	go out (of light) 85, 7
spendere *(tr)*	spend money 17
sperare di *(intr)*	hope (to) 3
sperimentare *(tr)*	experiment 3
***spettare a** *(intr)*	be up to, be the duty of *(Imp.)* 3
spezzare *(tr)*	snap, break 3
spiacere *(intr)*	mind (disinterest) 61
spiare *(tr)*	bug, spy on 13
spiccare *(tr)*	stand out (against background) 11
spiegare *(tr)*	explain, give reasons (for), open out (map), spread out (newspaper) 11
spingere a *(tr)*	push, shove, urge (to), jostle 86 **[M]**
splendere *(intr)*	shine (of sun) 17
splendere *(tr)*	flare 17
spogliare *(tr)*	strip, undress 13
***spogliarsi** *(intr/refl)*	get undressed 13, 7
spolverare *(tr)*	dust 3
sporcare *(tr)*	dirty 11
sporgere *(tr)*	project, jut out 80
***sporgersi** *(intr/refl)*	lean out 80, 7
sposare *(tr)*	marry 3
***sposarsi con** *(intr/refl)*	get married to 7
spostare *(tr)*	shift, move 3
sprangare *(tr)*	bar (door) 11
spremere *(tr)*	squeeze 4
spulciare *(tr)*	rid of fleas, examine, debug (IT) 12
spruzzare *(tr)*	splash, spray 3
spumeggiare *(intr)*	foam 12
spuntare *(tr)*	trim (hair) 3
sputare *(tr)*	spit 3
squadrare *(tr)*	square 3
squillare *(tr)*	blare 3
stabilire *(tr)*	appoint, fix, set up, establish 6
stabilire i prezzi di *(intr)*	price 6
stabilire relazioni *(intr)*	liaise (with) 6
***stabilirsi** *(intr/refl)*	settle, settle down 6, 7
stabilizzare *(tr)*	stabilize 3
staccare *(tr)*	detach, disconnect, unstick 11
stampare *(tr)*	print 3
***stancarsi di** *(intr/refl)*	tire of, get tired of 11, 7
standardizzare *(tr)*	standardize 3
***stare** *(intr)*	stay; stand; be 87 **[M]**
***stare attento** *(intr)*	look out, be careful 87
***stare bene** *(intr)*	keep well 87
***stare buono** *(intr)*	be good 87
***stare fermo** *(intr)*	be/keep still 87
***stare fresco** *(intr)*	be in for it 87
***stare fuori** *(intr)*	be outside, away from home 87

VERB INDEX

svalutare	*(tr)*	depreciate, devalue 3
*svanire	*(intr)*	vanish, die away, wear off (of sensation) 6
svantaggiare	*(tr)*	handicap 12
svegliare	*(tr)*	arouse, awaken, wake (s.one) 13
*svegliarsi	*(intr / refl)*	wake up 13, 7
svelare	*(tr)*	reveal, disclose 3
svendere	*(tr)*	sell off 4
*svenire	*(intr)*	pass out, faint 102
sviluppare	*(tr)*	develop 3
svitare	*(tr)*	unscrew 3
svolgere	*(tr)*	unfold 106

T

tacere	*(intr)*	be silent 90 **[M]**
tagliare	*(tr)*	cut, crop, shear 13
tagliare a fette	*(tr)*	slice 13
tamponare	*(tr)*	stop (wound) 3
tappare	*(tr)*	plug, stop up 3
tappezzare	*(tr)*	paper (wall) 3
tardare a	*(intr)*	delay (in doing sth.) 3
tassare	*(tr)*	tax 3
telefonare a	*(intr)*	ring up, telephone 3
temere di	*(tr)*	fear, dread 4
tendere	*(tr)*	stretch out; tend; strain (to limits), tense (muscles) 91 **[M]**
tendere a	*(intr)*	stretch out; tend to 91
tendere un'imboscata a	*(intr)*	ambush 91
tenere	*(tr)*	hold, keep, grasp 92 **[M]**
tenere a	*(intr)*	be eager to 92
tenere il broncio	*(tr)*	sulk 92
tenere un discorso a	*(tr)*	address, give a talk to 92
tenere a freno	*(tr)*	bridle 92
tenere conto di	*(tr)*	allow for 92
tenere in debito conto	*(tr)*	make allowance for 92
tenere indietro	*(tr)*	keep back, withhold 92
tenerci a	*(intr)*	care a lot about 92
*tenersi iontano	*(intr / refl)*	keep away, abstain 92, 7
tentare di	*(tr)*	attempt (to), try, tempt 3
†terminare	*(intr / tr)*	end, terminate 3
tessere	*(tr)*	weave (threads) 4
testimoniare	*(tr)*	bear witness, witness 13
timbrare	*(tr)*	stamp (letters) 3
tingere	*(tr)*	dye, tint 93 **[M]**
tirare	*(tr)*	draw, pull, haul, stretch, extend 3
tirare di scherma	*(intr)*	fence (sport) 3
tirare giù	*(tr)*	pull down, take down (tent etc.) 3
tirare in lungo	*(tr)*	linger 3
tirare vento	*(tr)*	be windy 3
toccare	*(tr)*	touch 11

*toccare a *(intr)*	take (turn), be up to *(Imp.)* 11
togliere *(tr)*	draw out, extract, remove, take off (clothes) 31
togliere il nocciolo a *(tr)*	stone (fruit) 31
togliere di mezzo *(tr)*	do away with 31
togliere la comunicazione *(tr)*	ring off 31
tollerare *(tr)*	tolerate 3
torcere *(tr)*	twist, wring 94 **[M]**
tormentare *(tr)*	harass, torment 3
*tornare (a casa) *(intr)*	go home, turn back 2
torturare *(tr)*	torture 3
tossire *(intr)*	cough 6
tracciare *(tr)*	plot, trace 12
tradire *(tr)*	betray 6
tradurre in / da *(tr)*	translate (into / from) 95 **[M]**
trafiggere *(tr)*	run through, pierce 19
*tramontare *(intr)*	set (of sun, moon) 3
trangugiare in fretta *(tr)*	gobble up 12
transigere *(intr)*	compromise 4, 25B
trapanare *(tr)*	drill a hole 3
trarre *(tr)*	draw, pull 96 **[M]**
trarre il massimo vantaggio da *(tr)*	make the best of 96
trasalire *(intr)*	start (startled) 77
trascinare *(tr)*	trail, drag 3
*trascorrere(intr)	pass (of time) 35
trascrivere *(tr)*	transcribe 81
trascurare *(tr)*	neglect 3
trasferire *(tr)*	transfer 6
trasformare in *(tr)*	transform (into) 3
trasgredire *(tr)*	infringe 6
traslocarsi *(intr / refl)*	move (house) 7
trasmettere *(tr)*	pass on, send on (orders), transmit 54
trasparire *(intr)*	shine through 23
trattare *(tr)*	use, treat (person) 3
trattare con *(intr)*	deal with 3
*trattarsi di *(intr / refl)*	be a matter of, be about 7
trattenere *(tr)*	detain 92
*trattenersi *(intr / refl)*	holdback, stay, remain 92, 7
travedere *(intr)*	be wrong 101
travestire *(tr)*	disguise 5
trebbiare *(tr)*	thresh 13
tremare *(intr)*	quiver, tremble 3
trionfare *(tr)*	triumph 3
tritare *(tr)*	mince 3
trovare *(tr)*	find, think out (a solution) 3
trovare per caso *(tr)*	chance upon 3
*trovarsi *(intr / refl)*	stand, be situated / located 7
*truccarsi *(intr / refl)*	make up (cosmetics) 11, 7

	*tuffarsi *(intr / refl)	plunge, dive 7
	tumultuare *(intr)*	riot 3
	tuonare *(intr)*	thunder 3
	turare *(tr)*	cork 3
U	ubbidire a *(intr)*	obey 6
	*ubriacarsi *(intr / refl)*	get drunk 11, 7
	uccidere *(tr)*	kill 97 **[M]**
	udire *(tr)*	hear 98 **[M]**
	uguagliare *(tr)*	equal, equalize 13
	umiliare *(tr)*	humiliate 13
	ungere *(tr)*	grease, oil 68
	unire *(tr)*	annex, join, combine, pool (resources), unite 6
	*unirsi a *(intr / refl)*	join, unite, team up, link up 6, 7
	urlare *(intr)*	roar, hoot, howl, scream 3
	usare *(tr)*	use 3
	*uscire *(intr)*	go / get / come out, exit 99 **[M]**
V	vagabondare *(intr)*	hike 3
	vagare *(intr)*	ramble, stray 11
	vagliare *(tr)*	sieve, riddle; screen 13
	*valere *(intr)*	be worth 100 **[M]**
	*valere la pena *(intr)*	be worth the trouble *(Imp.)* 100
	valutare *(tr)*	evaluate, rate, value 3
	*vantarsi di *(intr / refl)*	boast about 7
	variare *(tr)*	vary 13
	vedere *(tr)*	see, view 101 **[M]**
	non vedere l'ora di *(intr)*	look forward to 101
	veleggiare *(intr)*	sail 12
	vendere *(tr)*	sell, retail 4 **[M]**
	vendere al mercato *(tr)*	market 4
	venerare *(tr)*	worship, venerate 3
	*venire *(intr)*	come (motion) 102 **[M]**
	*venire a *(intr)*	come to, come and 102
	*venire a vedere *(intr)*	come and see 102
	*venire in mente *(intr)*	occur (of idea) 102
	ventilare *(tr)*	ventilate 3
	*vergognarsi di *(intr / refl)*	be ashamed of 7
	verificare *(tr)*	audit, check, verify 11
	verniciare *(tr)*	paint (house) 12
	versare *(tr)*	pour, shed, pay in (money) 3
	vestire *(tr)*	clothe 5
	*vestirsi *(intr / refl)*	dress, get dressed 5, 7
	vezzeggiare *(tr)*	fondle, pet child / animal 12
	viaggiare *(intr)*	travel 12
	vibrare *(tr)*	vibrate 3
	vietare di *(tr)*	forbid (to) 3
	vincere *(tr)*	win 103 **[M]**

violare *(tr)*	violate 3
violentare *(tr)*	rape 3
visitare *(tr)*	visit places 3
visualizzare *(tr)*	display (IT) 3
†**vivere** *(intr/tr)*	live, be alive 104 **[M]**
†**vivere di** *(intr/tr)*	live on 104
viziare *(tr)*	spoil (child) 13
vogare *(intr)*	stroke (of oars) 11
†**volare** *(intr/tr)*	fly 3
†**volare via** *(intr/tr)*	fly away 3
†**volere** *(intr/tr)*	want to, wish, like 105 **[M]**
†**voler bene a** *(intr/tr)*	be fond of, love 105
*__volerci__	take, require (time) 105
volgere *(tr)*	turn 106 **[M]**
*__volgersi__ *(intr/tr)*	turn around 106, 7
voltare *(tr)*	switch (direction) 3
*__voltarsi__ *(intr/refl)*	turn around 7
vomitare *(intr/tr)*	be sick, vomit 3
votare *(tr)*	vote 3
vuotare *(tr)*	empty 3

Z   **zoppicare** *(intr)*   limp 11